W9-ASD-791

NEW YORK CITY

TOP SIGHTS, AUTHENTIC EXPERIENCES

Ali Lemer, Regis St. Louis,
Robert Balkovich, Ray Bartlett

Contents

Plan Your Trip

Top Experiences.......................... 35

Dining Out....................................119

Treasure Hunt 141

Central **O** ﬧ Guggenheim Museum
Park   ﬧ Metropolitan Museum of Art

Roosevelt
Island

Museum of Modern Art
ﬧ
ﬧ Rockefeller Center

ﬧ Grand Central Terminal

Empire State Building

East River

wer East Side
nement Museum

wn

n Bridge

yn Bridge Park

t

O Prospect
Park

Coney Island
(6mi)

Hudson River

East River

Upper East Side
High-end boutiques,
sophisticated man-
sions and Museum
Mile – one of the
most cultured strips
in the world.
(Map p254)

**Union Square, Flatiron
District & Gramercy**
A bustling, vibrant park
binds surrounding areas
filled with good eats.
(Map p252)

**East Village &
Lower East Side**
Two of the city's hot-
test 'hoods that lure
students, bankers and
scruffier types alike.
(Map p248)

**Lower Manhattan &
the Financial District**
Iconic monuments,
riverfront access and
Wall St mingle at the
island's southern end.
(Map p246)

John F Kennedy
International ✈ *(5mi)*
→

Welcome to New York City

Epicenter of the arts. Dining and shopping capital. Center of international commerce. Trendsetter in fashion and design. One of the world's greatest cities, New York wears many crowns, and spreads an irresistible feast for all.

With its compact size and streets packed with eye candy of all sorts – architectural treasures, Old World cafes, atmospheric booksellers – NYC is a wanderer's delight. Crossing continents is as easy as walking a few avenues in this jumbled city of 200-plus nationalities. You can lose yourself in the crowds of Chinatown amid bright Buddhist temples and steaming noodle shops, then stroll up to Nolita for enticing boutiques and coffee tasting. Every neighborhood offers a dramatically different version of the city, from the 100-year-old Jewish delis of the Upper West Side to the meandering cobblestone lanes of Greenwich Village. And the best way to experience it is to walk its streets.

But if you want to see the real New York, you need to head to Brooklyn. These days, the name is shorthand for 'artsy cool' the world over, but there's far more here than hipster stereotypes. This sprawling borough (more than three times the size of Manhattan) is actually home to some of NYC's most interesting, historic and culturally diverse neighborhoods, with singularly fantastic dining, drinking, shopping and entertainment options – not to mention some of the best river views in the five boroughs.

*with eye candy of all sorts ...
NYC is a wanderer's delight*

Times Square (p62)
MARCIO JOSE BASTOS SILVA/SHUTTERSTOCK ©

★ NEW YORK CITY ★

Upper West Side & Central Park
Home to the premier performing arts center and the park that helps define the city. *(Map p254)*

Midtown
Times Square, Broadway theaters, canyons of skyscrapers, and bustling crowds that rarely thin. *(Map p252)*

Greenwich Village, Chelsea & Meatpacking District
Quaint, intimate streets plus trendy nightlife, shopping and art galleries galore. *(Map p248)*

SoHo & Chinatown
Soup dumpling parlors and hawkers selling bric-a-brac next door to cobblestone streets and stores with the biggest name brands in the world. *(Map p248)*

Lincoln Center

Broadway
Times Square
Pennsylvania (Penn) Station

Chelsea
Market

High Line

One World Trade Center

National September 11 Memorial & Museum

Liberty State Park

Ellis Island

Upper New York Bay

Governors Island

Statue of Liberty

L
T
China

Brookl

Brook

Hudson River

Brooklyn
These days, the name is shorthand for 'artsy cool' the world over, but there's far more here than hipster stereotypes. *(Map p256)*

N
0 —————— 2 km
0 —————— 1 mile

In Focus

Survival Guide

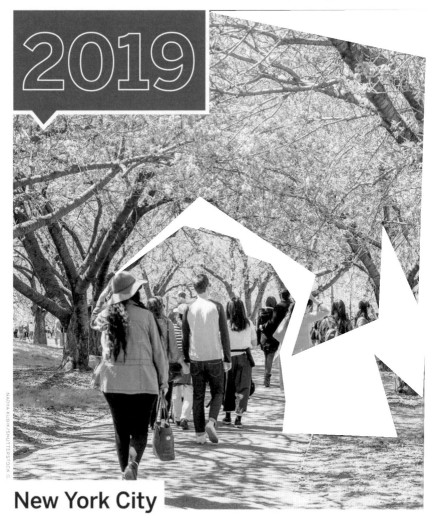

Plan Your Trip
This Year in New York City

2019

New York City

New York's event calendar is never empty, with numerous things on every month of the year – music and arts festivals, holiday markets, festive parades, sports tournaments, cultural carnivals and more. Make sure to plan ahead for the bigger events.

Clockwise from above: Cherry Blossom Festival (p9); Village Halloween Parade (p15); Independence Day fireworks (p12); SummerStage (p11)

NADYA KUBIK/SHUTTERSTOCK ©

★ **Top Festivals & Events**
Cherry Blossom Festival, late Apr
Shakespeare in the Park, late May–Aug
SummerStage, Jun–Aug
Independence Day, Jul 4
Village Halloween Parade, Oct 31

Plan Your Trip
This Year in New York City

January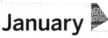

The winter doldrums arrive following the build-up of Christmas and New Year's Eve. Despite the long nights, New Yorkers take advantage of the frosty weather, with outdoor ice skating and weekend ski trips to the Catskills.

🏊 New Year's Day Swim　　Jan 1

What better way to greet the new year than with an icy dip in the Atlantic? Join the Coney Island Polar Bear Club for this annual brrrr fest (www.polarbearclub.org).

🏊 No Pants Subway Ride　　Jan 12

On the second Sunday in January, some 4000 New Yorkers spice things up with a bit of leg nudity on public transit. Anyone can join in, and there's usually an after-party for the cheeky participants. Check www.improveverywhere.com for meeting times and details.

☆ Winter Jazzfest　　mid Jan

In mid-January, this week-long music fest (www.winterjazzfest.com) brings over 100 acts playing at nearly a dozen venues across the city. Most of the action happens around the West Village.

☆ Broadway Week　　late Jan–early Feb

For about 2½ weeks from mid-January into early February (and again in September), you can buy two-for-one tickets to a whole host of top-notch Broadway musicals and plays, often including new productions. (www.nycgo.com/broadway-week)

Pictured: Broadway billboards in Times Square

✖ Restaurant Week　　late Jan–early Feb

For three weeks over January and February, some of the city's finest restaurants help take the chill off your wallet with discount meal deals during New York's Winter Restaurant Week (www.nycgo.com/restaurant-week). A three-course lunch costs around $30 ($42 for dinner).

OVIDIU HRUBARU/SHUTTERSTOCK ©

February

The odd blizzard and below-freezing temperatures make February a good time to stay indoors nursing a drink or a warm meal at a cozy bar.

✿ New York Fashion Week   Feb 8–16
The infamous New York Fashion Week (www.nyfw.com) is sadly not open to the public. But whether you're invited or not, being in the city could provide a vicarious thrill, especially if you can find the after-parties. Pictured: Prabal Gurung runway show

✕ Valentine's Day   Feb 14
If you're traveling with a special someone, you'll want to reserve well ahead for a Valentine's Day dinner. Many restaurants offer special prix-fixe menus, and it's quite the popular night for going out.

☆ Westminster Kennel Club Dog Show   mid Feb
New York goes to the dogs each February at this canine competition (www.

✿ Lunar (Chinese) New Year Festival   Feb 5
One of the biggest Chinese New Year celebrations in the country, this display of fireworks and dancing dragons draws mobs of thrill seekers into the streets of Chinatown. Consult www. explorechinatown.com for details.

westminsterkennelclub.org), where some 3200 dogs come from around the world to vie for top honors. The 'best in show' judging is held in Madison Square Garden.

☆ Off-Broadway Week   mid Feb–late Feb
In the second half of February (and again in October), get two-for-one tickets to various Off-Broadway shows around town, often including long-running productions like *Avenue Q* and *Stomp*. (www.nycgo.com/off-broadway-week)

Plan Your Trip
This Year in New York City

March

03

After months of freezing temperatures and thick winter coats, the odd warm spring day appears and everyone rejoices – though it's usually followed by a week of sub-zero drear as winter lingers on.

☆ Big East Basketball Tournament
early Mar

One of the largest men's college basketball tournaments (www.bigeast.com) has been held at Madison Square Garden for over 30 years. Ten eastern school teams compete for the title and a chance to play in the NCAA tournament later in the month.

⊙ Armory Show
mid Mar

New York's biggest contemporary art fair (www.thearmoryshow.com) sweeps into the city in March, showcasing the works of thousands of artists from around the world on two piers that jut into the Hudson River.

⊙ Macy's Flower Show
late Mar–early Apr

For two weeks in spring, Macy's department store is turned into a floral wonderland

✤ St Patrick's Day Parade
Mar 17

A massive audience, rowdy and wobbly from cups of green beer, lines Fifth Ave on March 17 for this popular parade of bagpipe blowers, floats and clusters of Irish-lovin' politicians. The parade, which was first held here in 1762, is the city's oldest and largest. (www.nycstpatricksparade.org)

(pictured above). The Herald Square flagship store hosts elaborate displays of blooms, lush mini-landscapes and clever blends of the natural and human-made environment.

April

Spring finally appears: optimistic alfresco joints have a sprinkling of street-side chairs as the city squares overflow with bright tulips and blossom-covered trees.

☆ Tribeca Film Festival
mid Apr–late Apr

Created in response to the tragic events of September 11, 2001, Robert De Niro's downtown film festival (www.tribecafilm.com) has quickly become a star on the indie movie circuit. You'll have to make some tough choices: over 150 films are screened during the 10-day fest.

🎎 Easter Bonnet Parade
Apr 21

Dating back to the 1870s, this parade features scores of nattily dressed, bonnet-wearing participants (pictured above)who show off their finery along Fifth Ave in Midtown (from 49th to 57th Sts). Bring your wildest hat and join in the action. It usually kicks off at 10am.

🎎 Earth Day
Apr 22

New York hosts a packed day of events at Union Square, with live

🎎 Cherry Blossom Festival
late Apr or early May

Known in Japanese as Sakura Matsuri, this annual tradition, held on one weekend in late April or early May, celebrates the magnificent flowering of cherry trees in the Brooklyn Botanic Garden (www.bbg.org). It's complete with entertainment and activities, plus refreshments and awe-inspiring beauty.

music, presentations on sustainability and hands-on activities for kids (www.earthdayinitiative.org). Grand Central Terminal also features displays on green initiatives.

Plan Your Trip
This Year in New York City

May

Brilliant bursts of blossoms adorn the flowering trees all around the city. The weather is warm and mild without the unpleasant humidity of summer.

🏃 TD Bank Five Boro Bike Tour   early May

Bike Month features two-wheelin' tours, parties and other events for pedal-pushing New Yorkers. TD Bank Five Boro Bike Tour (www.bikenewyork.org), the main event, sees thousands of cyclists hit the pavement for a 42-mile ride, much of it on roads closed to traffic or on waterfront paths.

🎊 Memorial Day   May 27

The last Monday of May is set aside to remember Americans who have died in combat. Each borough hosts a parade featuring marching bands, vintage cars and flag-waving veterans; the biggest is Queens' Little Neck–Douglaston Memorial Day Parade (www.lndmemorialday.org).

⊙ Fleet Week   late May

For one week (www.fleetweeknewyork. com) at the end of May, Manhattan

resembles a 1940s movie set as clusters of fresh-faced, uniformed sailors (pictured above) go 'on the town' to look for adventures. The ships they leave behind, docked in the Hudson River, invite the curious to hop aboard for tours.

June

Summer's definitely here and locals crawl out of their office cubicles to relax in the city's green spaces. Parades roll down the busiest streets and portable movie screens are strung up in several parks.

☆ Bryant Park Summer Film Festival Jun–Aug

June through August, Bryant Park (www.bryantpark.org) hosts free Monday-night outdoor screenings of classic Hollywood films, which kick off after sundown. Arrive early (folks line up by 4pm).

🐟 Mermaid Parade mid Jun

Celebrating sand, sea and summer is this wonderfully quirky afternoon parade (www.coneyisland.com). It's a flash of glitter and glamour, as elaborately costumed folks display their fishy finery along the Coney Island boardwalk. Held on the last Saturday of the month; all in costume are welcome.

🐟 NYC Pride Jun 30

Gay Pride Month culminates in a major march down Fifth Ave on the last Sunday of the month. NYC Pride (www.nycpride.org)

☆ SummerStage Jun–Aug

Central Park's SummerStage (www.cityparksfoundation.org/summerstage), which runs from June through August, features an incredible lineup of music and dance throughout summer. Django Django, Femi Kuti, Shuggie Otis and the Martha Graham Dance Company are among recent standouts.

is a five-hour spectacle involving representatives of every queer scene under the rainbow. This year is especially meaningful as 2019 is the 50th anniversary of the Stonewall Riots, the event that sparked the LGBT+ rights movement.

Queer culture in NYC's outer boroughs can feel worlds away from the Manhattan scene, and going to smaller, non-touristy celebrations can be a joyously unique experience. Queens Pride (www.queenspride.org), held the first Sunday in June, has a strong pan-Latin flavor. Brooklyn Pride (www.brooklynpride.org) kicks off the second Sunday in June and features a street fair and nighttime parade in Park Slope.
Pictured: Pride Parade participants

This Year in New York City

July

As the city swelters, locals flee to beachside escapes on Long Island. It's a busy month for tourism, however, as holidaying North Americans and Europeans fill the city.

☆ Nathan's Famous Hot Dog Eating Contest   Jul 4

This bizarre celebration of gluttony (www. nathansfamous.com) brings world-champion food inhalers to Coney Island each July 4. Ten-time winner Joey Chestnut currently holds the men's record, having scoffed 72 hot dogs (including buns!) in just 10 gut-busting minutes. (Four-time women's champion Miki Sudo's current record stands at 41.) Pictured: Musicians perform at the Hot Dog Eating Contest

☆ Lincoln Center Out of Doors   late Jul–mid Aug

New York City's performing arts power-house stages a festive program of concerts and dance parties at outdoor stages in the Lincoln Center complex (www.

lcoutofdoors.org). Afrobeat, Latin jazz and country are all part of the lineup, and there are special events for families.

☆ MoMA PS1 Warm Up   Jul–early Sep

Hang with the cool crowd on Saturdays from July through early September at this outdoor party at MoMA PS1 (www. momaps1.org/warmup) in Queens, which features a stellar lineup of DJs, bands and experimental musicians, all playing tunes under the summer sky.

08

August

Thick waves of summer heat slide between skyscrapers as everyone heads to the seashore or gulps cool blasts of air-conditioning. Myriad outdoor events and attractions add life to the languid urban heat.

🎏 Hong Kong Dragon Boat Festival   mid Aug

This Queens festival (www.hkdbf-ny.org) celebrates the fifth month of the Chinese lunar calendar with international music and dance, martial arts demonstrations, crafts and food – and the main event of 200 dragon boat teams racing across the lake in Flushing Meadows Corona Park.

Pictured: Dragon boat racers

☆ Jazz Age Lawn Party   late Aug

Be the cat's pajamas in summery 1920s attire at this Governors Island party, a full day of big band jazz, Charleston dancing and pre-Prohibition cocktails (www.jazzage lawnparty.com). Buy your tickets as early as possible – this event always sells out. Also happens in June.

☆ US Open   late Aug–early Sep

In late August, Queens' Arthur Ashe Stadium takes center stage in sports as the world's top tennis players compete in the final Grand Slam tournament of the year (www.usopen.org). If you can't find tickets, you can watch the matches screened in sports bars all around town.

☆ Charlie Parker Jazz Festival   late Aug

This open-air two-day fest (www.cityparks foundation.org) is a great day out for music fans. Incredible jazz talents take to the stage in Marcus Garvey Park in Harlem and in Tompkins Square Park in the East Village.

Plan Your Trip
This Year in New York City

September

Labor Day officially marks the end of the Hamptons' share-house season as the blistering heat of summer fades to more tolerable levels. As locals return to work, the cultural calendar ramps up.

☆ Electric Zoo   early Sep
Celebrated over the Labor Day weekend, Electric Zoo (www.electriczoofestival.com) is New York's electronic music festival held in sprawling Randall's Island Park. Past headliners have included Moby, Afrojack, David Guetta, Martin Solveig and The Chemical Brothers. Pictured: DJ Armin van Buuren performs

✲ West Indian American Day Carnival   Sep 2
This exuberant parade and carnival (www. wiadcacarnival.org) down Eastern Pkwy every September celebrates Caribbean culture and the West Indian community of Crown Heights, with reggae music, steel-drum bands and glittering, feathered-and-beaded costumes of every color in the rainbow.

✲ Atlantic Antic   late Sep
New York's best street festival offers live music, a cornucopia of food and drink, and numerous craft and clothing vendors. Climb aboard some vintage buses at the New York Transit Museum's display. It runs along Brooklyn's Atlantic Ave (www. atlanticave.org) between Fourth Ave and the waterfront, usually on the fourth Sunday in September.

☆ BAM's Next Wave Festival   Sep–Dec
Celebrated for over 30 years, the Brooklyn Academy of Music's Next Wave Festival (www.bam.org), which runs through December, showcases world-class avant-garde theater, music and dance.

TOP: LEV RADIN/SHUTTERSTOCK ©. BOTTOM: LEV RADIN/SHUTTERSTOCK ©

10

October

Brilliant bursts of color fill the trees as temperatures cool and alfresco cafes finally shutter their windows. Along with May, October is one of the most pleasant and scenic months to visit NYC.

🏃 Comic Con   early Oct

Enthusiasts from near and far gather at this annual beacon of nerd-dom (www. newyorkcomiccon.com) to dress up as their favorite characters and cavort with like-minded anime aficionados. Pictured: A model wears a costume by artist Ryan Novelline

🎊 Blessing of the Animals   early Oct

In honor of the Feast Day of St Francis, which falls early in the month, pet owners flock to the grand Cathedral Church of St John the Divine for the annual Blessing of the Animals (www.stjohndivine.org) with their sidekicks – poodles, lizards, parrots, llamas, you name it.

👁 Open House New York   mid Oct

The country's largest architecture and design event, Open House New York (www.

🎊 Village Halloween Parade   Oct 31

On Halloween, New Yorkers don their wildest costumes for a night of revelry. See the most outrageous displays at the Village Halloween Parade (www. halloween-nyc.com) that runs up Sixth Ave in the West Village. It's fun to watch, but even better to join in.

ohny.org) features special architect-led tours, plus lectures, design workshops, studio visits and site-specific performances all over the city.

Plan Your Trip
This Year in New York City

November

As the leaves tumble, light jackets are replaced by wool and down. A headliner marathon is tucked into the final days of prehibernation weather, then families gather to give thanks.

☉ New York City Marathon early Nov
Held in the first week of November, this annual 26-mile run (www.nycmarathon. org; pictured above) draws thousands of athletes from around the world, and many more excited viewers line the streets to cheer the runners on.

☆ New York Comedy Festival early Nov
Funny-makers take the city by storm during the New York Comedy Festival (www.ny comedyfestival.com) with stand-up sessions, improv nights and big-ticket shows hosted by the likes of Rosie O'Donnell and Ricky Gervais.

☉ Thanksgiving Day Parade Nov 28
Massive helium-filled balloons soar overhead, high-school marching bands rattle their snares and millions of onlookers

bundle up with scarves and coats to celebrate Thanksgiving (the fourth Thursday in November) with Macy's world-famous 2.5-mile-long parade (www.macys.com).

☉ Christmas Tree Lighting Ceremony late Nov or early Dec
The flick of a switch ignites the massive Christmas tree in Rockefeller Center (www. rockefellercenter.com/holidays), officially ushering in the holiday season. Bedecked with over 25,000 lights, it is NYC's unofficial Yuletide headquarters and a must-see for anyone visiting the city during December.

🏃 Ice Skating Nov–Mar
New Yorkers make the most of the winter by taking advantage of outdoor rinks across the city. These usually open in November and run until late March, with top choices including Central Park, Bryant Park, Prospect Park and Rockefeller Center.

2019

12

December

Winter's definitely here, but there's plenty of holiday cheer to warm the spirit. Fairy lights adorn most buildings and department stores create elaborate worlds within their storefront windows.

🔒 Holiday Markets   Dec 1–24

In the month before Christmas, New York becomes a wonderland of holiday markets (pictured above), selling crafts, jewelry, clothing and accessories, ceramics, toys and more. Get a steaming cup of hot chocolate and stroll the aisles. The biggest markets can be found at Union Square, Bryant Park and Grand Central Terminal.

🏃 New York Road Runners Midnight Run   Dec 31

Want to start 2020 off with a bang? Join other runners on a 4-mile dash through Central Park at midnight (the festivities and fireworks kick off beforehand). Sign up with New York Road Runners (www.nyrr.org).

🎊 New Year's Eve   Dec 31

The ultimate place to ring in the New Year, Times Square (www.timessquarenyc.org/

☆ Radio City Christmas Spectacular   Nov–Dec

Radio City Music Hall in Midtown stages this extravagant show (www.radiocity christmas.com) every year, featuring the high-kicking Rockettes and a visit from Santa Claus. It's a crowd-pleasing family show that younger kids will love.

nye) swarms with millions who come to stand squashed together like sardines, swig booze, freeze in subarctic temperatures, witness the annual dropping of the ball and chant the '10...9...8...' countdown in perfect unison.

Plan Your Trip
Need to Know

Daily Costs

Budget:
Less than $100

- Dorm bed: $40–70
- Slice of pizza: around $4
- Food-truck taco: from $3
- Bus or subway ride: $3

Midrange:
$100–300

- Double room in a mid-range hotel: from around $200
- Brunch for two at a mid-range restaurant: $70
- Dinner for two at a mid-range eatery: $130
- Craft cocktail at a lounge: $14–19
- Discount TKTS ticket to a Broadway show: $80

Top End:
More than $300

- Luxury stay at the NoMad Hotel: $325–850
- Tasting menu at a top-end restaurant: $90–325
- A 1½-hour massage at the Great Jones Spa: $200
- Metropolitan Opera orchestra seats: $100–390

Advance Planning

Two months before Book hotel reservations as soon as possible – prices increase the closer you get to your arrival date. Snag tickets to your favorite Broadway blockbuster.

Three weeks before If you haven't done so already, score a table at your top-choice high-end restaurant.

One week before Surf the web and scan blogs and Twitter for the latest restaurant and bar openings, plus upcoming art exhibitions.

Useful Websites

NYC: The Official Guide (www.nycgo.com) New York City's official tourism portal.

Explore Brooklyn (www.explorebk.com) Brooklyn-specific events and listings.

New York Magazine (www.nymag.com) Comprehensive, current listings for bars, restaurants, entertainment and shopping.

New York Times (www.nytimes.com) Excellent local news coverage and theater listings.

Lonely Planet (www.lonelyplanet.com/usa/new-york-city) Destination information, hotel bookings, traveler forum and more.

Arriving in NYC

John F Kennedy International Airport The AirTrain ($5) links to the subway ($2.75), which makes the one-hour journey into Manhattan. Express bus to Grand Central or Port Authority

Currency

US dollar ($)

Language

English

Visas

The US Visa Waiver Program allows nationals of 38 countries to enter the US without a visa, but you must fill out an ESTA application before departing.

Money

ATMs widely available; credit cards accepted at most hotels, stores and restaurants. Farmers markets, food trucks and some restaurants and bars are cash-only.

Cell Phones

International travelers can use local SIM cards in a smartphone provided it is unlocked. Alternatively, you can buy a cheap US phone and load it up with prepaid minutes.

Time

Eastern Standard Time (EST) – five hours behind Greenwich Mean Time (London) and three hours ahead of Pacific Standard Time (California).

For more, see the **Survival Guide** (p229)

When to Go

Summers can be scorching hot; winters are cold and sometimes snowy. Spring or autumn are the best times to explore.

New York City

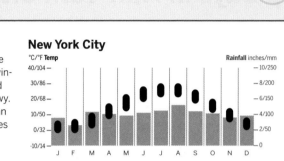

costs $18. Taxis cost a flat $52 excluding tolls, tip and rush-hour surcharge.

LaGuardia Airport The closest airport to Manhattan but least accessible by public transit: take the Q70 express bus from the airport to the 74th St–Broadway subway station. Express bus to Midtown costs $15. Taxis range from $34 to $53, excluding tolls and tip.

Newark Liberty International Airport Take the AirTrain to Newark Airport train station, and board any train bound for New York's Penn Station ($13). Taxis range from $60 to $80 (plus $15 toll and tip). Allow 45 minutes to one hour of travel time.

Getting Around

Check the Metropolitan Transportation Authority website (www.mta.info) for public transportation information (buses and subway). Delays have increased as ridership has expanded.

Subway Inexpensive, somewhat efficient and operates around the clock, though can be confusing. Single ride is $2.75 with a MetroCard.

Bus Convenient during off hours – especially when transferring between the city's eastern and western sides. Uses the MetroCard; same price as the subway.

Taxi Meters start at $2.50 and increase roughly $5 for every 20 blocks. See www.nyc.gov/taxi.

Bicycle The city's popular bike share Citi Bike provides excellent access to most parts of Manhattan.

Inter-borough ferry The New York City Ferry (www.ferry.nyc) provides handy transportation between waterside stops in Manhattan, Brooklyn and Queens.

Top Tips

○ MetroCards are valid on subways, buses, ferries and the tramway to Roosevelt Island. If staying a while, buy a 7-Day Unlimited Pass.

○ Subway lines run both local and express trains. Local trains stop at all stations, express trains do not.

○ If the number on a taxi's top light is lit, it's available. Note that green Boro taxis can't make pick-ups south of W 110th St and E 96th St.

○ When giving an address, always include the nearest cross street/s (eg 700 Sixth Ave *at* 22nd St).

○ The TKTS Booth in Times Square (p59) sells half-price, same-day tickets to selected shows and musicals. The South Street Seaport and Downtown Brooklyn branches also sell next-day matinee tickets.

Plan Your Trip

Top Days in New York City

Lower Manhattan & Brooklyn

Leave behind the concrete canyons for a day of broad horizons and river views, not to mention a stroll over an iconic bridge. Be sure to book advance tickets for the Statue of Liberty and Ellis Island, and One World Trade Center.

❶ Statue of Liberty & Ellis Island (p40)

Book tickets in advance and arrive for your ferry early. Ellis Island will likely occupy most of the morning. Food options are poor on the islands, so bring snacks.

➡ Statue Cruises ferry dock to Brookfield Place

🏃 After returning to Battery Park, walk 1 mile north along the Battery Park Esplanade to Brookfield Place.

❷ Brookfield Place lunch (p124)

Inside Brookfield Place two sprawling food halls offer a wide range of delicacies, including sushi, gourmet tacos and savory French crepes. Grab a window seat for river views.

➡ Brookfield Place to One World Trade Center

🏃 Walk a block north to Vesey St and cross busy West St via the covered pedestrian overpass. You'll exit at the foot of One World Trade Center.

❸ One World Trade Center (p94)

Step into NYC's tallest building and ride up to the One World Observatory for

Day 01

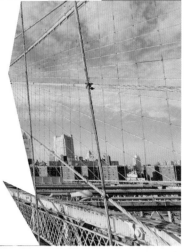

JURI1108/SHUTTERSTOCK ©

astounding views over NYC. Reserve tickets in advance.

⊙ One World Trade Center to the National September 11 Memorial & Museum

🏃 Walk south to the memorial, located next to the building.

❹ National September 11 Memorial & Museum (p90)

One of New York's most powerful sites, this memorial pays moving tribute to the victims of the 2001 terrorist attack. Visit the adjoining museum to learn more about that day's tragic events.

⊙ National September 11 Memorial to Brooklyn Bridge

🏃 Walk east on Vesey St, cross Broadway, and then continue up Park Row. The walkway entrance is across from City Hall Park.

❺ Brooklyn Bridge (p46)

Join the hordes of other visitors making this magical pilgrimage over one of the city's most beautiful landmarks.

⊙ Brooklyn Bridge to Empire Fulton Ferry State Park

🏃 Walk over the bridge from Manhattan to Brooklyn. Take the stairs and turn left at the bottom. Walk downhill to the waterfront.

❻ Empire Fulton Ferry State Park (p47)

This lovely park has staggering views of Manhattan and the Brooklyn Bridge, and a fully restored 1922 carousel. Dumbo's atmospheric brick streets are sprinkled with cafes, shops and 19th-century warehouses.

⊙ Empire Fulton Ferry State Park to Juliana's

🏃 Walk west on Water St to Old Fulton St; turn left and walk east toward Front St.

❼ Dinner at Juliana's (p139)

Enjoy pizza maestro Patsy Grimaldi's legendary thin-crust pies – the classic margherita is one of NYC's best.

From left: Statue of Liberty (p40); Brooklyn Bridge (p46)

Top Days in New York City

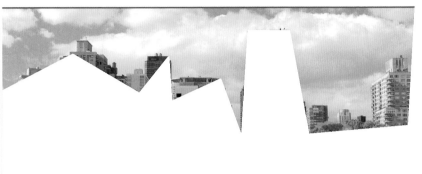

SONGQUAN DENG/SHUTTERSTOCK ©

Upper East Side & Midtown

Landmarks, highlights, big-ticket items: on this itinerary you'll experience the NYC of everyone's collective imagination, including the city's most famous museum and park. Take in the mythic landscape of Midtown's skyscrapers from amid the clouds at Rockefeller Center.

Day

02

❶ Breakfast at the Neue Galerie (p69)

Start the morning uptown at Café Sabarsky, an elegant Viennese-style dining room inside the Neue Galerie. Afterwards, head upstairs into the museum for a look at gorgeous paintings by Gustav Klimt, Paul Klee and other famous Central European artists.

➲ Neue Galerie to Metropolitan Museum of Art

🚶 Walk four blocks south along Fifth Ave.

❷ Metropolitan Museum of Art (p66)

Head to this world-class museum and delve into the sprawling Ancient Greek and Roman collections. Check out the Egyptian Wing (which includes an ancient temple), then take in works by European masters on the 2nd floor. Head up to the Cantor Roof Garden in season for park views.

➲ Metropolitan Museum of Art to Central Park

🚶 Walk into Central Park at the 79th St entrance.

ANDREY BAYDA/SHUTTERSTOCK ©

❸ Central Park (p36)

Get some fresh air in Central Park, the city's spectacular public backyard. Walk south to Conservatory Water, where toy boats sail the pond.

➲ Central Park to Times Square

🚕 Exit the park on Fifth Ave however far south you'd like, and grab a cab for Times Square.

❹ Times Square (p62)

Soak up the bright lights and crowded streets of Times Square from the TKTS Booth's stadium seating at the northern end, where you can take in the dazzling tableau. Purchase discounted tickets for a show that night.

➲ Times Square to Rockefeller Center

🏃 Walk west to Sixth Ave and then north to 49th St.

❺ Top of the Rock (p84)

Buy a ticket for the open-air observation deck at Rockefeller Center's Top of the Rock for stunning midtown vistas.

➲ Rockefeller Center to ViceVersa

🏃 It's a half-mile walk west along 51st (or grab a taxi if you're weary).

❻ Dinner at ViceVersa (p135)

Take a pre-show dinner at this polished Italian eatery with a relaxing back patio.

➲ ViceVersa to a Broadway show

🏃 Walk east to the theater.

❼ Broadway Show (p56)

Enjoy a blockbuster musical for an only-in-New-York spectacle. Afterwards, swig cocktails late into the night at the Edison Hotel's restored piano bar, Rum House (p173).

From left: Central Park (p36); Times Square (p62)

Plan Your Trip
Top Days in New York City

Chelsea & Upper West Side

The best in American art, a famed elevated green space, market adventures and some spectacular dinosaurs set the stage for a fun day's ramble on the West Side. Cap off the day at Lincoln Center, one of the country's top performance spaces.

Day

03

❶ Whitney Museum of American Art (p55)

Start your day perusing the spacious galleries here, with great American artists such as O'Keeffe, Rothko and Hopper.

○ Whitney Museum of American Art to the High Line

🚶 Enter the High Line at its southern end on Gansevoort St, just outside the museum.

❷ The High Line (p52)

The stroll-worthy High Line is an abandoned railway 30ft above the street and one of New York's favorite downtown destinations. Enter at the southern end and meander north for views of the Hudson River and the city streets below.

○ The High Line to Chelsea Market

🚶 Exit at the 16th St stairway for the Tenth Ave entrance of Chelsea Market.

❸ Chelsea Market lunch (p114)

The main concourse of this former cookie factory is packed with food stalls slinging

OPIS ZAGREB/SHUTTERSTOCK ©

everything from spicy Korean noodle soups to Aussie-style sausage rolls.

➜ Chelsea Market to American Museum of Natural History

[S] Grab an uptown C train at Eighth Ave and 14th St and take it to 86th and Central Park West.

❹ American Museum of Natural History (p79)

No matter what your age, you'll experience childlike wonder at the dinosaur fossils in the exceptional American Museum of Natural History. Don't miss the Rose Center for Earth & Space, a unique architectural gem.

➜ American Museum of Natural History to Boulud Sud

🚌 Take the bus down Columbus Ave, walk or grab a cab the 0.8 miles south to W 64th.

❺ Dinner at Boulud Sud (p137)

Celebrity chef Daniel Boulud presents his take on Mediterranean cuisines in a mid-century modern setting. The pre-theater prix fixe meal is a bargain.

➜ Boulud Sud to Lincoln Center

🚶 Cross Broadway and Columbus Ave to Lincoln Center.

❻ A Show at Lincoln Center (p76)

Head across to Lincoln Center for opera at the Metropolitan Opera House (the largest in the world), a symphony in Avery Fisher Hall, or ballet or a play at one of its two theaters – all great shows in architecturally mesmerizing settings.

➜ Lincoln Center to Manhattan Cricket Club

[S] Take the 1 train two stops to 79th St and walk half a block east.

❼ Manhattan Cricket Club (p177)

This swanky spot is accessed through a hidden staircase inside the Burke & Wills restaurant (ask the host for access). While away the night on a chesterfield with cocktail in hand.

From left: Chelsea Market (p114); Metropolitan Opera House (p78), Lincoln Center

Top Days in New York City

MICHELE VACCHIANO/SHUTTERSTOCK ©

Lower East Side & the East Village

Gain insight into immigrant history, grab ethnic eats, check out cutting-edge art and theater (as well as cheap booze and live music), and walk up and down tiny blocks to peek into stylish boutiques. As a general rule, the further east you go the looser things get.

Day

04

❶ Lower East Side Tenement Museum (p98)

Gain fantastic insight into the shockingly cramped living conditions of 19th- and early-20th-century immigrants at this brilliantly curated museum.

◗ Lower East Side Tenement Museum to Little Italy

🏃 Walk west on Delancey St through Sara D Roosevelt Park to Mulberry St.

❷ Little Italy (p89)

It feels more like a theme park than an authentic Italian strip, but Mulberry St is still the heart of the 'hood. Stroll up Mulberry to the boutiques and hip little cafes of Nolita.

◗ Little Italy to the Butcher's Daughter

🏃 Walk two blocks north along Mulberry and turn right onto Kenmare St; it's another two blocks further.

❸ Lunch at the Butcher's Daughter (p126)

Grab a bite at this delightful earth-friendly eatery in Nolita. The vegetarian cafe serves

ED ROONEY/ALAMY STOCK PHOTO ©

up creative, healthy dishes that also happen to be delicious. Wash them down with a craft beer or bespoke mimosa.

○ The Butcher's Daughter to the New Museum of Contemporary Art

🏃 Walk several blocks east to Bowery and turn north.

❹ New Museum of Contemporary Art (p101)

Symbolic of the once-gritty Bowery's transformation, this ultramodern museum has a steady menu of edgy works in new forms.

○ New Museum of Contemporary Art to Chinatown

🏃 Turn right on Delancey St, then left on Mott St and continue until you reach Canal St.

❺ Chinatown (p86)

Take an afternoon stroll through one of New York's most vibrant districts. Chinatown's teeming streets are lined with dumpling houses, bakeries, fish markets, vegetable stands, massage parlors and colorful shops selling everything under the sun.

○ Chinatown to Joe's Pub

S Take the 6 train from Canal St three stops to Astor Pl.

❻ Joe's Pub (p184)

Catch some live music or comedy from top performers at this intimate cabaret bar, or see a contemporary play at the Public Theater, in the same building.

○ Joe's Pub to Degustation

🏃 It's an easy stroll around the corner to Degustation on E 5th St.

❼ Dinner at Degustation (p128)

A snug eatery with a strong local following, Degustation is the place for decadent flavors that blend old-world recipes with new-world creativity. Afterwards, you're well-placed for exploring the East Village bar scene.

From left: Little Italy (p89);
The Butcher's Daughter (p126)

Plan Your Trip
Hot Spots For...

CULTURE VULTURES

⊙ **MoMA** NYC's darling museum has brilliantly curated spaces boasting the best of the world's modern art. (pictured above; p48)

⊙ **Metropolitan Museum of Art** The most encyclopedic museum in the Americas. (p66)

✕ **Cookshop** Great indoor-outdoor dining spot near the heart of Chelsea's gallery scene. (p129)

♟ **La Compagnie des Vins Surnaturels** A sophisticated wine bar in Nolita, with hundreds of vintages. (p168)

☆ **Brooklyn Academy of Music** This hallowed theater hosts cutting-edge works, particularly during its celebrated Next Wave Festival. (p192)

GLITZ & GLAMOUR

☆ **Broadway** Book seats to an award-winning show starring some of the best actors in show business. (pictured below; p56)

⊙ **Frick Collection** This Gilded Age mansion has Vermeers, El Grecos and Goyas and a stunning courtyard fountain. (p69)

🔒 **Barneys** The fashionista's aspirational closet comes with a hefty price tag. (p153)

✕ **Eleven Madison Park** Arresting, cutting-edge cuisine laced with unexpected whimsy. (p133)

♟ **Bar SixtyFive** Raise a glass to the glittering views over Manhattan from this elegant spot in Rockefeller Center. (p173)

HISTORY BUFFS

👁 **Lower East Side Tenement Museum** Gain fascinating insight into the lives of 19th- and early-20th century immigrants on a tour of a preserved tenement. (p98)

👁 **Ellis Island** The gateway to freedom and opportunity for so many of America's immigrants. (p41)

☆ **Hamilton** A popular Broadway musical that offers an American history lesson set to urban rhythms. (p59)

✕ **Chumley's** A former speakeasy with Prohibition-era decor and a first-rate seasonal menu. (p132)

🍷 **Lantern's Keep** Classic, elegant libations in a historic Midtown hotel. (p174)

ROMANCE

👁 **Metropolitan Opera** Dress to the nines and have a fancy night out at Lincoln Center. (p78)

👁 **Brooklyn Heights Promenade** Gorgeous views of Manhattan and the Brooklyn Bridge – a stunner at sunset. (p109)

✕ **Le Bernardin** Book in advance for a very special meal at this Michelin-starred treat. (p134)

🍷 **Little Branch** A hidden gem of a jazz bar with low lighting and excellent cocktails. (p171)

🏊 **Loeb Boathouse** Spend some alone time out on the lake in Central Park. (pictured above; p201)

ACTIVE OUTDOORS

👁 **The High Line** Wild plants and towering weeds steal the show. (p52)

👁 **Prospect Park** Escape the crowds at Brooklyn's gorgeous park, with trails, hills, a canal, lake and meadows. (p102)

🏊 **Downtown Boathouse** Free kayaking for the entire family out on the Hudson River. (p202)

🛍 **Union Square Greenmarket** Assemble a picnic from the lovely produce and gourmet goodies at this outdoor market. (pictured above; p152)

✕ **The Butcher's Daughter** Healthful, plant-based meals accompanied by fresh-pressed juices. (p126)

Plan Your Trip
What's New

Stonewall National Monument

In 2016 outgoing President Obama designated 7.7 acres of the West Village as a US National Monument, the first such designation in American history to honor the LGBTQ+ civil rights movement.

NYC by Ferry

New York is once again embracing ferries, with routes linking Manhattan, Brooklyn and Queens – a scenic sail across the East River for the same price as a subway ride.

Eating Green

The hunger for vegetarian and vegan dining continues to grow. You'll find meat-free restaurants all across the city, including hot spots such as the Seasoned Vegan (p137) in Harlem and Michelin-starred Nix (p129) in Greenwich Village.

Sounds of Harlem

Harlem has become one of the best places to hear eclectic global sounds thanks to several new live music spots: Silvana (p177) and Shrine (p177) host a stellar lineup of bands and singers every night of the week.

Food, Glorious Food

The casual dining scene just keeps getting better, with many new food halls around the city. DeKalb Market Hall (p138) is the latest, with dozens of tempting culinary stalls.

Chefs Club

At this new space (p126) in Nolita, celebrated chefs from around the globe take over the kitchen for anywhere from a few weeks to several months.

Above: Pickle stand in the DeKalb Market Hall (p138)

Plan Your Trip
For Free

Summertime

From June through early September, SummerStage (p11) features over 100 free performances at 17 parks around the city. You'll have to be tenacious to get tickets to Shakespeare in the Park (p10), held in Central Park, but it's well worth the effort. Top actors like Meryl Streep and Al Pacino have taken the stage in the past. Prospect Park has the Celebrate Brooklyn! (www.bricartsmedia.org) summer concert series.

Summertime also sees free film screenings in the River to River Festival (www.rivertorivernyc.com), and the Bryant Park Summer Film Festival (p11) on Monday nights.

Museums

The following times are free or pay-what-you-wish:

○ MoMA (p48) 4pm to 9pm Friday

○ Guggenheim Museum (p80) 5:45pm to 7:45pm Saturday

○ Whitney Museum of American Art (p55) 7pm to 10pm Friday

○ Frick Collection (p69) 2pm to 6pm Wednesday and 6pm to 9pm first Friday of month

○ New Museum of Contemporary Art (p101) 7pm to 9pm Thursday

On the Water

The free Staten Island Ferry (p238) provides magical views of the Statue of Liberty, and you can enjoy it with a cold beer (available on the boat). From May to October, you can also take a ferry (free on summer weekend mornings, $2 at other times) to Governors Island (www.govisland.com), a car-free oasis with priceless views.

For a bit more adventure, take out a free kayak, available at the Downtown Boathouse (p202) and Manhattan Community Boathouse (p202).

Resources

Find free and discounted events through **Club Free Time** (www.clubfreetime.com) and **The Skint** (www.theskint.com), with daily listings of free tours, concerts, talks, workshops, art openings, book readings and more.

Above: Whitney Museum of American Art (p55)

Plan Your Trip
Family Travel

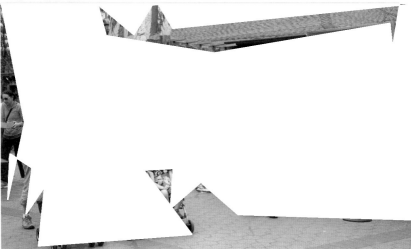

LITTLENYSTOCK/SHUTTERSTOCK ©

Need to Know

Car Seats Children under seven can ride on an adult's lap in a taxi or you can use your own car seat. Ride-sharing services may have available car seats.

Strollers Not allowed on public buses unless folded.

Babysitters Contact the Baby Sitters' Guild (www.babysittersguild.com).

Resources Check out Time Out New York Kids (www.timeout.com/new-york-kids) and Mommy Poppins (www.mommypoppins.com).

Subway Children under 44 inches (110cm) ride free.

Sights & Activities

For many kids, some of New York City's top attractions are a world of fun. For tots aged one to five, hit the **Children's Museum of the Arts** (www.cmany.org) in West SoHo and the **Brooklyn Children's Museum** (www.brooklynkids.org) in Crown Heights. Both have story times, art classes, craft hours and painting sessions. Bigger kids can clamber on vintage subway cars at the **New York Transit Museum** (www.mta. info/mta/museum) or slide down a pole at the **New York City Fire Museum** (www. nycfiremuseum.org).

The city has several zoos, but the best by far is the **Bronx Zoo** (www.bronxzoo. com), which is known for its well-designed habitats. If you're pressed for time, **Central Park Zoo** (www.centralparkzoo.com) is great for a short visit.

The **boat ride** (☑877-523-9849; www. statuecruises.com; adult/child from $18.50/9; ☺departures 8:30am-4pm; ⓢ4/5 to Bowling Green; R/W to Whitehall St; 1 to South Ferry) to the **Statue of Liberty** (p40) offers the opportunity to chug around New York Harbor and get to know an icon that most kids only know from textbooks. If you can't make it there, the free **Staten Island Ferry** (p238) is great, too.

A glass-roofed elevator leads to the **Top of the Rock** (p84), a lookout that offers glittering views of New York.

STU99/GETTY IMAGES ©

Hot dogs. Ice cream. Amusement-park rides. **Coney Island** (p116) is just the ticket if you're in need of some low-brow summertime entertainment.

Transportation

A startling number of subway stations lack elevators and will have you lugging strollers up and down flights of stairs (though you can avoid the turnstile by getting buzzed through an easy-access gate); visit http://web.mta.info/accessibility/stations.htm for a guide to stations with elevators. Regarding fares, anyone over 44 inches is supposed to pay full fare, but the rule is rarely enforced.

Babysitting

While most major hotels (and a handful of boutique-style places) offer on-site babysitting services, or can at least provide you with referrals, you can also call the **Baby Sitters' Guild** (www.babysittersguild. com). Established in 1940 specifically to serve travelers who are staying in hotels with children, it has a stable of sitters who speak a range of 16 languages. All are carefully screened, most are CPR–certified and many have nursing backgrounds; they'll come to your hotel room and even bring games and arts-and-crafts projects. Prices start at $40 per hour.

From left: Bronx Zoo; Wollman Skating Rink (p200)

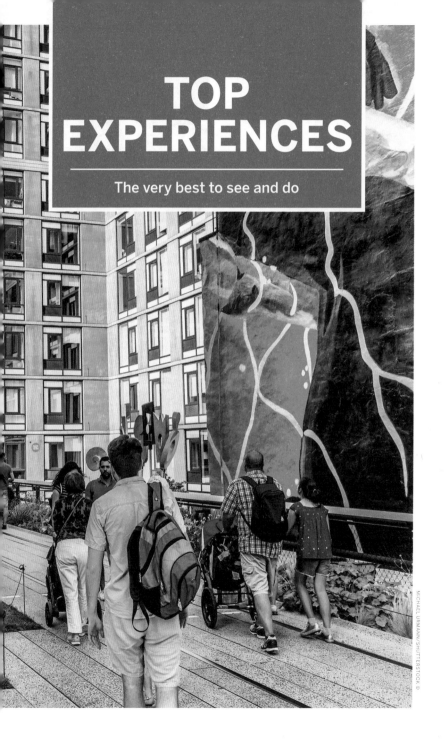

TOP EXPERIENCES

The very best to see and do

The Pond, Central Park

Central Park

Lush lawns, cool forests, flowering gardens, glassy bodies of water and meandering, wooded paths provide a dose of serene nature amid the urban rush of New York City. Today, this 'people's park' is still one of the city's most popular attractions, beckoning throngs of New Yorkers with concerts, events and wildlife.

Great For...

ⓘ Need to Know

Map p254; www.centralparknyc.org; 59th to 110th Sts, btwn Central Park West & Fifth Ave; ⊘6am-1am; ♿

★ **Top Tip**

To escape the crowds, try the North Meadow (north of 97th St) or the Harlem Meer.

PAVEL GAUL/GETTY IMAGES ©

Like the city's subway system, the vast and majestic Central Park, an 843-acre rectangle of open space in the middle of Manhattan, is a great class leveler – which is exactly what it was envisioned to be. Created in the 1860s and '70s by Frederick Law Olmsted and Calvert Vaux on the marshy northern fringe of the city, the immense park was designed as a leisure space for all New Yorkers, regardless of color, class or creed.

Olmsted and Vaux (who also created Prospect Park in Brooklyn) were determined to keep foot and road traffic separate and cleverly designed the crosstown transverses under elevated roads to do so.

Throughout the year, visitors find free outdoor concerts at the Great Lawn, precious animals at the Central Park Wildlife Center and, each summer, top-notch drama at the annual Shakespeare in the Park productions, held at the open-air Delacorte Theater. Some other recommended stops include the ornate Bethesda Fountain, which edges the Lake, and its Loeb Boathouse, where you can rent rowboats or enjoy lunch at an outdoor cafe; the Shakespeare Garden (west side between 79th and 80th Sts), which has lush plantings and excellent skyline views; and the Ramble (mid-park from 73rd to 79th Sts), a wooded thicket that's popular with birdwatchers. While parts of the park swarm with joggers, in-line skaters, musicians and tourists on warm weekends, it's quieter on weekday afternoons – but especially in less well-trodden spots above 72nd St such as the Harlem Meer and the North Meadow (north of 97th St).

Folks flock to the park even in winter, when snowstorms can inspire cross-country skiing and sledding or a simple stroll through

'Imagine' mosaic, Strawberry Fields

the white wonderland, and crowds turn out every New Year's Eve for a midnight run. The **Central Park Conservancy** (Map p254; ☎212-310-6600; www.centralparknyc.org/tours; 14 E 60th St, btwn Madison & Fifth Aves; [S]N/R/W to 5th Ave-59th St) offers guided tours of the park, including those that focus on public art, wildlife and places of interest to kids.

Strawberry Fields

This tear-shaped garden serves as a memorial to former Beatle John Lennon. It is composed of a grove of stately elms and a tiled mosaic that reads, simply, 'Imagine.' Find it at the level of 72nd St on the west side.

☑ Don't Miss

Free and inexpensive tours with the **Central Park Conservancy** (www.centralparknyc.org/tours).

IGOR TALEVSKI/SHUTTERSTOCK ©

Bethesda Terrace & Mall

The arched walkways of Bethesda Terrace, crowned by the magnificent Bethesda Fountain, have long been a gathering area for New Yorkers of all flavors. To the south is the Mall (featured in countless movies), a promenade shrouded in mature North American elms. The southern stretch, known as Literary Walk, is flanked by statues of famous authors.

Conservatory Water & Around

At the level of 74th St is the Conservatory Water, where model sailboats drift lazily and kids scramble about on a toadstool-studded Alice in Wonderland statue. There are Saturday story hours at the Hans Christian Andersen statue to the west of the water (at 11am, June to September).

Great Lawn & Around

The Great Lawn is a massive emerald carpet at the center of the park – between 79th and 86th Sts – and is surrounded by ball fields and London plane trees. Immediately to the southeast is the Delacorte Theater, home to the annual Shakespeare in the Park festival, as well as Belvedere Castle, a lookout.

What's Nearby?

American Folk Art Museum Museum
(Map p254; ☎212-595-9533; www.folkartmuseum.org; 2 Lincoln Sq, Columbus Ave, btwn 65th & 66th Sts; [FREE] This tiny institution contains a couple of centuries' worth of folk and outsider art treasures, including pieces by Henry Darger (known for his girl-filled battlescapes) and Martín Ramírez (producer of hallucinatory *caballeros* on horseback). There is also an array of wood carvings, paintings, hand-tinted photographs and decorative objects.

🍴 Take a Break

Class things up with an afternoon martini at the **Loeb Boathouse** (Map p254; ☎212-517-2233; www.thecentralparkboathouse.com).

FRANK SCHIEFELBEIN/EYEEM/GETTY IMAGES ©

Statue of Liberty & Ellis Island

Stellar skyline views, a scenic ferry ride, a lookout from Lady Liberty's crown, and a moving tribute to America's immigrants at Ellis Island – unmissable is an understatement.

Great For...

☑ Don't Miss

The breathtaking views from Lady Liberty's crown (remember to reserve tickets well in advance).

Statue of Liberty

A Powerful Symbol

Lady Liberty has been gazing sternly toward 'unenlightened Europe' since 1886. Dubbed the 'Mother of Exiles,' the statue symbolically admonishes the rigid social structures of the old world. 'Give me your tired, your poor, your huddled masses yearning to breathe free, the wretched refuse of your teeming shore' she declares in Emma Lazarus' famous 1883 poem 'The New Colossus.'

History of the Statue

Conceived as early as 1865 by French intellectual Édouard de Laboulaye as a monument to the republican principles shared by France and the USA, the Statue of Liberty is still generally recognized as a

symbol for at least the ideals of opportunity and freedom. French sculptor Frédéric-Auguste Bartholdi traveled to New York in 1871 to select the site, then spent more than 10 years in Paris designing and making the 151ft-tall figure Liberty Enlightening the World. It was then shipped to New York, erected on a small island in the harbor and unveiled in 1886. Structurally, it consists of an iron skeleton (designed by Gustave Eiffel) with a copper skin attached to it by stiff but flexible metal bars.

Visiting the Statue

Access to the crown is limited, so reservations are required. Book as far in advance as possible (additional $3). Pedestal access is also limited, so reserve in advance (no additional fee). Keep in mind, there's no elevator and the climb from the base is equal to a 22-story building. Otherwise, a

visit means you can wander the grounds and enjoy the view of Lady Liberty from all sides (plus the great views of Manhattan). A free audioguide (available upon arrival to the island) provides historical details and little-known facts about the statue.

The trip to Liberty Island, via ferry, is usually made in conjunction with nearby Ellis Island. Ferries leave from **Battery Park** (Map p246; www.nycgovparks.org; Broadway, at Battery Pl; ⊘sunrise-1am; Ⓢ4/5 to Bowling Green; R/W to Whitehall St; 1 to South Ferry) and tickets include admission to both sights. Reserve in advance to cut down on long wait times.

Ellis Island

America's most famous and historically important gateway is **Ellis Island** (☏212-363-3200, tickets 877-523-9849; www.nps.gov/elis; ferry incl Statue of Liberty adult/child $18.50/9; ⊘8:30am-6pm, hours vary by season; Ⓢ1 to South Ferry or 4/5 to Bowling Green, then 🚢to Ellis Island) – the very spot where old-world despair met new-world promise. Between 1892 and 1924, more than 12 million immigrants passed through this processing station, their dreams in tow. An estimated 40% of Americans today have at least one ancestor who was processed here, confirming the major role this tiny harbor island has played in the making of modern America.

Main Building Architecture

With their Main Building, architects Edward Lippincott Tilton and William A Boring created a suitably impressive and imposing 'prologue' to America. The designing duo won the contract after the original wooden building burnt down in 1897. Having attended the École des Beaux-Arts in Paris, it's not surprising that they opted for a beaux-arts aesthetic for the project. The building evokes a grand train station, with majestic triple-arched entrances, decorative Flemish bond brickwork, and granite quoins (cornerstones) and belvederes.

Inside, it's the 2nd-floor, 338ft-long Registry Room (also known as the Great Hall) that takes the breath away. It was under its beautiful vaulted ceiling that the newly arrived lined up to have their documents checked, and that the polygamists, paupers, criminals and anarchists were turned back. The original plaster ceiling was severely damaged by an explosion of munition barges at nearby Black Tom Wharf. It was a blessing in disguise, with the rebuilt version adorned with striking, herringbone-patterned tiles by Rafael Guastavino. The Catalan-born engineer was also behind the beautiful tiled ceiling at the Grand Central Oyster Bar & Restaurant at Grand Central Terminal.

Main Building Restoration

After a $160 million restoration, the Main Building was reopened to the public as the Ellis Island Immigration Museum in 1990. Now anybody who rides the ferry to the island can experience a cleaned-up, modern version of the historic new-arrival experience, the museum's interactive exhibits paying homage to the hope, jubilation and sometimes bitter disappointment of the millions who came here in search of a new beginning. Among them were Hungarian Erik Weisz (Harry Houdini), Rodolfo Guglielmi (Rudolph Valentino) and Brit Archibald Alexander Leach (Cary Grant).

ALIJA/GETTY IMAGES ©

Immigration Museum Exhibits

The museum's exhibits are spread over three levels. To get the most out of your visit, opt for the 50-minute self-guided audio tour (free with ferry ticket, available from the museum lobby). Featuring narratives from a number of sources, including historians, architects and the immigrants themselves, the tour brings to life the museum's hefty collection of personal objects, official documents, photographs and film footage. It's an evocative experience to relive personal memories – both good and bad – in the very halls and corridors in which they occurred.

The collection itself is divided into a number of permanent and temporary exhibitions. If you're very short on time, skip the 'Journeys: The Peopling of America 1550–1890' exhibit on the 1st floor and focus on the 2nd floor. It's here that you'll find the two most fascinating exhibitions. The first, 'Through America's Gate,' examines the step-by-step process faced by the newly arrived, including the chalk-marking of those suspected of illness, a wince-inducing eye examination, and 29 questions in the beautiful, vaulted Registry Room. The second, 'Peak Immigration Years,' explores the motives behind the immigrants' journeys and the challenges they faced once free to begin their new American lives. Particularly interesting is the collection of old photographs, which offers intimate glimpses into the daily lives of these courageous new Americans.

For a history of the rise, fall and resurrection of the building itself, make time for the 'Restoring a Landmark' exhibition on the 3rd floor; its tableaux of trashed desks, chairs and other abandoned possessions are strangely haunting. Best of all, the audio tour offers optional, in-depth coverage for those wanting to delve deeper into the collections and the island's history. If you don't feel like opting for the audio tour, you can always pick up one of the phones in each display area and listen to the recorded, yet affecting memories of real Ellis Island immigrants, taped in the 1980s. Another option is the free, 45-minute guided tour with a park ranger. If booked three weeks in advance by phone, the tour is also available in American sign language.

American Immigrant Wall of Honor & Fort Gibson Ruins

Accessible from the 1st-floor 'Journeys: The Peopling of America 1550–1890' exhibit is the outdoor American Immigrant Wall of Honor, inscribed with the names of more than 700,000 immigrants. Believed to be the world's longest wall of names, it's a fund-raising project, allowing any American to have an immigrant relative's name recorded for the cost of a donation. Construction of the wall in the 1990s uncovered the remains of the island's original structure, Fort Gibson – you can see the ruins at the southwestern corner of the memorial. Built in 1808, the fortification was part of a harbor-defense system against the British that also included Castle Clinton in Battery Park and Castle Williams on Governors Island. During this time, Ellis Island measured a modest 3.3 acres of sand and slush. Between 1892 and 1934, the island expanded dramatically thanks to landfill brought in from the ballast of ships and construction of the city's subway system.

What's Nearby?

Ferries depart from Battery Park. Nearby attractions include the following museums.

Museum of Jewish Heritage — Museum

(Map p246; ☎646-437-4202; www.mjhnyc.org; 36 Battery Pl; adult/child $12/free, 4-8pm Wed free; 🕐10am-6pm Sun-Tue, to 8pm Wed & Thu, to 5pm Fri mid-Mar–mid-Nov, to 3pm Fri rest of year, closed Sat; 👪; [S]4/5 to Bowling Green; R/W to Whitehall St) An evocative waterfront museum, exploring all aspects of modern Jewish identity and culture, from religious traditions to artistic accomplishments. The museum's core exhibition includes a detailed exploration of the Holocaust, with personal artifacts, photographs and documentary films providing a personal, moving experience. Outdoors is the Garden of Stones installation. Created by artist Andy Goldsworthy and dedicated to those who lost loved ones in the Holocaust, its 18 boulders form a narrow pathway for contemplating the fragility of life.

The building itself consists of six sides and three tiers to symbolize the Star of David and the six million Jews who perished in WWII. Exhibitions aside, the venue also hosts films, music concerts, ongoing lecture series and special holiday performances. Frequent, free workshops for families with children are also on offer, while the on-site, kosher cafe serves light food.

National Museum of the American Indian

National Museum
of the American Indian   Museum

(Map p246; 212-514-3700; www.nmai.si.edu; 1 Bowling Green; 10am-5pm Fri-Wed, to 8pm Thu; S 4/5 to Bowling Green; R/W to Whitehall St) FREE
An affiliate of the Smithsonian Institution, this elegant tribute to Native American culture is set in Cass Gilbert's spectacular 1907 Custom House, one of NYC's finest beaux-arts buildings. Beyond a vast elliptical rotunda, sleek galleries play host to changing exhibitions documenting Native American art, culture, life and beliefs. The museum's permanent collection includes stunning decorative arts, textiles and ceremonial objects that document the diverse native cultures across the Americas.

The four giant female sculptures outside the building are the work of Daniel Chester French, who would go on to sculpt the seated Abraham Lincoln at Washington, DC's Lincoln Memorial. Representing (from left to right) Asia, North America, Europe and Africa, the figures offer a revealing look at America's world view at the beginning of the 20th century; Asia 'bound' by its religions, America 'youthful and virile,' Europe 'wise yet decaying' and Africa 'asleep and barbaric.' The museum also hosts a range of cultural programs, including dance and music performances, readings for children, craft demonstrations, films and workshops.

★ Mayor in the House

One of NYC's most famous mayors worked at Ellis Island before going into politics. Fluent in Italian, Croatian and Yiddish, Fiorello La Guardia worked as a translator while attending NYU law school at night.

TTSTUDIO/SHUTTERSTOCK ©

Brooklyn Bridge

Even before its completion, the world's first suspension bridge inspired poet Walt Whitman, and later Jack Kerouac too. But perhaps most evocative is Marianne Moore's description of it as a 'climactic ornament, a double rainbow'.

A New York icon, the Brooklyn Bridge was the world's first steel suspension bridge. Indeed, when it opened in 1883, the 1596ft span between its two support towers was the longest in history. Although its construction was fraught with disaster, the bridge became a magnificent example of urban design, inspiring poets, writers and painters. Today, its pedestrian walkway – which begins just east of City Hall – delivers a soul-stirring view of lower Manhattan.

Construction

Ironically, one man deprived of this view was the bridge's very designer, John Roebling. The Prussian-born engineer was knocked off a pier in Fulton Landing in June 1869, dying of tetanus poisoning before construction of the Brooklyn Bridge even began. Consequently, his son, Washington

Great For...

☑ Don't Miss

An early morning stroll over the bridge – a magical time to take in the view.

❶ Need to Know

Map p246; Ⓢ 4/5/6 to Brooklyn Bridge-City Hall; J/Z to Chambers St; R/W to City Hall

✕ Take a Break

For classic and specialty coal-fired thin-crust pizzas, head to Juliana's (p139).

★ Top Tip

Crowds can be thick. Don't try riding a bike across the bridge unless going in the early morning or at night.

than two abreast or else you're in danger of colliding with runners and speeding cyclists. And take care to stay on the side of the walkway marked for folks on foot, and not in the bike lane.

The bridge walk is 1.3 miles, but allow around an hour in either direction to stop and soak up the views.

What's Nearby?

Just north of the Manhattan-side access to the bridge lies Chinatown (p86). On the Brooklyn side, you're a short stroll from Dumbo and Brooklyn Bridge Park (p106).

Dumbo   Neighborhood
Dumbo's nickname is an acronym for its location, 'Down Under the Manhattan Bridge Overpass,' and while this north Brooklyn slice of waterfront used to be strictly for industry, it's now the domain of high-end condos, furniture shops and art galleries. Several highly regarded performing-arts spaces are located in the cobblestone streets and the **Empire Fulton Ferry State Park** hugs the waterfront and offers picture-postcard Manhattan views.

Roebling, supervised its construction, which lasted 14 years and managed to survive budget overruns and the deaths of 20 workers. The younger Roebling himself suffered from the bends while helping to excavate the riverbed for the bridge's western tower and remained bedridden for much of the project; his wife, Emily, oversaw construction in his stead. There was one final tragedy to come in June 1883, when the bridge opened to pedestrian traffic. Someone in the crowd shouted, perhaps as a joke, that the bridge was collapsing into the river, setting off a mad rush in which 12 people were trampled to death.

Crossing the Bridge

Walking across the grand Brooklyn Bridge is a rite of passage for New Yorkers and visitors alike – with this in mind, walk no more

The Museum of Modern Art

Museum of Modern Art

Quite possibly the greatest hoarder of modern master-pieces on earth, the Museum of Modern Art (MoMA) is a cultural promised land. The MoMA is a thrilling crash course in all that is beautiful and addictive about art.

Great For...

☑ **Don't Miss**

The sculpture garden makes a fine retreat when you have gallery fatigue.

Since its founding in 1929, MoMA has amassed over 150,000 artworks, doc-umenting the emerging creative ideas and movements of the late 19th century through to those that dominate today. For art buffs, it's Valhalla.

Visiting MoMA

It's easy to get lost in MoMA's vast collec-tion. To maximize your time and create a plan of attack, download the museum's free smartphone app from the website beforehand. MoMA's permanent collection spans four levels, with prints, illustrated books and the unmissable Contemporary Galleries on level two; architecture, design, drawings and photography on level three; and painting and sculpture on levels four and five. Many of the big hitters are on these last two levels, so tackle the museum

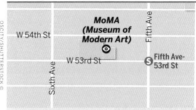

❶ Need to Know

MoMA; Map p254; 📞212-708-9400; www.
moma.org; 11 W 53rd St, btwn Fifth & Sixth
Aves; adult/child 16yr & under $25/free, 4-9pm
Fri free; ⏱10:30am-5:30pm Sat-Thu, to 9pm
Fri; 🚻; Ⓢ E/M to 5th Ave-53rd St; F to 57th St;
E/B/D to 7th Ave-57th St

★ Top Tip

Keep your museum ticket handy, as it
also provides free entry to film screenings and **MoMA PS1** (📞718-784-2084;
www.momaps1.org; 22-25 Jackson Ave, Long
Island City; suggested donation adult/child
$10/free, free with MoMA ticket, Warm Up party
online/at venue $18/22; ⏱noon-6pm Thu-
Mon, Warm Up parties noon-9pm Sat Jul-Aug;
Ⓢ E, M to Court Sq-23rd St; G, 7 to Court Sq).

from the top down before the fatigue sets
in. Must-sees include Van Gogh's *Starry
Night*, Cézanne's *The Bather*, Picasso's *Les
Demoiselles d'Avignon* and Henri Rous-
seau's *The Sleeping Gypsy*, not to mention
iconic American works such as Warhol's
Campbell's Soup Cans and *Gold Marilyn
Monroe*, Lichtenstein's equally poptastic
Girl With Ball and Hopper's haunting *House
by the Railroad*.

Abstract Expressionism

One of the greatest strengths of MoMA's
collections is abstract expressionism, a
radical movement that emerged in New
York in the 1940s and boomed a decade
later. Defined by its penchant for irreverent individualism and monumentally
scaled works, this so-called 'New York
School' helped turn the metropolis into *the*

epicenter of Western contemporary art.
Among the stars are Rothko's *Magenta,
Black, Green on Orange*, Pollock's *One
(Number 31, 1950)* and de Kooning's
Painting.

Lunchtime Talks

To delve a little deeper into MoMA's collection, join one of the museum's lunchtime
talks and readings, which see writers,
artists, curators and designers offering
expert insight into specific works and exhibitions on view. The talks take place daily at
11:30am and 1:30pm. To check upcoming
topics, click the 'Exhibitions & Events' link
on the MoMA website.

Film Screenings

Not only a palace of visual art, MoMA
screens an incredibly well-rounded selection of celluloid gems from its collection
of over 22,000 films, including the works

of the Maysles Brothers and every Pixar animation film ever produced. Expect anything from Academy Award–nominated documentary shorts and Hollywood classics, to experimental works and international retrospectives. Best of all, your museum ticket will get you in for free.

What's Nearby
Radio City
Music Hall   Historic Building
(Map p254; www.radiocity.com; 1260 Sixth Ave, at W 51st St; tours adult/child $27/20; ⊘tours 9:30am-5pm; ➌; Ⓢ B/D/F/M to 47th-50th Sts-Rockefeller Center) This spectacular Moderne movie palace was the brainchild of vaudeville producer Samuel Lionel 'Roxy' Rothafel. Never one for understatement, Roxy launched his venue on

December 23, 1932 with an over-the-top extravaganza that included camp dance troupe the Roxyettes (mercifully renamed the Rockettes). Guided tours (75 minutes) of the sumptuous interiors include the glorious auditorium, Witold Gordon's classically inspired mural *History of Cosmetics* in the Women's Downstairs Lounge, and the *très* exclusive VIP Roxy Suite.

As far as catching a show here goes, be warned: the vibe doesn't quite match the theater's glamour these days. That said, there are often some fabulous talents in the lineup, with past performers including Rufus Wainwright, Aretha Franklin and Dolly Parton. And while the word 'Rockettes' provokes eye rolling from most self-consciously cynical New Yorkers, fans of glitz and kitsch might just get a

thrill from the troupe's annual Christmas Spectacular.

Same-day tour tickets are available at the candy store beside the Sixth Ave entrance, though it's worth considering paying the extra $5 to book your ticket online given that tours can sell out quickly, particularly on rainy days.

St Patrick's Cathedral Cathedral

(Map p254; ☎212-753-2261; www.saintpatrickscathedral.org; Fifth Ave, btwn E 50th & 51st Sts; 🕒6:30am-8:45pm; [S]B/D/F/M to 47th-50th Sts-Rockefeller Center, E/M to 5th Ave-53rd St)
Fresh from a major restoration, America's largest Catholic cathedral graces Fifth Ave with its Gothic Revival splendor. Built at a cost of nearly $2 million during the Civil War, the building did not originally include the two front spires; those were added in 1888. Step inside to appreciate the Louis Tiffany–designed altar and Charles Connick's stunning Rose Window, the latter gleaming above a 7000-pipe church organ.

A basement crypt behind the altar contains the coffins of every New York cardinal and the remains of Pierre Toussaint, a champion of the poor and the first African American nominated for sainthood.

🍴 **Take a Break**

For a casual vibe, nosh on Italian-inspired fare at MoMA's **Cafe 2** (Map p254; ☎212-333-1299; www.momacafes.com; Museum of Modern Art, 11 W 53rd St, btwn Fifth & Sixth Aves, 2nd fl; sandwiches & salads $8-14, mains $12-18; 🕒11am-5pm, to 7:30pm Fri; 📶; [S]E, M to 5th Ave-53rd St).

LITTLENYSTOCK/SHUTTERSTOCK ©

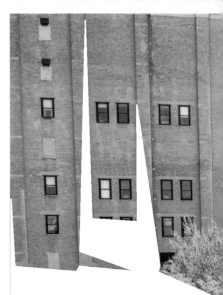

The High Line

A resounding triumph of urban renewal, the High Line is a remarkable linear public park built along a disused elevated rail line. Each year, this aerial greenway attracts millions of visitors who come for stunning vistas of the Hudson River, public art installations, willowy stretches of native-inspired landscaping and a thoroughly unique perspective on the neighborhood streets below.

Great For...

ⓘ Need to Know

Map p248; ☑212-500-6035; www.thehighline.org; Gansevoort St, Meatpacking District; ☉7am-11pm Jun-Sep, to 10pm Apr, May, Oct & Nov, to 7pm Dec-Mar; ☐M11 to Washington St; M11, M14 to 9th Ave; M23, M34 to 10th Ave, ⓢA/C/E, L to 8th Ave-14th St; 1, C/E to 23rd St

★ **Top Tip**

Entrances are at Gansevoort, 14th, 16th, 18th, 20th, 23rd, 26th, 30th and 34th Sts.

History

It's hard to believe that the High Line was once a disused railway that anchored a rather unsavory district of ramshackle domestic dwellings and slaughterhouses. The viaduct that would one day become the High Line was commissioned in 1929 when the municipal government decided to raise the street-level tracks after years of deadly accidents.

By the 1980s, the rails became obsolete (thanks to a rise in truck transportation). Petitions were signed by local residents to remove the eyesores, but in 1999 a committee called the Friends of the High Line was formed to save the tracks and transform them into a public open space. Community support grew and, on June 9, 2009, part one of the celebrated project opened with much ado.

Along the Way

The main things to do on the High Line are stroll, sit and picnic in a park 30ft above the city. Along the park's length you'll pass through willowy stretches of native-inspired landscaping, lounge chairs for soaking up the view and some surprising vantage points over the bustling streets – especially at the cool Gansevoort Overlook, where bleacher-like seating faces a huge pane of glass that allows you to view the traffic, buildings and pedestrians beyond as living works of urban art.

Information, Tours, Events & Eats

As you walk along the High Line you'll find staffers wearing shirts with the signature double-H logo who can point you in the right direction or offer you additional information about the converted rails. There are also myriad staffers behind the scenes organizing public art exhibitions and activity sessions, including warm-weather family events such as story time, science and craft projects.

Free tours take place periodically and explore a variety of topics: history, horticulture, design, art and food. Check the event schedule on the website for the latest details.

To top it all off, the High Line also invites various gastronomic establishments from around the city to set up vending carts and stalls so that strollers can enjoy to-go items on the green. Expect a showing of the finest coffee and ice-cream establishments during the warmer months.

What's Nearby?

Whitney Museum of American Art
Museum

(Map p248; ☏212-570-3600; www.whitney.org; 99 Gansevoort St, at Washington St, West Village; adult/child $25/free, pay-what-you-wish 7-10pm Fri; ⊙10:30am-6pm Mon, Wed, Thu & Sun, to 10pm Fri & Sat; ⓈA/C/E, L to 8th Ave-14th St) After years of construction, the Whitney's new downtown location opened to much fanfare in 2015. Perched near the foot of the High Line, this architecturally stunning building – designed by Renzo Piano – makes a suitable introduction to the museum's superb collection. Inside the spacious, light-filled galleries, you'll find works by all the great American artists, including Edward Hopper, Jasper Johns, Georgia O'Keeffe and Mark Rothko.

Chelsea Galleries

Chelsea is home to the highest concentration of art galleries in NYC. Most lie in the 20s, on the blocks between Tenth and Eleventh Aves. By subway, take the C or E line to 23rd St. Most galleries are open Tuesday through Sunday, but double-check opening hours. Openings for new shows typically take place on Thursday evenings, with wine and a festive art-minded crowd.

Pick up Art Info's *Gallery Guide* (with map) for free at most galleries, or visit www.chelseagalleries.nyc.

✖ Take a Break

A cache of eateries is stashed within Chelsea Market (p114) at the 14th St exit.

Richard Rodgers Theatre

Broadway

Broadway is NYC's dream factory – a place where romance, betrayal, murder and triumph come with dazzling costumes, toe-tapping tunes and stirring scores. The lineup is truly staggering here, with a wide range of musicals, dramas and comedies – and plenty of blurring between genres. Reserve well ahead for top shows, which sell out months in advance.

Great For...

❶ Need to Know

Theatermania (www.theatermania. com) provides listings, reviews and ticketing for any form of theater.

★ **Top Tip**

Many shows offer discounted, day-of 'rush' tickets, available each morning when the box office opens; expect queues.

Broadway Beginnings

The neighborhood's first playhouse was the long-gone Empire, opened in 1893 and located on Broadway between 40th and 41st Sts. Two years later, cigar manufacturer and part-time comedy scribe Oscar Hammerstein opened the Olympia, also on Broadway, before opening the Republic (now children's theater New Victory; p189) in 1900. This led to a string of new venues, among them the still-beating **New Amsterdam Theatre** (Map p252; ☎844-483-9008; www.newamsterdamtheatre.com; 214 W 42nd St, btwn Seventh & Eighth Aves; 👪; [S]N/Q/R/W, S, 1/2/3, 7 to Times Sq-42nd St; A/C/E to 42nd St-Port Authority Bus Terminal) and **Lyceum Theatre** (Map p254; www.shubert.nyc/theatres/lyceum; 149 W 45th St, btwn Sixth & Seventh Aves; [S]N/R/W to 49th St).

The Broadway of the 1920s was well-known for its lighthearted musicals, commonly fusing vaudeville and music-hall traditions, and producing classic tunes like Cole Porter's *Let's Misbehave*. At the same time, Midtown's theater district was evolving as a platform for new American dramatists. One of the greatest was Eugene O'Neill. Born in Times Square at the long-gone Barrett Hotel (1500 Broadway) in 1888, the playwright debuted many of his works here, including Pulitzer Prize winners *Beyond the Horizon* and *Anna Christie*. O'Neill's success on Broadway paved the way for other American greats like Tennessee Williams, Arthur Miller and Edward Albee – a surge of serious talent that led to the establishment of the annual Tony Awards in 1947.

These days, New York's Theater District covers an area stretching roughly from 40th St to 54th St between Sixth and Eighth Aves, with dozens of Broadway and off-Broadway theaters spanning block-buster musicals to new and classic drama.

Getting a Ticket

Unless there's a specific show you're after, the best – and cheapest – way to score tickets in the area is at the **TKTS Booth** (www.tdf.org/tkts; Broadway, at W 47th St; ⏱3-8pm Mon & Fri, 2-8pm Tue, 10am-2pm & 3-8pm Wed & Sat, 10am-2pm Thu, 11am-7pm Sun; ⓢN/Q/R/W, S, 1/2/3, 7 to Times Sq-42nd St), where you can line up and get same-day discounted tickets for top Broadway and off-Broadway shows. Smartphone users can download the free TKTS app, which offers rundowns of both Broadway and off-Broadway shows, as well as real-time updates of what's available on that day. Always have a back-up choice in case your first preference sells out, and never buy from scalpers on the street.

The TKTS Booth is an attraction in its own right, with its illuminated roof of 27 ruby-red steps rising a panoramic 16ft 1in above the 47th St sidewalk.

> ### ★ Did You Know?
>
> The term 'Off-Broadway' is not a geographical one – it simply refers to theaters that are smaller in size (200 to 500 seats) and usually have less of a glitzy production budget than the Broadway big hitters.

What's On?

Musicals rule the marquees on Broadway, blending song and dance in star-studded productions. But there are always plays on too, for those less musically inclined.

Hamilton

Lin-Manuel Miranda's acclaimed new musical is Broadway's hottest ticket, using contemporary hip-hop beats to recount the story of America's founding father, Alexander Hamilton. Inspired by Ron Chernow's biography *Alexander Hamilton*, the musical has won a swath of awards, including top honors at the Drama Desk Awards and New York Drama Critics' Circle Awards and a whopping 11 Tony Awards.

Harry Potter & the Cursed Child

This two-part stage play based on JK Rowling's wizarding world sees the now-adult Harry, Ron, Hermione and Ginny dealing with their own teenage children's experiences at Hogwarts. It's been nominated for 10 Tony Awards, including Best Play.

PITK/SHUTTERSTOCK ©

> ### ☆ Tony Awards
>
> The Tony Awards are the Oscars of the theater world, bestowing awards across a host of categories (best direction, costume design, etc). Check out the latest winners on www.tonyawards.com.

Book of Mormon

Subversive, obscene and ridiculously hilarious, this cutting musical satire is the work of *South Park* creators Trey Parker and Matt Stone and *Avenue Q* composer Robert Lopez. Winner of nine Tony Awards, it tells the story of two naive Mormons on a mission to 'save' a Ugandan village.

Kinky Boots

Adapted from a 2005 British indie film, Harvey Fierstein and Cyndi Lauper's smash hit tells the story of a doomed English shoe factory unexpectedly saved by Lola, a business-savvy drag queen. It garnered six Tony Awards, including Best Musical.

Dear Evan Hansen

This poignant contemporary musical about an anxious high-school student trying to fit in has been both a critics' darling and an audience favorite. Penned by Oscar-winning songwriters Benj Pasek and Justin Paul *(La La Land),* the show won six Tony Awards in 2017, including Best Musical and Best Score, and a 2018 Grammy Award for Best Musical Theater Album.

Frozen

Disney's smash-hit animated film about a young princess's quest to save her older sister and their kingdom has been adapted into a new live-action musical. Dazzling costumes and sets and newly added songs – as well as every child's favorite earworm, 'Let It Go' – make this a great family show.

The Lion King

A top choice for families with kids, Disney's blockbuster musical tells the tale of a lion cub's journey to adulthood and the throne of the animal kingdom. The spectacular sets, costumes and African chants are worth the ticket alone.

Chicago

This beloved Bob Fosse/Kander & Ebb classic tells the story of showgirl Velma Kelly, wannabe Roxie Hart, lawyer Billy Flynn and the fabulously sordid goings-on of the Chicago underworld with sassy, infectious energy. It's also easier to get tickets to than some of the newer shows.

Wicked

An extravagant prequel to *The Wizard of Oz*, this long-running, pop-rock musical gives the story's witches a turn to tell the tale. The musical is based on Gregory Maguire's 1995 novel.

Aladdin

Based on the 1992 Disney animation, this witty dervish of a musical recounts the tale of a street urchin who falls in love with the daughter of a sultan. The stage version includes songs from the film as well as numerous numbers that didn't make the final cut, and new material written specifically for the live production.

Intrepid Sea, Air & Space Museum

What's Nearby?
Intrepid Sea, Air & Space Museum   Museum

(☎877-957-7447; www.intrepidmuseum.org; Pier 86, Twelfth Ave at W 46th St; adult/child $33/21, discounted for NYC residents; ☻10am-5pm Mon-Fri, to 6pm Sat & Sun Apr-Oct, 10am-5pm Mon-Sun Nov-Mar; 🚾; 🚌westbound M42, M50 to 12th Ave, ⓢA/C/E to 42nd St-Port Authority Bus Terminal)
The USS *Intrepid* survived both a WWII bomb and kamikaze attacks. Thankfully, this hulking aircraft carrier is now a lot less stressed, playing host to a multimillion dollar interactive military museum that tells its tale through videos, historical artifacts and frozen-in-time living quarters. The flight deck features fighter planes and military helicopters, which might inspire you to try the museum's high-tech flight simulators.

The rides include the G Force Encounter, allowing you to experience the virtual thrill of flying a supersonic jet plane, and the Transporter FX, a flight simulator promising six full minutes of 'complete sensory overload.' The museum is also home to the guided-missile submarine *Growler* (not for the claustrophobic), a decommissioned Concorde, and the former NASA space shuttle *Enterprise*.

✗ Take a Break
Stiff drinks and a whiff of nostalgia await at the no-bull bar **Jimmy's Corner** (Map p254; ☎212-221-9510; 140 W 44th St, btwn Sixth & Seventh Aves; ☻11:30am-2:30am Mon-Thu, to 4am Fri, 12:30pm-4am Sat, 3pm-2:30am Sun; ⓢN/Q/R/W, 1/2/3, 7 to 42nd St-Times Sq; B/D/F/M to 42nd St-Bryant Park).

Times Square

Love it or hate it, the intersection of Broadway and Seventh Ave, better known as Times Square, is New York City's hyperactive heart: a restless, hypnotic torrent of glittering lights, bombastic billboards and raw urban energy. For feeling the great pulse of this burgeoning metropolis – its disparate crowds, rushing taxi cabs and skyscraper-studded backdrop – there's no better place to start than Times Square.

Great For...

ⓘ Need to Know

Map p254; www.timessquarenyc.org; Broadway, at Seventh Ave; Ⓢ N/Q/R/W, S, 1/2/3, 7 to Times Sq-42nd St

★ **Top Tip**

In the museum, write your dreams onto a piece of ready-to-flutter New Year's Eve confetti.

NYC Icons

Times Square is not hip or fashionable, and it couldn't care less. It's too busy pumping out iconic, mass-marketed NYC – yellow cabs, soaring skyscrapers and razzle-dazzle Broadway marquees. This is the New York of collective fantasies – the place where Al Jolson 'makes it' in the 1927 film *The Jazz Singer*, where photojournalist Alfred Eisenstaedt famously captured a lip-locked sailor and nurse on VJ Day in 1945, and where Alicia Keys and Jay-Z waxed lyrically about this 'concrete jungle where dreams are made.'

For several decades, the dream here was a sordid, wet one. The economic crash of the early 1970s led to a mass exodus of corporations from Times Square. Billboard niches went dark, stores shut and once-grand hotels were converted into SRO (single-room occupancy) dives. While the adjoining Theater District survived, its respectable playhouses shared the streets with porn cinemas and strip clubs. That all changed with tough-talking Mayor Rudolph Giuliani, who, in the 1990s, boosted police numbers and lured a wave of 'respectable' retail chains, restaurants and attractions. By the new millennium, Times Square had gone from 'X-rated' to 'G-rated,' drawing almost 40 million visitors annually.

Get a Drink with a View

For a panoramic overview of the square, order a drink at the Renaissance Hotel's **R Lounge** (Map p254; ☎212-261-5200; www.rloungetimessquare.com; 714 Seventh Ave, at W 48th St), the floor-to-ceiling windows of which overlook the neon-lit spectacle.

Diamond District

A Subway & A Newspaper

At the turn of last century, Times Square was known as Longacre Sq, an unremarkable intersection far from the commercial epicenter of Lower Manhattan. This would change with a deal made between subway pioneer August Belmont and *New York Times* publisher Adolph Ochs.

Belmont approached Ochs, and convinced him that moving the *New York Times* to the intersection of Broadway and 42nd St would be a win-win – an in-house subway station meant faster newspaper distribution and the influx of commuters would also mean more sales right outside its headquarters. Belmont even convinced New York Mayor George B McClellan Jr to rename the square in honor of the broadsheet. It was an irresistible offer and, in the winter of 1904–05, both subway station and the *Times*' new headquarters at One Times Sq made their debut.

☑ Don't Miss

The view from the bleachers overlooking the frenzy. Take a seat and enjoy some of the finest people-watching on earth.

CHRISTIAN MUELLER/SHUTTERSTOCK ©

What's Nearby?

Museum of Arts & Design Museum

(MAD; Map p254; ☎212-299-7777; www.madmuseum.org; 2 Columbus Circle, btwn Eighth Ave & Broadway; adult/18yr & under $16/free, by donation 6-9pm Thu; 🕐10am-6pm Tue-Sun, to 9pm Thu; 👪; [S]A/C, B/D, 1 to 59th St-Columbus Circle) MAD offers four floors of superlative design and handicrafts, from blown glass and carved wood to elaborate metal jewelry. Its temporary exhibitions are top notch and innovative: one past show explored the art of scent. The museum gift shop sells some fantastic contemporary jewelry, while the 9th-floor restaurant/bar Robert (p174) is perfect for panoramic cocktails.

Diamond District Area

(Map p254; www.diamonddistrict.org; W 47th St, btwn Fifth & Sixth Aves; [S]B/D/F/M to 47th-50th Sts-Rockefeller Center) Like Diagon Alley in *Harry Potter*, the Diamond District is a world unto itself. Best experienced on weekdays, it's an industrious whirl of Hasidic Jewish traders, pesky hawkers and love-struck couples looking for the perfect rock. It's home to more than 2600 businesses (at street level and on upper floors) cutting, polishing, appraising or showcasing all manner of diamonds. In fact, the strip handles approximately 90% of the cut diamonds sold in the country. Marilyn, eat your heart out!

🍴 Take a Break

Grab a legendary cubano sandwich from nearby **Margon** (Map p254; ☎212-354-5013; 136 W 46th St, btwn Sixth & Seventh Aves; sandwiches $11-12, mains from $11; 🕐6am-5pm Mon-Fri, from 7am Sat; [S]B/D/F/M to 47th-50th Sts-Rockefeller Center).

Metropolitan Museum of Art

This museum of encyclopedic proportions has more than two million objects in its permanent collection, and many of its treasures are showcased in no less than 17 acres' worth of galleries. You could spend weeks exploring the Met and still not see it all.

This sprawling museum, founded in 1870, houses one of the biggest art collections in the world. Its permanent collection has everything from Egyptian temples to American paintings. Known colloquially as 'The Met,' the museum draws over six million visitors a year to its galleries – making it the largest single-site attraction in New York City. In other words, plan on spending some time here.

Great For...

☑ Don't Miss

The hieroglyphic-covered Temple of Dendur, complete with reflecting pond and Central Park views.

Egyptian Art

The museum has an unrivaled collection of ancient Egyptian art, some of which dates back to the Paleolithic era. Located to the north of the Great Hall, the 39 Egyptian galleries open dramatically with one of the Met's prized pieces: the Mastaba Tomb of Perneb (c 2300 BC), an Old Kingdom burial chamber crafted from limestone.

Madame X (Madame Pierre Gautreau), Gallery 771

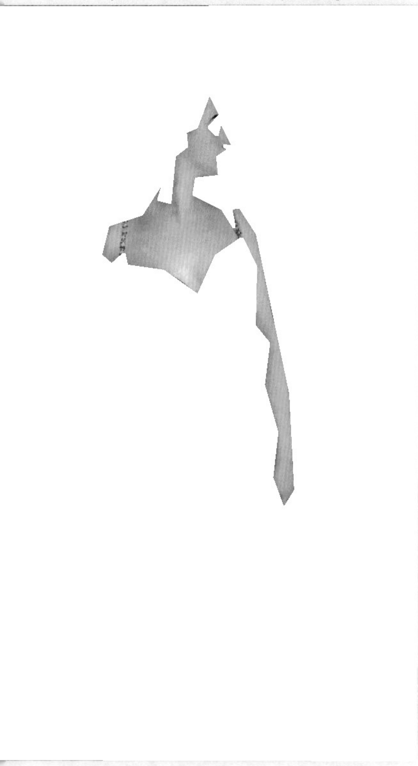

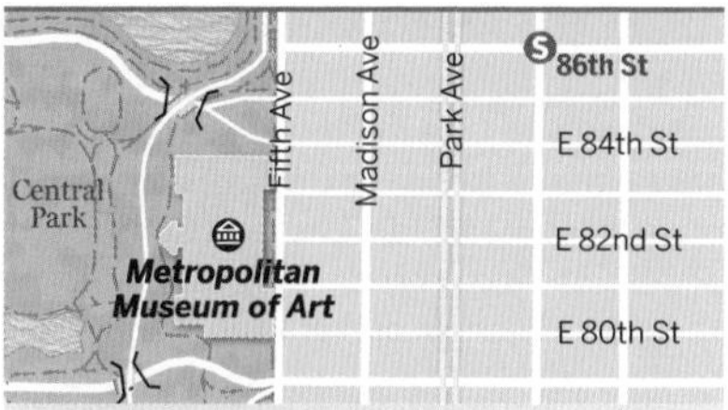

Need to Know

Map p254; ☎212-535-7710; www.metmuseum.org; 1000 Fifth Ave, cnr E 82nd St; 3-day pass adult/senior/child $25/$17/free; 🕐10am-5:30pm Sun-Thu, to 9pm Fri & Sat; 👪; [S]4/5/6, Q to 86th St

🍴 Take a Break

The casual Petrie Court cafe serves good lunch and drink options in a pretty setting.

★ Top Tip

Docents offer free guided tours of specific galleries. Check the website or information desk for details.

From here, a web of rooms is cluttered with funerary stelae, carved reliefs and fragments of pyramids. (Don't miss the intriguing Models of Meketre, clay figurines meant to help in the afterlife, in Gallery 105.) These eventually lead to the Temple of Dendur (Gallery 131), a sandstone temple to the goddess Isis that resides in a sunny atrium gallery with a reflecting pool.

Greek & Roman Art

The 27 galleries devoted to classical antiquity are another Met doozy. From the Great Hall, a passageway takes viewers through a barrel-vaulted room flanked by the chiseled torsos of Greek figures. This spills right into one of the Met's loveliest spaces: the airy Roman sculpture court (Gallery 162), full of marble carvings of gods and historical figures. The statue of a bearded Hercules from AD 68–98, with a lion's skin draped about him, is particularly awe-inspiring.

European Paintings

Want Renaissance? The Met's got it. On the museum's 2nd floor, the European Paintings' galleries display a stunning collection of masterworks. This includes more than 1700 canvases from the roughly 500-year-period starting in the 13th century, with works by every important painter from Duccio to Rembrandt. In fact, everything here is, literally, a masterpiece. In Gallery 621 there are several Caravaggios, including the masterfully painted *The Denial of St Peter*. Gallery 611, to the west, is packed with Spanish treasures, including El Greco's famed *View of Toledo*. Continue south to Gallery 632 to see various Vermeers, including *Young Woman with a Water Pitcher*. Nearby, in Gallery 634, gaze at several Rembrandts, including a 1660 *Self-Portrait*.

Art of the Arab Lands

On the 2nd floor you'll find the Islamic galleries with 15 incredible rooms showcasing the museum's extensive collection of art from the Middle East and Central and South Asia. In addition to garments, secular decorative objects and manuscripts, you'll find gilded and enameled glassware (Gallery 452) and a magnificent 14th-century *mihrab* (prayer niche) lined with elaborately patterned polychrome tile-work (Gallery 455).

American Wing

In the northwestern corner, the American galleries showcase a wide variety of decorative and fine art from throughout US history. These include everything from colonial portraiture to Hudson River

School masterpieces to John Singer Sargent's unbearably sexy *Madame X* (Gallery 771) – not to mention Emanuel Leutze's massive canvas of *Washington Crossing the Delaware* (Gallery 760).

The Roof Garden

One of the best spots in the entire museum is the roof garden, which features rotating sculpture installations by contemporary and 20th-century artists (Jeff Koons, Andy Goldsworthy and Imran Qureshi have all shown here). But its best feature is the view that it offers of the city and Central Park. It's also home to the Cantor Roof Garden Bar (p175), an ideal spot for a drink, especially at sunset. The roof garden is open from mid-April to October.

Coffins and Mummy of the Lady Nephthys, Gallery 112

What's Nearby?

Frick Collection Gallery

(Map p254; ☎212-288-0700; www.frick.org; 1 E 70th St, cnr Fifth Ave; adult/student $22/12, pay-what-you-wish 2-6pm Wed, first Fri of month excl Jan & Sep; 🕐10am-6pm Tue-Sat, 11am-5pm Sun; [S]6 to 68th St-Hunter College) This spectacular art collection sits in a mansion built by prickly steel magnate Henry Clay Frick, one of the many such residences that made up Millionaires' Row. The museum has over a dozen splendid rooms that display masterpieces by Titian, Vermeer, Gilbert Stuart, El Greco and Goya.

The museum is a treat for a number of reasons. One, it resides in a lovely, rambling beaux-arts structure built from 1913 to 1914 by Carrère and Hastings. Two, it's generally not crowded (one exception being during popular shows). And, three, it feels refreshingly intimate, with a trickling indoor courtyard fountain and gardens that can be explored on warmer days. A demure Portico Gallery displays decorative works and sculpture.

A worthwhile audio tour (available in several languages) is included in the price of admission. Classical music fans will enjoy the frequent piano and violin concerts that take place on Sunday.

Neue Galerie Museum

(Map p254; ☎212-628-6200; www.neuegalerie.org; 1048 Fifth Ave, cnr E 86th St; adult/student $20/10, 6-8pm 1st Fri of the month free; 🕐11am-6pm Thu-Mon; [S]4/5/6 to 86th St) This restored Carrère and Hastings mansion from 1914 is a resplendent showcase for German and Austrian art, featuring works by Paul Klee, Ernst Ludwig Kirchner and Egon Schiele. In pride of place on the 2nd floor is Gustav Klimt's golden 1907 *Portrait of Adele Bloch-Bauer I*, which was acquired for the museum by cosmetics magnate Ronald Lauder for a whopping $135 million.

This is a small but beautiful place with winding staircases and wrought-iron banisters. It also boasts a lovely, street-level eatery, Café Sabarsky (p135). Avoid weekends (and the free first Friday of the month) if you don't want to deal with gallery-clogging crowds.

★ For Kids

The Met hosts plenty of kid-centric happenings (check the website) and distributes a special museum brochure and map created specifically for the tykes.

ROGERS FUND, 1911 ©

☆ Deeper Knowledge

You'll find over 300 audio and visual posts on the Met audioguide. Hire one for $7, or download the free smartphone app (the Met app).

Empire State Building

The striking art-deco skyscraper has appeared in dozens of films and still provides one of the best views in town – particularly around sunset when the twinkling lights of the city switch on. Although the crowds are substantial, no one regrets making the journey to the top. There's no other view quite like it, with the great metropolis spread out before you in all its complicated beauty.

Great For...

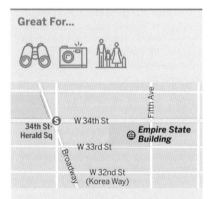

❶ Need to Know

Map p252; www.esbnyc.com; 350 Fifth Ave, at W 34th St; 86th-fl observation deck adult/child $34/27, incl 102nd-fl observation deck $54/47; ⊗8am-2am, last elevators up 1:15am; Ⓢ4, 6 to 33rd St; Blue and Orange PATH to 33rd St; B/D/F/M, N/Q/R/W to 34th St-Herald Sq

★ Top Tip

To beat the crowds, buy tickets online (well worth the extra $2 convenience fee).

The Chrysler Building may be prettier and One World Trade Center and 432 Park Avenue may be taller, but the Queen Bee of the New York skyline remains the Empire State Building. NYC's tallest star, it has enjoyed close-ups in around 100 films, from *King Kong* to *Independence Day*. Heading up to the top is a quintessential NYC experience.

Observation Decks

There are two observation decks. The open-air 86th-floor deck offers an alfresco experience, with coin-operated telescopes for close-up glimpses of the metropolis in action. Further up, the enclosed 102nd-floor deck is New York's second-highest observation deck, trumped only by the observation deck at One World Trade Center. Needless to say, the views over the city's five boroughs (and five neighboring states, weather permitting) are spectacular. Particularly memorable are the views at sunset, when the city dons its nighttime cloak in dusk's afterglow. For a little of that Burt Bacharach magic, head to the 86th floor between 9pm and 1am from Thursday to Saturday, when the twinkling sea of lights is accompanied by a soundtrack of live sax (yes, requests are taken). Alas, the passage to heaven will involve a trip through purgatory: the queues to the top are notorious. Getting here very early or very late will help you avoid delays – as will buying your tickets online, ahead of time.

By the Numbers

The statistics are astonishing: 10 million bricks, 60,000 tons of steel, 6400 windows and 328,000 sq ft of marble. Built

Shake Shack, Madison Square Park

on the original site of the Waldorf-Astoria, construction took a record-setting 410 days, using seven million hours of labor and costing a mere $41 million. It might sound like a lot, but it fell well below its $50 million budget (just as well, given it went up during the Great Depression). Coming in at 102 stories and 1472ft from bottom to top, the limestone monolith opened for business on May 1, 1931.

Language of Light

Since 1976, the building's top 30 floors have been floodlit in a spectrum of colors each night, reflecting seasonal and holiday hues. Famous combos include orange,

white and green for St Patrick's Day; blue and white for Chanukah; white, red and green for Christmas; and the rainbow colors for Gay Pride weekend in June. For a full rundown of the color schemes, check the website.

What's Nearby?
Madison Square Park   Park

(Map p252; ☑212-520-7600; www.madison squarepark.org; E 23rd to 26th Sts, btwn Fifth & Madison Aves, Flatiron District; ⊙6am-11pm; ☝; ⓢR/W, F/M, 6 to 23rd St) This park defined the northern reaches of Manhattan until the island's population exploded after the Civil War. These days it's a much-welcome oasis from Manhattan's relentless pace, with a popular children's playground, dog-run area and **Shake Shack** (Map p252; ☑646-889-6600; www.shakeshack.com; Madison Square Park, cnr E 23rd St & Madison Ave, Flatiron District; burgers $4.20-9.50; ⊙7:30am-11pm Mon-Fri, from 8:30am Sat & Sun; ⓢR/W, F/M, 6 to 23rd St) burger joint. It's also one of the city's most cultured parks, with specially commissioned art installations and (in the warmer months) activities ranging from literary discussions to live music gigs. See the website for more information.

The park is also the perfect spot from which to gaze up at the landmarks that surround it, including the Flatiron Building to the southwest, the moderne Metropolitan Life Tower to the southeast and the New York Life Insurance Building, topped with a gilded spire, to the northeast.

Between 1876 and 1882 the torch-bearing arm of the Statue of Liberty was on display here, and in 1879 the first Madison Square Garden arena was constructed at Madison Ave and 26th St. At the southeastern corner of the park, you'll find one of the city's few self-cleaning, coin-operated toilets.

DW LABS INCORPORATED/SHUTTERSTOCK ©

✕ Take a Break

Feast on dumplings, barbecue and kimchi in nearby restaurant-lined Koreatown (32nd St between Fifth & Sixth Aves).

Iconic Architecture

Midtown is home to some of New York's grandest monuments, with artful works of architecture soaring above the concrete canyons. This walk provides a mix of perspectives – with godlike views from up high and street-side exploring amid the raw energy of the whirling city.

Start Grand Central Terminal
Finish Rockefeller Center
Distance 2 miles
Duration 3 hours

5 Between Sixth and Fifth Aves is the **Diamond District** (p65), where more than 2600 businesses sell gems and jewelry.

4 The soaring **Bank of America Tower** (Sixth Ave, btwn W 42nd & 43rd Sts) is NYC's fourth-tallest building and one of its most ecofriendly.

7 Nearby is the **Rockefeller Center** (p85), a magnificent complex of art-deco skyscrapers and sculptures.

8 Head to the GE Building's 70th floor for an unforgettable vista at the **Top of the Rock** (p84).

Ⓢ Fifth Ave-53rd St

W 51st St

Rockefeller Plaza

W 50th St

W 49th St

8 **7**
FINISH

Fifth Ave

Madison Ave

Ⓢ 47th-50th Sts-Rockefeller Center

5

W 46th St

Sixth Ave (Avenue of the Americas)

W 45th St

W 44th St

W 43rd St

4 42nd St-Bryant Park

5th Ave

Ⓢ Ⓢ W 42nd St
42nd St-Times Sq

Bryant Park

3

W 40th St

Take a Break...

In Bryant Park, stop in for a tasty snack or meal at **Bryant Park Grill** (www.arkrestaurants.com/bryant_park; mains $19.50-45; ⏲11:30am-11pm).

3 Step inside the **New York Public Library** (www.nypl.org) to peek at its spectacular Rose Reading Room.

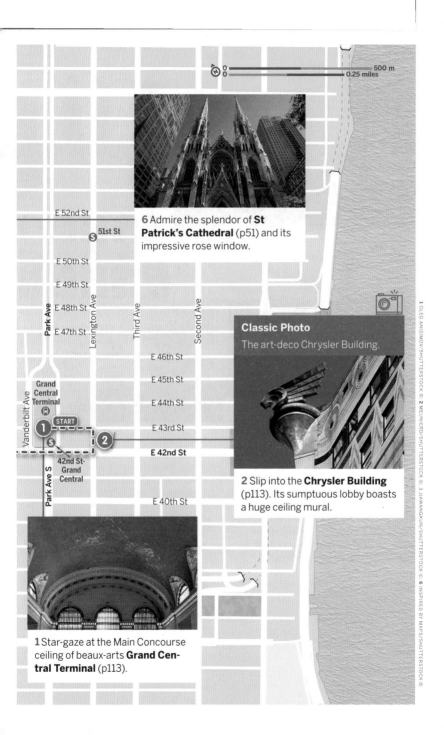

500 m
0.25 miles

E 52nd St

51st St

E 50th St

E 49th St

E 48th St

E 47th St

Park Ave

Lexington Ave

Third Ave

Second Ave

6 Admire the splendor of **St Patrick's Cathedral** (p51) and its impressive rose window.

E 46th St

E 45th St

E 44th St

E 43rd St

E 42nd St

Grand Central Terminal

Vanderbilt Ave

START

1

2

42nd St-Grand Central

Park Ave S

E 40th St

Classic Photo
The art-deco Chrysler Building.

2 Slip into the **Chrysler Building** (p113). Its sumptuous lobby boasts a huge ceiling mural.

1 Star-gaze at the Main Concourse ceiling of beaux-arts **Grand Central Terminal** (p113).

1 OLEG ANISIMOV/SHUTTERSTOCK ©; 2 MEUNIERD/SHUTTERSTOCK ©; 3 JIAWANGKUN/SHUTTERSTOCK ©; 6 INSPIRED BY MAPS/SHUTTERSTOCK ©

Lincoln Center

This vast cultural complex is the epicenter of high art in Manhattan. Famed venues are spread around the 16-acre campus and include concert halls, an opera house, film screening centers and the renowned Juilliard School. The big draw here is seeing one of the Met's lavish opera productions.

This stark arrangement of gleaming modernist temples contains some of Manhattan's most important performance spaces: Avery Fisher Hall (home to the New York Philharmonic), David H Koch Theater (home of the New York City ballet), and the iconic Metropolitan Opera House, the interior walls of which are dressed with brightly saturated murals by painter Marc Chagall.

A History of Building & Rebuilding

Built in the 1960s, this imposing campus replaced a group of tenements called San Juan Hill, a predominantly African American neighborhood where the exterior shots for the movie *West Side Story* were filmed. In addition to being a controversial urban planning move, Lincoln Center wasn't exactly well received at an architectural level – it was relentlessly criticized for its

---

Great For...

☑ **Don't Miss**

A lush production at the world-famous Metropolitan Opera House.

Map p254;

❶ Need to Know

Map p254; ☎212-875-5456, tours 212-875-5350; www.lincolncenter.org; Columbus Ave, btwn W 62nd & 66th Sts; tours adult/student $25/20; ⊙tours 11:30am & 1:30pm Mon-Sat, 3pm Sun; 👪; ⓢ1 to 66th St-Lincoln Center **FREE**

★ Top Tip

You can get discounted (25% to 50% off) tickets at the **David Rubenstein Atrium** (Map p254; ☎212-721-6500; http://atrium.lincolncenter.org; 61 W 62nd St, at Broadway; ⊙atrium 8am-10pm Mon-Fri, 9am-10pm Sat & Sun, ticket box office noon-7pm Tue-Sat, to 5pm Sun; ⓢ1 to 66th St-Lincoln Center) ticket booth.

conservative design, fortress-like aspect and poor acoustics. For the center's 50th anniversary (2009–10), Diller Scofidio + Renfro and other architects gave the complex a much-needed and critically acclaimed freshening up.

Highlights

A survey of the three classic buildings surrounding Revson Fountain is a must. These include the Metropolitan Opera, Avery Fisher Hall and the David H Koch Theater, the latter designed by Philip Johnson. (These are all located on the main plaza at Columbus Ave, between 62nd and 65th Sts.) The fountain is spectacular in the evenings when it puts on Las Vegas–like light shows.

Of the refurbished structures, there are a number that are worth examining, including Alice Tully Hall, now displaying a very contemporary translucent, angled facade, and the David Rubenstein Atrium, a public space offering a lounge area, a cafe, an information desk and a ticket vendor plying day-of discount tickets to Lincoln Center performances. Free events are held here on Thursday evenings, with a wide-ranging roster including eclectic global sounds (such as Indian classical music or Afro-Cuban jazz), prog rock, chamber music, opera and ballet.

Performances & Screenings

On any given night, there are at least 10 performances happening throughout Lincoln Center – and even more in summer, when Lincoln Center Out of Doors (a series of dance and music concerts) and Midsummer Night Swing (ballroom dancing under the stars) lure those who love parks and culture. For details on seasons, tickets and programming – which runs the gamut from opera to dance to theater to ballet – check the website.

Metropolitan Opera House

New York's premier opera company, the **Metropolitan Opera** (Map p254; 🎫 tickets 212-362-6000, tours 212-769-7028; www. metopera.org) is the place to see classics such as *Carmen, Madame Butterfly* and *Macbeth,* not to mention Wagner's *Ring Cycle.* The Opera also hosts premieres and revivals of more contemporary works, such as Peter Sellars' *Nixon in China.* The season runs from September to April.

Ticket prices start around $35 and can get close to $500. Note that the box seats can be a bargain, but unless you're in boxes right over the stage, the views are dreadful. Seeing the stage requires sitting with your head cocked over a handrail – a literal pain in the neck.

New York City Ballet

This prestigious **ballet company** (Map p254; 🎫 212-496-0600; www.nycballet.com) was first directed by renowned Russian-born choreographer George Balanchine back in the 1940s. Today, the company has 90 dancers and is the largest ballet organization in the US, performing 23 weeks a year at Lincoln Center's David H Koch Theater. During the holidays the troop is best known for its annual production of *The Nutcracker.*

New York Philharmonic

The oldest professional orchestra in the US (dating back to 1842) holds its season every year at Avery Fisher Hall. Directed by Alan Gilbert, the son of two Philharmonic

American Museum of Natural History

musicians, the **orchestra** (Map p254; ☑212-875-5656; www.nyphil.org) plays a mix of classics (Tchaikovsky, Mahler, Haydn) and contemporary works, as well as concerts geared toward children.

What's Nearby?

American Museum of Natural History
Museum

(Map p254; ☑212-769-5100; www.amnh.org; Central Park West, at W 79th St; suggested admission adult/child $23/13; ☺10am-5:45pm; ☒; ⓢB, C to 81st St-Museum of Natural History; 1 to 79th St) Founded in 1869, this classic museum contains a veritable wonderland of more than 30 million artifacts, including lots of menacing dinosaur skeletons, as well as the Rose Center for Earth & Space, with its cutting-edge planetarium. From September to May, the museum is home to the Butterfly Conservatory, a glasshouse featuring 500-plus butterflies from all over the world.

On the natural history side, the museum is perhaps best known for its Fossil Halls containing nearly 600 specimens, including the skeletons of a massive mammoth and a fearsome *Tyrannosaurus rex*.

There are also plentiful animal exhibits (the stuffed Alaskan brown bears are popular), galleries devoted to gems and an IMAX theater. The Milstein Hall of Ocean Life contains dioramas showcasing ecologies, weather and conservation, as well as a beloved 94ft replica of a blue whale. At the 77th St Lobby Gallery, visitors are greeted by a 63ft canoe carved by the Haida people of British Columbia in the middle of the 19th century.

For the space set, it's the Rose Center that is the star of the show. Its mesmerizing glass-box facade – home to space-show theaters and the planetarium – is indeed an otherworldly setting. Every half-hour between 10:30am and 4:30pm you can drop yourself into a cushy seat to view *Dark Universe,* narrated by famed astrophysicist Neil deGrasse Tyson, which explores the mysteries and wonders of the cosmos.

Celebrities provide narration for some of the other films: Meryl Streep gives us the evolutionary lowdown on vertebrates on the 4th floor, while Liam Neeson narrates the four-minute *Big Bang,* which provides a fine introduction to exploring the rest of the Rose Center.

☑ **Don't Miss**

The gift shop is full of operatic bric-a-brac, including Met curtain cuff links and Rhinemaidens soap. (Seriously.)

SONGQUAN DENG/SHUTTERSTOCK ©

☆ **Behind the Scenes**

For a behind-the-scenes look at the Opera House, tours ($25) are offered weekdays at 3pm and Sundays at 10:30am and 1:30pm during the performance season. Other tours of the complex are also available.

Guggenheim Museum

A sculpture in its own right, architect Frank Lloyd Wright's swirling white building is one of New York's most photogenic museums. Although the permanent collection on display is small, the Guggenheim stages some exceptional shows, with critically acclaimed retrospectives and thought-provoking site-specific installations by some of the greatest artists of the 20th and 21st centuries.

Great For...

ⓘ Need to Know

Map p254; ☏212-423-3500; www.guggenheim.org; 1071 Fifth Ave, cnr E 89th St; adult/child $25/free, pay-what-you-wish 5:45-7:45pm Sat; ⊙10am-5:45pm Sun-Wed & Fri, to 7:45pm Sat, closed Thu; ♿; §4/5/6 to 86th St

★ **Top Tip**
Entrance lines can be brutal; save time by purchasing tickets online in advance.

THE SOLOMON R GUC   MUSEU

Architect Frank Lloyd Wright's elegant curvilinear building almost overshadows the collection of 20th-century art that it houses. Completed in 1959, the inverted ziggurat structure was derided by some critics but hailed by others, who welcomed it as a beloved architectural icon. Since it first opened, this unusual structure has appeared on countless postcards, TV programs and films.

Abstract Roots

The Guggenheim came out of the collection of Solomon R Guggenheim, a New York mining magnate who began acquiring abstract art in his sixties at the behest of his art adviser, an eccentric German baroness named Hilla Rebay. In 1939, with Rebay serving as director, Guggenheim opened a temporary museum on 54th

St titled the Museum of Non-Objective Painting. (Incredibly, it had gray velour walls, piped-in classical music and burning incense.) Four years later, the pair commissioned Wright to construct a permanent home for the collection.

Years in the Making

Like any development in New York City, the project took forever to come to fruition. Construction was delayed for almost 13 years due to budget constraints, the outbreak of WWII and outraged neighbors, who weren't all that excited to see an architectural spaceship land in their midst. Construction was completed in 1959, after both Wright and Guggenheim had passed away.

When the Guggenheim finally opened its doors in October 1959, the ticket price was

View of the interior ramp, topped by a skylight

50¢ and the works on view included pieces by Wassily Kandinsky, Alexander Calder and abstract expressionists Franz Kline and Willem de Kooning.

Visiting Today

A renovation in the early 1990s added an eight-story tower to the east, which provided an extra 50,000 sq ft of exhibition space. These galleries show the permanent collection and other exhibits, while the museum's ascending ramps are occupied by rotating exhibitions of modern and contemporary art. Though Wright intended visitors to go to the top and wind their way down, the cramped, single elevator doesn't allow for this. Exhibitions, therefore, are installed from bottom to top.

Alongside works by Picasso and Jackson Pollock, the museum's permanent holdings include paintings by Monet, Van Gogh and Degas, photographs by Robert Mapplethorpe, and key surrealist works donated by Guggenheim's niece Peggy.

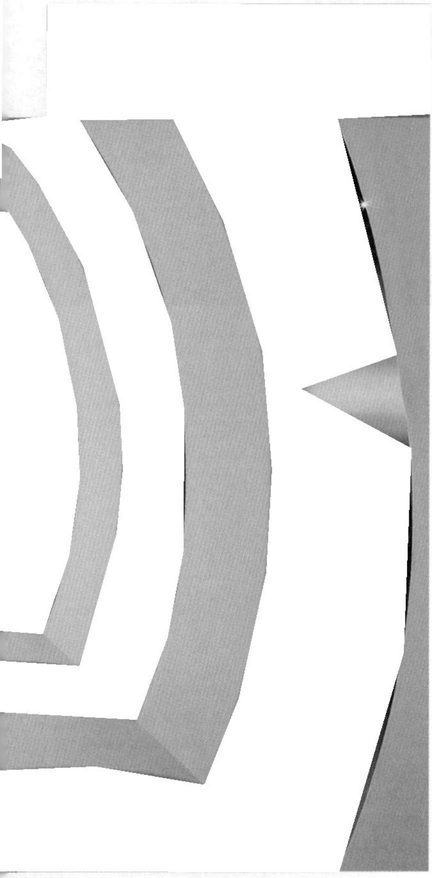

INTERIOR OF THE SOLOMON R. GUGGENHEIM MUSEUM, NEW YORK. ©SRGF, NY. USED WITH PERMISSION. GARDEL BERTRAND/GETTY IMAGES ©

What's Nearby?

Cooper-Hewitt National Design Museum Museum

(Map p254; ☎212-849-8400; www.cooperhewitt.org; 2 E 91st St, cnr Fifth Ave; adult/child $18/free, pay-what-you-wish 6-9pm Sat; 🕒10am-6pm Sun-Fri, to 9pm Sat; [S]4/5/6 to 86th St) Part of the Smithsonian Institution in Washington, DC, this house of culture is the only museum in the country that's dedicated to both historic and contemporary design. The collection, which spans 3000 years, is housed in the 64-room mansion built by billionaire Andrew Carnegie in 1901.

Jewish Museum Museum

(Map p254; ☎212-423-3200; www.thejewishmuseum.org; 1109 Fifth Ave, btwn E 92nd & 93rd Sts; adult/child $15/free, Sat free, pay-what-you-wish 5-8pm Thu; 🕒11am-5:45pm Sat-Tue, to 8pm Thu, to 4pm Fri; 👪; [S]6, Q to 96th St) This New York City gem is tucked into a French-Gothic mansion from 1908, housing 30,000 items of Judaica, as well as sculpture, painting and decorative arts. It hosts excellent temporary exhibits, featuring retrospectives on influential figures such as Art Spiegelman, as well as world-class shows on the likes of Marc Chagall, Édouard Vuillard and Man Ray, among other past luminaries.

🍴 Take a Break

The **Wright** (Map p254; ☎212-427-5690; mains $23-28; 🕒11:30am-3:30pm Mon-Wed & Fri, from 11am Sat & Sun), at ground level, is a space-age eatery serving modern American brunch and lunch dishes.

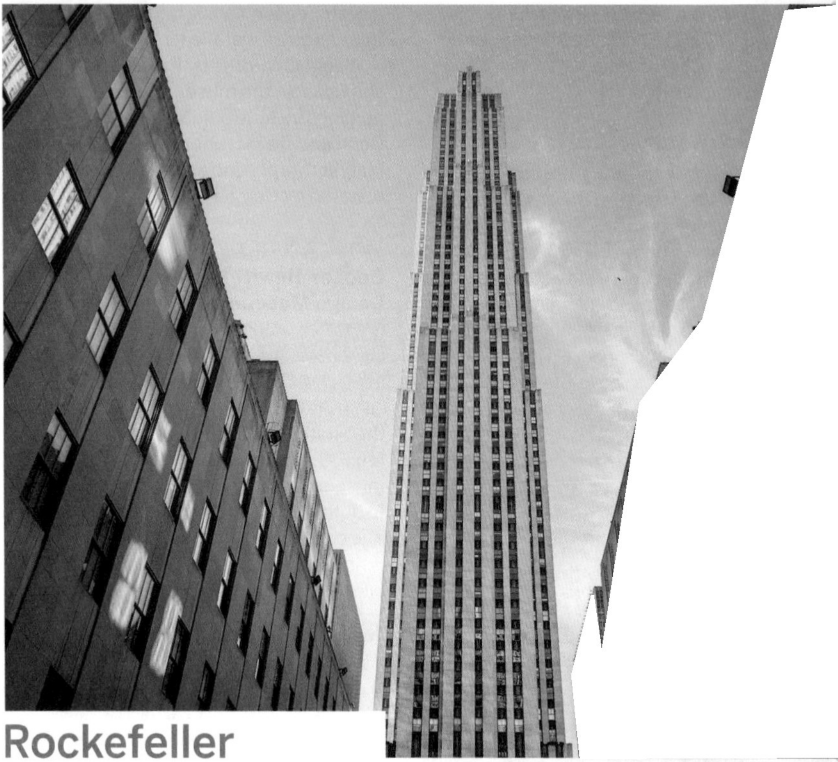

ASIM VERMA/SHUTTERSTOCK ©

Rockefeller Center

Always a hive of activity, Rockefeller Center has wide-ranging appeal, with art-deco towers, a sky-high viewing platform and a famed ice rink in winter.

Great For...

🔭 📷 👪

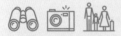

☑ Don't Miss

Drinks with panoramic views at Bar SixtyFive (p173).

This 22-acre 'city within a city' debuted at the height of the Great Depression. Taking nine years to build, it was America's first multiuse retail, entertainment and office space – a modernist sprawl of 19 buildings (14 of which are the original art-deco structures), outdoor plazas and big-name tenants. Developer John D Rockefeller Jr may have sweated over the cost (a mere $100 million), but it was all worth it; the Center was declared a National Landmark in 1987.

Top of the Rock

There are views, and then there's *the* view from the **Top of the Rock** (Map p254; ☎212-698-2000, toll free 877-692-7625; www.topoftherocknyc.com; 30 Rockefeller Plaza, entrance on W 50th St, btwn Fifth & Sixth Aves; adult/child $37/31, sunrise/sunset combo $54/43; 🕒8am-midnight, last elevator at 11pm; [S]B/D/F/M

Atlas by Lee Lawrie and Rene Paul Chambellan

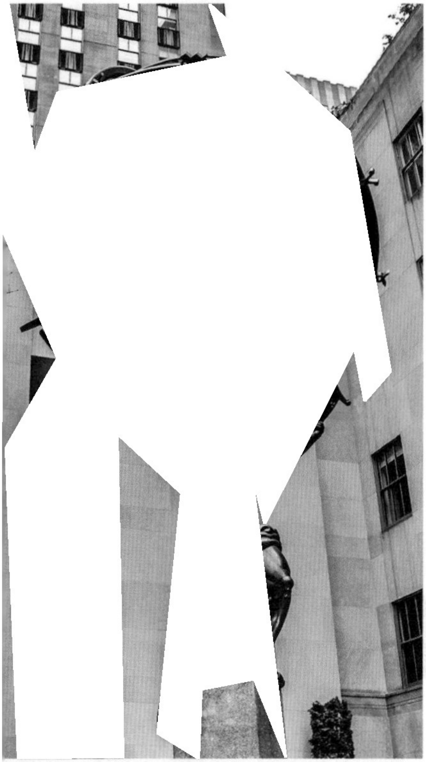

GORAN VRHOVAC/GETTY IMAGES ©

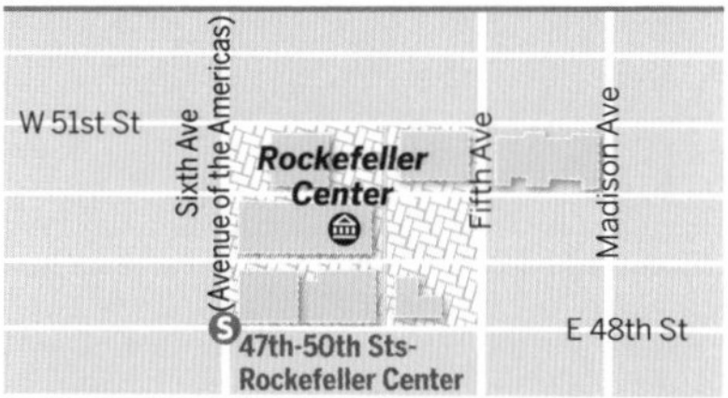
W 51st St
Sixth Ave
(Avenue of the Americas)
Rockefeller Center
Fifth Ave
Madison Ave
E 48th St
47th-50th Sts-Rockefeller Center

Need to Know

Map p254; ☎212-332-6868; www.rockefellercenter.com; Fifth to Sixth Aves, btwn W 48th & 51st Sts; [S]B/D/F/M to 47th-50th Sts-Rockefeller Center

🍴 Take a Break

Grab a bite at Burger Joint (p134), well concealed inside Le Parker Meridien hotel.

★ Top Tip

To beat the wintertime ice-skating crowds, come at the first skating period (8:30am) to avoid a long wait.

to 47th-50th Sts-Rockefeller Center). Crowning the GE Building, 70 stories above Midtown, its blockbuster vista includes one icon that you won't see from atop the Empire State Building – *the* Empire State Building. If possible, head up just before sunset to see the city transform from day to glittering night (if you're already in the area and the queues aren't long, purchase your tickets in advance to avoid the late-afternoon rush). Alternatively, if you don't have under-21s in tow, ditch Top of the Rock for the 65th-floor cocktail bar (p173), where the same spectacular views come with well-mixed drinks… at a cheaper price than the Top of the Rock admission.

Public Artworks

Rockefeller Center features the work of 30 great artists, commissioned around the theme 'Man at the Crossroads Looks Uncertainly But Hopefully at the Future.' Paul Manship contributed *Prometheus*, overlooking the sunken plaza, and *Atlas*, in front of the International Building (630 Fifth Ave). Isamu Noguchi's *News* sits above the entrance to the Associated Press Building (50 Rockefeller Plaza), while José Maria Sert's oil *American Progress* awaits in the lobby of the GE Building. The latter work replaced Mexican artist Diego Rivera's original painting, rejected by the Rockefellers for containing 'communist imagery.'

Rockefeller Plaza

Come the festive season, Rockefeller Plaza is where you'll find New York's most famous Christmas tree. Ceremoniously lit just after Thanksgiving, it's a tradition that dates back to the 1930s, when construction workers set up a small tree on the site. In its shadow, Rink at Rockefeller Center (p201) is the city's most famous (and infamously crowded) ice-skating rink.

Lunar New Year Parade in Chinatown

Chinatown

Take a trip to Asia without leaving the US mainland on a wander through the narrow lanes of Chinatown. It's pure sensory overload amid fast-talking street vendors, neon-lit noodle parlors and colorful storefronts packed with eye candy from the Far East.

Great For...

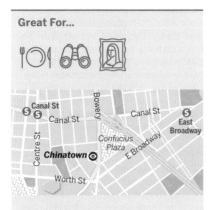

ⓘ Need to Know

Map p248; www.explorechinatown.com; south of Broome St & east of Broadway; ⓢ N/Q/R/W, J/Z, 6 to Canal St; B/D to Grand St; F to East Broadway

★ **Top Tip**

Don't forget to wander down the back alleys for a technicolor assortment of spices and herbs to perfect your own Eastern dishes.

Endless exotic moments await in New York City's most colorfully cramped community, where a walk through the neighborhood is never the same, no matter how many times you pass through. Catch the whiff of fresh fish and ripe persimmons, hear the clacking of mah-jongg tiles on makeshift tables, and shop for everything imaginable, from rice-paper lanterns and embroidered slippers to a pound of pressed nutmeg.

Museum of Chinese in America

In a space designed by architect Maya Lin, **MOCA** (Map p248; 212-619-4785; www.mocanyc.org; 215 Centre St, btwn Grand & Howard Sts; adult/child $10/5, 1st Thu of month free; 11am-6pm Tue, Wed & Fri-Sun, to 9pm Thu; N/Q/R/W, J/Z, 6 to Canal St) is a multifaceted space whose engaging permanent and temporary exhibitions shed light on Chinese American life, both past and present. Browse interactive multimedia exhibits, maps, timelines, photos, letters, films and artifacts. The museum's anchor exhibit provides an often intimate glimpse into topics including immigration, cultural identity and racial stereotyping.

Foodie Adventures

The most rewarding experience for Chinatown neophytes is to access this wild and wonderful world through their taste buds. Chinatown's menus sport wonderfully low prices, uninflated by ambience, hype or reputation. The neighborhood is rife with family recipes passed across generations and continents, and steaming street stalls clutter the sidewalk serving pork buns and other finger-friendly food.

Traditional Chinese dragon, Lunar New Year Parade

Buddhist Temples

Chinatown is home to Buddhist temples large and small, public and obscure. They are easily stumbled upon during a full-on stroll of the neighborhood, and at least two such temples are considered landmarks. The **Eastern States Buddhist Temple** (Map p248; 212-966-6229; 64 Mott St, btwn Bayard & Canal Sts; 8:30am-6pm; S N/Q/R/W, J/Z, 6 to Canal St) is filled with hundreds of Buddhas, while the **Mahayana Temple** (Map p248; 212-925-8787; http://en.mahayana. us; 133 Canal St, at Manhattan Bridge Plaza; 8:30am-6pm; S B/D to Grand St; J/Z to Bowery; 6 to Canal St) holds one golden, 16ft-high Buddha, sitting on a lotus and edged with

offerings of fresh oranges, apples and flowers. Mahayana is the largest Buddhist temple in Chinatown, and its entrance, which overlooks the frenzied vehicle entrance to the Manhattan Bridge, is guarded by two proud and handsome golden lions. Step inside and you'll find a simple interior of wooden floor and red paper lanterns, dramatically upstaged by the temple's magnificent Buddha.

Canal Street

Walking down Canal St is like a game of Frogger played on the streets of Shanghai. This is Chinatown's spine, where you'll dodge oncoming human traffic as you scurry into side streets to scout treasures from the Far East. You'll pass stinky seafood stalls hawking slippery fish; mysterious herb shops peddling a witch's cauldron's worth of roots and potions; storefront bakeries with steamy windows and the tastiest 80¢ pork buns you've ever had; restaurants with whole, roasted ducks hanging by their skinny necks in the windows; and produce markets piled high with fresh lychee, bok choy and Asian pears.

What's Nearby?
Little Italy   Area
(Map p248; S N/Q/R/W, J/Z, 6 to Canal St; B/D to Grand St) This once-strong Italian neighborhood (film director Martin Scorsese grew up on Elizabeth St) saw an exodus in the mid-20th century when many of its residents moved to more suburban neighborhoods in Brooklyn and beyond. Today, it's mostly concentrated on Mulberry St between Broome and Canal Sts, a stretch packed with checkerboard tablecloths and (mainly mediocre) Italian fare. If you're in town in late September, be sure to check out the raucous **San Gennaro Festival** (www.sangennaro.org; Sep), which honors the patron saint of Naples.

MANDRITOIU/SHUTTERSTOCK®

✖ Take a Break
Indulge in arguably the best Peking duck around at Peking Duck House (p126).

Reflecting Pool

MATTHEW T CARROLL/GETTY IMAGES ©

National September 11 Memorial & Museum

An evocative museum and North America's largest artificial waterfalls are as much a symbol of hope and renewal as they are a tribute to the victims of terrorism.

Great For...

☑ Don't Miss

Santiago Calatrava's dramatic WTC Transportation Hub, located next to the museum, which was inspired by the image of a child releasing a dove.

The National September 11 Memorial and Museum is a dignified tribute to the victims of the worst terrorist attack on American soil. Titled *Reflecting Absence*, the memorial's two massive reflecting pools are a symbol of renewal and commemorate the thousands who lost their lives. Beside them stands the Memorial Museum, a striking, solemn space documenting that horrific fall day in 2001.

Reflecting Pools

Surrounded by a plaza planted with 400 swamp white oak trees, the 9/11 Memorial's reflecting pools occupy the very footprints of the ill-fated twin towers. From their rim, a steady cascade of water pours 30ft down toward a central void. The flow of the water is richly symbolic, beginning as hundreds of smaller

National September 11 Memorial & Museum

National
September 11
Memorial &
Museum

Vesey St

West St (West Side Hwy)

Brookfield
Place

Memorial
Pool

Chambers St-
WTC

Church St

World Trade Center
Transportation Hub

Cortlandt St

ⓘ Need to Know

Map p246; www.911memorial.org; 180 Green-
wich St; ⏰7:30am-9pm; Ⓢ E to World Trade
Center; R/W to Cortlandt St; 2/3 to Park Pl
FREE

✕ Take a Break

Head up to Tribeca for great dining
options such as Locanda Verde (p124).

★ Top Tip

To minimize queuing, purchase
tickets online or at one of the vending
machines outside the museum building.

streams, merging into a massive torrent
of collective confusion, and ending with
a slow journey toward an abyss. Bronze
panels frame the pools, inscribed with the
names of those who died in the terrorist
attacks of September 11, 2001, and in
the World Trade Center car bombing on
February 26, 1993. Designed by Michael
Arad and Peter Walker, the pools are both
striking and deeply poignant.

Memorial Museum

The contemplative energy of the memorial
is further enhanced by the **National September 11 Memorial Museum** (Map p246;
www.911memorial.org/museum; 180 Greenwich
St; memorial free, museum adult/child $24/15,
5-8pm Tue free; ⏰9am-8pm Sun-Thu, to 9pm Fri
& Sat, last entry 2hr before close; Ⓢ E to World
Trade Center; R/W to Cortlandt St; 2/3 to Park Pl).

Standing between the reflective pools,
the museum's glass entrance pavilion
eerily evokes a toppled tower. Inside the
entrance, an escalator leads down to the
museum's main subterranean lobby. On
the descent, visitors stand in the shadow
of two steel tridents, originally embedded
in the bedrock at the base of the North
Tower. Each standing over 80ft tall and
weighing 50 tons, they once provided the
structural support that allowed the towers
to soar over 1360ft into the sky. In the
subsequent sea of rubble, they remained
standing, becoming immediate symbols
of resilience.

The tridents are two of more than
10,300 objects in the museum's collection. Among these are the Vesey Street
Stairs; dubbed the 'survivors staircase,'
they allowed hundreds of workers to flee
the WTC site on the morning of 9/11. At
the bottom of these stairs is the moving
In Memoriam gallery, its walls lined with
the photographs and names of those who
perished. Interactive touch screens and a

central reflection room shed light on the victims' lives. Their humanity is further fleshed out by the numerous personal effects on display. Among these is a dust-covered wallet belonging to Robert Joseph Gschaar, an insurance underwriter working on level 92 of the South Tower. The wallet's contents include a photograph of Gschaar's wife, Myrta, and a $2 bill, twin to the one given to Myrta by Gschaar as a symbol of their second chance at happiness.

Around the corner from the In Memoriam gallery is the New York City Fire Department's Engine Company 21. One of the largest artifacts on display, its burnt-out cab is testament to the inferno faced by those at the scene. The fire engine stands at the entrance to the museum's main Historical Exhibition. Divided into three sections – Events of the Day, Before 9/11 and After 9/11 – its collection of videos, real-time audio recordings, images, objects and testimonies provide a rich, meditative exploration of the tragedy, the events that preceded it (including the WTC bombing of 1993), and the stories of grief, resilience and hope that followed.

The Historical Exhibition spills into the monumental Foundation Hall, flanked by a massive section of the original slurry wall, built to hold back the waters of the Hudson River during the towers' construction. It's also home to the last steel column removed during the clean-up, adorned with the messages and mementos of recovery workers, responders and loved ones of the victims.

What's Nearby?

St Paul's Chapel Church

(Map p246; ☏212-602-0800; www.trinitywall
street.org; 209 Broadway, at Fulton St; ⊙10am-6pm
Mon-Sat, 7am-6pm Sun, churchyard closes 4pm;
Ⓢ A/C, J/Z, 2/3, 4/5 to Fulton St; R/W to Cortlandt
St; E to Chambers St) After his inauguration
in 1789, George Washington worshipped
at this classic revival brownstone chapel,
which found new fame in the aftermath of
September 11. With the World Trade Center
destruction occurring just a block away,
the mighty structure became a spiritual
support and volunteer center, movingly
documented in its exhibition 'Unwavering
Spirit: Hope & Healing at Ground Zero.'

Through photographs, personal objects
and messages of support, the exhibition
honors both the victims and the volunteers
who worked round the clock, serving meals,
setting up beds, doling out massages and
counseling rescue workers.

Trinity Church Church

(Map p246; ☏212-602-0800; www.trinitywall
street.org; 75 Broadway, at Wall St; ⊙7am-6pm;
Ⓢ 1, R/W to Rector St; 2/3, 4/5 to Wall St) New
York City's tallest building upon completion
in 1846, Trinity Church features a 280ft-high
bell tower and a richly colored stained-glass
window over the altar. Famous residents
of its serene cemetery include Founding Father Alexander Hamilton, while its
excellent music series includes Concerts at
One (1pm Thursdays) and magnificent choir
concerts, including an annual December
rendition of Handel's *Messiah*.

African Burial Ground National Monument Memorial

(☏212-637-2019; www.nps.gov/afbg; 290
Broadway, btwn Duane & Reade Sts; ⊙memo-
rial 10am-4pm Tue-Sat Apr-Oct, visitor center
10am-4pm Tue-Sat year-round; Ⓢ J/Z to Chambers
St; R/W to City Hall; 4/5/6 to Brooklyn Bridge-City
Hall) **FREE** In 1991, construction workers
here uncovered more than 400 stacked
wooden caskets, just 16ft to 28ft below
street level. The boxes contained the
remains of both enslaved and free African
Americans from the 17th and 18th centuries
(nearby Trinity Church would not allow
them to be buried in its graveyard). Today, a
poignant memorial site and a visitor center
with educational displays honor the estimated 15,000 men, women and children
buried here.

☑ Don't Miss

In the museum, look out for the so-called
'Angel of 9/11,' the eerie outline of a
woman's anguished face on a twisted
girder believed to originate from the
point where American Airlines Flight 11
slammed into the North Tower.

TONY SHI PHOTOGRAPHY/GETTY IMAGES ©

✗ Take a Break

Inside Brookfield Place (p124), you'll
find a string of chef-driven dining spots
and a French food emporium.

JUNTASK/GETTY IMAGES ©

One World Trade Center

Soaring above the city skyline is this shimmering tower, a symbol of Lower Manhattan's rebirth. Its observation decks offer mesmerizing views over the vast metropolis (and surrounding states).

Filling what was a sore and glaring gap in the Lower Manhattan skyline, One World Trade Center symbolizes rebirth, determination and a city's resilience. More than just another super-tall building, this tower is a richly symbolic giant, well aware of the past yet firmly focused on the future. For lovers of New York, it's also the hot new stop for dizzying, unforgettable urban views.

The Building

Leaping up from the northwest corner of the World Trade Center site, the 104-floor tower is architect David M Childs' redesign of Daniel Libeskind's original 2002 concept. Not only the loftiest building in America, this tapered giant is currently the tallest building in the Western Hemisphere, not to mention the fourth tallest in the world by pinnacle height. The tower soars skywards

---

Great For...

☑ **Don't Miss**

The staggering view from the base of the tower looking skyward.

ℹ Need to Know

One WTC; Map p246; cnr West & Vesey Sts; Ⓢ E to World Trade Center; 2/3 to Park Pl; A/C, J/Z, 4/5 to Fulton St; R/W to Cortlandt St

☆ Famous Residents

The building's most famous tenant is Condé Nast Publications, which made the move from 4 Times Square in 2014.

★ Top Tip

You can save a bit of time in line by pre-purchasing your tickets online (www.oneworldobservatory.com).

One thing that wasn't foreseen by the architects and engineers was the antenna's noisy disposition; the strong winds that race through its lattice design produce a haunting, howling sound known to keep some locals up at night.

One World Observatory

Not one to downplay its assets, the skyscraper is home to **One World Observatory** (Map p246; ☏ 844-696-1776; www.oneworldobservatory.com; cnr West & Vesey Sts; adult/child $34/28; ⊙ 9am-8pm, last ticket sold at 7:15pm; Ⓢ E to World Trade Center; 2/3 to Park Pl; A/C, J/Z, 4/5 to Fulton St; R/W to Cortlandt St), the city's loftiest observation deck. While the observatory spans levels 100 to 102, the experience begins at the ground-floor Global Welcome Center, where an electronic world map highlights the homeland of visitors (data relayed from ticket scans). The bitter bickering that plagued much of the project's development is all but forgotten in the adjoining Voices exhibition, where architects and construction workers wax lyrically about the tower's formation on 144 video screens.

with chamfered edges. The result is a series of isosceles triangles that, seen from the building's base, reach to infinity.

Crowning the structure is a 408ft cabled-stayed spire. Co-designed by sculptor Kenneth Snelson, it brings the building's total height to 1776ft, a symbolic reference to the year of American independence. Indeed, symbolism feeds several aspects of the building: the tower's footprint is equal to those of the twin towers, while the observation decks match the heights of those in the old complex. Unlike the original towers, however, One WTC was built with a whole new level of safety in mind, its precautionary features including a 200ft-high blast-resistant base (clad in over 2000 pieces of glimmering prismatic glass) and 1m-thick concrete walls encasing all elevators, stairwells, and communication and safety systems.

After a quick rundown of the site's geology, the real thrills begin as you step inside one of five Sky Pod elevators, among the fastest in the world. As the elevators begin their 1250ft skyward journey, LED wall panels kick into action. Suddenly, you're in a veritable time machine, watching Manhattan's evolution from forested island to teeming concrete jungle. Forty-seven seconds (and 500 years) later, you're on level 102, where another short presentation ends with a spectacular reveal.

Skip the overpriced eateries on level 101 and continue down to the real highlight: level 100. Waiting for you is an epic, 360-degree panorama guaranteed to keep your index finger busy pointing out landmarks, from the Brooklyn and Manhattan Bridges, to Lady Liberty and the Woolworth, Empire State and Chrysler Buildings. If you need a hand, interactive mobile tablets are available for hire ($15). As expected, the view is extraordinary (choose a clear day!), taking in all five boroughs and adjoining states.

What's Nearby?

Woolworth Building Notable Building
(Map p246; ☎203-966-9663; www.woolworth tours.com; 233 Broadway, at Park Pl; 30/60/90min tours $20/30/45; ⓢR/W to City Hall; 2/3 to Park Pl; 4/5/6 to Brooklyn Bridge-City Hall) The world's tallest building upon completion in 1913, Cass Gilbert's 60-story, 792ft-tall Woolworth Building is a neo-Gothic marvel, elegantly clad in masonry and terracotta. Surpassed in height by the Chrysler Building in 1930, its landmarked lobby

Woolworth Building

is a breathtaking spectacle of dazzling, Byzantine-like mosaics. The lobby is only accessible on prebooked guided tours, which also offer insight into the building's more curious original features, among them a dedicated subway entrance and a secret swimming pool.

At its dedication, the building was described as a 'cathedral of commerce'; though meant as an insult, FW Woolworth, head of the five-and-dime chain-store empire headquartered there, took the comment as a compliment and began throwing the term around himself.

★ Did You Know?

One World Trade Center has green credentials, including a gray-water system that collects and uses rainwater and building materials made substantially of post-industrial recycled content.

Federal Reserve Bank of New York Notable Building

(Map p246; ☎212-720-6130; www.newyorkfed.org; 33 Liberty St, at Nassau St, entrance at 44 Maiden Lane; reservation required; 🕑guided tours 1pm & 2pm Mon-Fri; [S]A/C, J/Z, 2/3, 4/5 to Fulton St)

[FREE] The best reason to visit the Federal Reserve Bank is the chance to (briefly) ogle at its high-security vault – more than 10,000 tons of gold reserves reside here, 80ft below ground. You'll only see a small part of that fortune, but signing on to a free tour (the only way down; book several months ahead) is worth the effort.

While you don't need to join a guided tour to browse the bank's interactive museum, which delves into the bank's history and research, you will still need to book a time online. Bring your passport or other official ID.

LITTLENYSTOCK/SHUTTERSTOCK ©

Lower East Side Tenement Museum

In a neighborhood once teeming with immigrants, this museum opens a window to the past on guided tours through meticulously preserved tenements. You'll learn all about real people who lived on these densely packed streets.

Great For...

❶ Need to Know

Map p248; ☎877-975-3786; www.tenement. org; 103 Orchard St, btwn Broome & Delancey Sts, Lower East Side; tours adult/student & senior $25/20; ⊙10am-6:30pm Fri-Wed, to 8:30pm Thu; ⓢB/D to Grand St; J/M/Z to Essex St; F to Delancey St

★ **Top Tip**

Watch the free 30-minute film shown in the visitor center that gives an overview of immigrant life in NYC.

There's no museum in New York that humanizes the city's colorful past quite like the Lower East Side Tenement Museum, which puts the neighborhood's heart-breaking but inspiring heritage on full display in several re-creations of former tenements. Always evolving and expand-ing, the museum has a variety of tours and talks beyond the museum's walls – a must for anyone interested in old New York.

Inside the Tenement

A wide range of tenement tours lead visitors into the building where hundreds of immigrants lived and worked over the years. Hard Times, one of the most popular tours, visits apartments from two different time periods – the 1870s and the 1930s. There you'll see the squalid conditions tenants faced – in the early days there was a wretched communal outhouse, and no electricity or running water – and what life was like for the families who lived there. Other tours focus on Irish immigrants and the harsh discrimination they faced, sweatshop workers and 'shop life' (with a tour through a re-created 1870s German beer hall).

103 Orchard Street

The visitor center at 103 Orchard St has a museum shop and a small screening room that plays an original film. Several evenings a month, the museum hosts talks here, often relating to the present immigrant experience in America. The building itself was, naturally, a tenement, too – ask the staff about the interesting families of East European and Italian descent that once dwelled here.

Meet Victoria

Travel back to 1916 and meet Victoria Confino, a 14-year-old girl from a Greek Sephardic family. Played by a costumed interpreter, Victoria interacts with visitors answering questions about what her life was like in those days. It's especially rec-ommended for kids, as visitors are free to handle household objects.

Neighborhood Tours

A great way to understand the immigrant experience is on a walking tour around the neighborhood. These tours, ranging from 75 minutes to two hours, explore a variety of topics. Foods of the Lower East Side looks at the ways traditional foods have shaped American cuisine; Then & Now explores the way the neighborhood has changed over the decades; and Outside the Home looks at life beyond the apartment – where immigrants stored (and lost) their life savings, the churches and synagogues so integral to community life, and the meeting halls where poorly paid workers gathered to fight for better conditions.

What's Nearby?

New Museum of
Contemporary Art   Museum

(Map p248; ☑212-219-1222; www.newmuseum.org; 235 Bowery, btwn Stanton & Rivington Sts, Lower East Side; adult/child $18/free, 7-9pm Thu by dona-tion; ⏰11am-6pm Tue, Wed & Fri-Sun, to 9pm Thu; ⓢR/W to Prince St; F to 2nd Ave; J/Z to Bowery; 6 to Spring St) Rising above the neighborhood, the New Museum of Contemporary Art is a sight to behold: a seven-story stack of off-kilter, white, ethereal boxes designed by Tokyo-based architects Kazuyo Sejima and Ryue Nishizawa of SANAA and the New York–based firm Gensler. It was a long-awaited breath of fresh air along what was a completely gritty Bowery strip when it arrived back in 2007 – though since its opening, many glossy new constructions have joined it, quickly transforming this once down-and-out avenue.

Founded in 1977 by Marcia Tucker and housed in five different locations over the years, the museum's mission statement is simple: 'New art, new ideas.' The institution gave gallery space to artists Keith Haring, Jeff Koons, Joan Jonas, Mary Kelly and Andres Serrano at the beginning of their careers, and continues to show contem-porary heavy hitters. In fact, the city's sole museum dedicated to contemporary art has brought a steady menu of edgy works in new forms.

☑ **Don't Miss**

A peek into the 1870s and the 1930s on the Hard Times tour.

BUYENLARGE/CONTRIBUTOR/GETTY IMAGES ©

✕ **Take a Break**

Take a bite out of history at famed Jewish deli Russ & Daughters (p150), in business since 1914.

Audubon Center Boathouse (p105)

Prospect Park

Brooklyn's favorite green space is a grassy wonderland of rolling meadows, babbling brooks, hillside overlooks, flower-strewn trails and an open lake. It's a fantastic place for running, walking, picnicking, skating or just getting a dose of the great outdoors.

Great For...

ⓘ Need to Know

Map p256; ☎718-965-8951; www.prospect park.org; Grand Army Plaza; ⏱5am-1am; Ⓢ2/3 to Grand Army Plaza; F to 15th St-Pros-pect Park; B, Q to Prospect Park

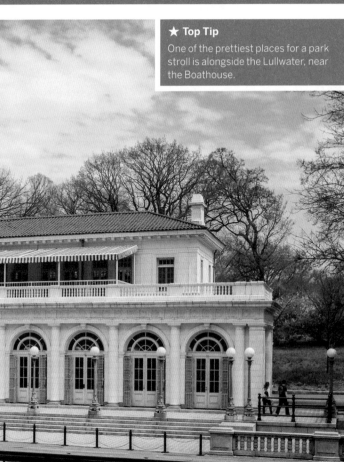

★ Top Tip

One of the prettiest places for a park stroll is alongside the Lullwater, near the Boathouse.

The creators of the 585-acre Prospect Park, Calvert Vaux and Frederick Law Olmsted, considered this an improvement on their other New York project, Central Park. Created in 1866, Prospect Park has many of the same features: a gorgeous meadow, a scenic lake, forested pathways and rambling hills that are straddled with leafy walkways. It receives roughly 10 million visitors a year.

Grand Army Plaza

A large, landscaped traffic circle with a massive ceremonial arch sits at the intersection of Flatbush Ave and Prospect Park West. This marks the beginning of Eastern Parkway and the entrance to Prospect Park. The arch, which was built in the 1890s, is a memorial to Union soldiers who fought in the Civil War.

Long Meadow

The 90-acre Long Meadow, which is bigger than Central Park's Great Lawn, lies to the south of the park's formal entrance at Grand Army Plaza. It's a super strolling and lounging spot, filled with pick-up ball games and families flying kites. On the south end is the Picnic House, with a snack stand and public bathrooms.

Children's Corner

Near Flatbush Ave, the Children's Corner contains a terrific 1912 carousel, originally from Coney Island, and the **Prospect Park Zoo** (Map p256; ☏718-399-7339; www.prospect parkzoo.com; 450 Flatbush Ave; adult/child $8/5; ☉10am-5pm Mon-Fri Apr-Oct, to 4:30pm Nov-Mar; 👬; Ⓢ B, Q to Prospect Park; 2/3 to Grand Army Plaza), featuring sea lions, baboons, wallabies and a small petting

Soldiers and Sailors Memorial Arch, Grand Army Plaza

zoo. To the northeast of the carousel is the 18th-century **Lefferts Historic House** (Map p256; ☏718-789-2822; www.prospectpark. org/lefferts; near Flatbush Ave & Empire Blvd; suggested donation $3; ☉hours vary, closed Jan-Mar; ♿; SB, Q to Prospect Park), which has plenty of old-fashioned toys to goof around with.

Audubon Center Boathouse

Sitting on a northern finger of Prospect Park Lake, the photogenic boathouse hosts a range of activities throughout the year (guided bird-watching sessions, free yoga classes, nature-themed art exhibitions, hands-on craft activities for kids). From here, there is a trailhead for 2.5 miles of woodsy nature trails. Check the website or ask at the boathouse for details.

Lakeside

Prospect Park's newest attraction continues to turn heads. The 26-acre LeFrak Center at Lakeside (p201) complex features skating rinks, as well as a cafe, new walking trails and a small concert space.

What's Nearby?

Brooklyn Botanic Garden   Gardens
(Map p256; ☏718-623-7200; www.bbg.org; 150 Eastern Pkwy; adult/student/child $15/8/ free, 10am-noon Fri free, Tue-Fri Dec-Feb free; ☉8am-6pm Tue-Fri, from 10am Sat & Sun Mar-Oct, hours vary rest of year; ♿; S2/3 to Eastern Pkwy-Brooklyn Museum; B, Q to Prospect Park) One of Brooklyn's most picturesque attractions, this 52-acre garden is home to thousands of plants and trees, as well as a Japanese garden where river turtles swim alongside a Shinto shrine. The best time to visit is late April or early May, when the blooming cherry trees (a gift from Japan) are celebrated in Sakura Matsuri, the Cherry Blossom Festival.

Brooklyn Museum   Museum
(Map p256; ☏718-638-5000; www.brooklyn museum.org; 200 Eastern Pkwy; suggested admission adult/child $16/free; ☉11am-6pm Wed & Fri-Sun, to 10pm Thu, to 11pm 1st Sat of month Oct-Aug; ♿; S2/3 to Eastern Pkwy-Brooklyn Museum) This encyclopedic museum is housed in a five-story, 560,000-sq-ft beaux-arts building designed by McKim, Mead & White. Today, the building houses more than 1.5 million objects, including ancient artifacts, 19th-century period rooms, and sculptures and paintings from across several centuries. The museum offers a great alternative to the packed-to-the-gills institutions in Manhattan.

🍴 **Take a Break**

Near the park's north entrance, friendly Cheryl's Global Soul (p139) is a neighborhood favorite.

Brooklyn Bridge Park

The pride and joy of Brooklyn, this revitalized waterfront park offers loads of amusement, with playgrounds, walkways, and lawns with plenty of summertime outdoor entertainment, including live music and open-air cinema, not to mention grand views of Manhattan skyscrapers across the river.

Great For...

❶ Need to Know

Map p256; ☎718-222-9939; www.brooklyn bridgepark.org; East River Waterfront, btwn Atlantic Ave & John St, Brooklyn Heights/ Dumbo; ⊙6am-1am, some sections to 11pm, playgrounds to dusk; 👪; 🚌B63 to Pier 6/ Brooklyn Bridge Park; B25 to Old Fulton St/ Elizabeth Pl, 🚢East River or South Brooklyn routes to Dumbo/Pier 1, 🚇A/C to High St; 2/3 to Clark St; F to York St FREE

★ **Top Tip**

Be sure to check out what's on when you're in town: the website lists outdoor yoga and dance classes, theater and cinema, family activities and more.

This 85-acre park, nearing completion, is one of Brooklyn's most talked-about new sights. Wrapping around a bend on the East River, it runs for 1.3 miles from Jay St in Dumbo to the west end of Atlantic Ave in Cobble Hill. It has revitalized a once-barren stretch of shoreline, turning a series of abandoned piers into public parkland.

Empire Fulton Ferry

Just east of the Brooklyn Bridge, in the northern section of Dumbo, you'll find a state park with a grassy lawn that faces the East River. Near the water is **Jane's Carousel** (Map p256; ☎718-222-2502; www.janescarousel.com; Old Dock St, Brooklyn Bridge Park, Dumbo; tickets $2; 🕐11am-7pm Wed-Mon mid-May–mid-Sep, to 6pm Thu-Sun mid-Sep–mid-May; 👪; [S]F to York St; A/C to High St), a lovingly restored 1922 carousel set inside a glass pavilion designed by Pritzker Prize–winning architect Jean Nouvel. The park is bordered on one side by the **Empire Stores & Tobacco Warehouse** (Map p256; www.empirestoresdumbo.com; 53-83 Water St, near Main St, Dumbo; 🕐8am-7:30pm; 🚌B25 to Water/Main Sts, [S]F to York St; A/C to High St), a series of Civil War–era structures that house restaurants, shops and a theater. Keep heading up to the Manhattan Bridge to find a new bouldering wall. There's also a much-loved playground, which resembles a pirate ship.

Pier 1

A 9-acre pier just south of the Empire Fulton Ferry is home to a stretch of park featuring a playground, walkways and the Harbor View and Bridge View Lawns, both of which overlook the river. On the

View from Brooklyn Heights Promenade

Bridge View Lawn, you'll find artist Mark di Suvero's 30ft kinetic sculpture *Yoga* (1991). From July through August, free outdoor films are screened on the Harbor View Lawn against a stunning backdrop of Manhattan. Other free open-air events happen throughout the summer. The seasonal Brooklyn Bridge Garden Bar (brooklynbridgegardenbar.com) can be found on the pier's north end. You can also catch the East River Ferry (www.eastriverferry.com) from the north end of the pier.

Pier 2 & Pier 4

At Pier 2, you'll find courts for basketball, handball and bocce, plus a skating rink.

☑ Don't Miss

The views of Manhattan from Empire Fulton Ferry at sunset.

DROP OF LIGHT/SHUTTERSTOCK ©

Nearby, there's a tiny beach at Pier 4. Though swimming is not allowed, you can hire stand-up paddleboards here. If you want to head up to Brooklyn Heights, you can take a bouncy pedestrian bridge (access near Pier 2).

Pier 5 & Pier 6

At the southern end of the park, off Atlantic Ave, Pier 6 has a fantastic playground and a small water play area for tots (if you're bringing kids, pack swimsuits and towels). Neighboring Pier 5, just north, has walkways, sand volleyball courts, soccer fields and barbecue grills. There's also a few seasonal concessions (May to October), including wood-fired pizza, beer and Italian treats at **Fornino** (Map p256; ☎718-422-1107; www.fornino.com; Pier 6, Brooklyn Bridge Park, Brooklyn Heights; pizzas $10-26; 🕐10am-midnight Memorial Day–mid-Sep, weather permitting Apr, May & Oct; 🚌B63 to Brooklyn Bridge Park/Pier 6, [S]2/3, 4/5 to Borough Hall; R to Court St), which has wood-fired pizzas and rooftop dining at picnic tables with panoramic views. A free seasonal ferry runs on weekends from Pier 6 to **Governors Island** (☎212-825-3045; www.govisland.com; 🕐10am-6pm Mon-Fri, to 7pm Sat & Sun May-Oct; [S]4/5 to Bowling Green; 1 to South Ferry) [FREE].

Still in the works are plans to transform the west end of Pier 6 with meadows, trees and a triangular platform with unrivaled views of Lower Manhattan.

What's Nearby?

Brooklyn Heights Promenade Viewpoint

(Map p256; www.nyharborparks.org; btwn Orange & Remsen Sts, Brooklyn Heights; 🕐24hr; [S]N/R/W to Court St; 2/3 to Clark St; A/C to High St) All of the east–west lanes of Brooklyn Heights (such as Clark and Pineapple Sts) lead to the neighborhood's number-one attraction: a narrow park with breathtaking views of Lower Manhattan and New York Harbor. Though it hangs over the busy Brooklyn–Queens Expressway (BQE), this little slice of urban beauty is a great spot for a sunset walk.

West Village Wandering

Of all the neighborhoods in New York City, the West Village is easily the most walkable, its cobbled corners straying from the signature gridiron that unfurls across the rest of the island. An afternoon stroll is not to be missed; hidden landmarks and quaint cafes abound.

Start Cherry Lane Theater
Finish Washington Sq Park
Distance 1 mile
Duration 1 hour

4 To the north of **Christopher Park** is the **Stonewall Inn** (p225), the starting place of the LGBTIQ+ revolution.

3 For another TV landmark, head to **66 Perry St**, Carrie Bradshaw's apartment in *Sex and the City*.

2 The apartment block at **90 Bedford** was the fictitious home of the cast of *Friends*.

1 Established in 1924, **Cherry Lane Theater** (p186) is the city's longest continuously running off-Broadway establishment.

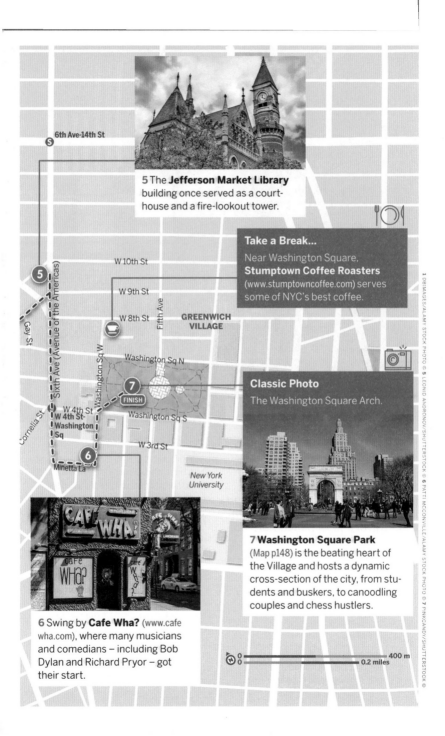

5 The **Jefferson Market Library** building once served as a courthouse and a fire-lookout tower.

Take a Break...

Near Washington Square, **Stumptown Coffee Roasters** (www.stumptowncoffee.com) serves some of NYC's best coffee.

Classic Photo

The Washington Square Arch.

7 **Washington Square Park** (Map p148) is the beating heart of the Village and hosts a dynamic cross-section of the city, from students and buskers, to canoodling couples and chess hustlers.

6 Swing by **Cafe Wha?** (www.cafe wha.com), where many musicians and comedians – including Bob Dylan and Richard Pryor – got their start.

6th Ave-14th St

W 10th St
W 9th St
W 8th St
GREENWICH VILLAGE
Washington Sq N
Washington Sq S
W 4th St
W 4th St-Washington Sq
W 3rd St
Minetta La
New York University
Gay St
Sixth Ave (Avenue of the Americas)
Washington Sq W
Fifth Ave
Cornelia St

7 FINISH
5

0   400 m
0   0.2 miles

1 DBIMAGES/ALAMY STOCK PHOTO © 5 LEONID ANDRONOV/SHUTTERSTOCK © 6 PATTI MCCONVILLE/ALAMY STOCK PHOTO © 7 PINKCANDY/SHUTTERSTOCK ©

Grand Central Terminal

This cathedral of transportation is New York's most breathtaking beaux-arts building. Its chandeliers, marble and historic bars and restaurants are from an era when train travel and romance were not mutually exclusive.

Great For...

☑ Don't Miss

Mouthwatering morsels await at Grand Central Market, a 240ft corridor lined with fresh produce and artisan treats.

42nd Street Facade

Clad in Connecticut Stony Creek granite at its base and Indiana limestone on top, Grand Central's showpiece facade is crowned by America's greatest monumental sculpture, *The Glory of Commerce*. Designed by the French sculptor Jules Coutan, the piece was executed in Long Island City by local carvers Donnelly and Ricci. Once completed, it was hoisted up, piece by piece, in 1914. Its protagonist is a wing-capped Mercury, the Roman god of travel and commerce. To the left is Hercules in an unusually placid stance, while looking down on the mayhem of 42nd St is Minerva, the ancient guardian of cities. The clock beneath Mercury's foot contains the largest example of Tiffany glass in the world.

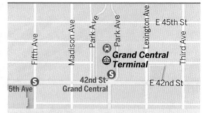

❶ Need to Know

Map p254; www.grandcentralterminal.com; 89 E 42nd St, at Park Ave; ◷5:30am-2am; 🆂S, 4/5/6, 7 to Grand Central-42nd St

✕ Take a Break

Stop by The Campbell (p173) for a top-shelf cocktail in swanky surrounds.

★ Top Tip

Come back at night, when the calmness gives the hallways an almost sacred vibe.

again. Enter renovation architects Beyer Blinder Belle, who restored the work, but left a tiny patch of soot (in the northwest corner) as testament to just what a fine job they did.

Main Concourse

Grand Central's trump card is more akin to a glorious ballroom than a thoroughfare. The marble floors are Tennessee pink, while the vintage ticket counters are Italian Bottocino marble. The vaulted ceiling is (quite literally) heavenly, its turquoise and gold-leaf mural depicting eight constellations...backwards. A mistake? Apparently not. Its French designer, painter Paul César Helleu, wished to depict the stars from God's point of view – from the out, looking in. The original, frescoed execution of Helleu's design was by New York–based artists J Monroe Hewlett and Charles Basing. Moisture damage saw it faithfully repainted (alas, not in fresco form) by Charles Gulbrandsen in 1944. By the 1990s, however, the mural was in ruins

What's Nearby?

Chrysler Building   Historic Building
(Map p254; 405 Lexington Ave, at E 42nd St; ◷lobby 8am-6pm Mon-Fri; 🆂S, 4/5/6, 7 to Grand Central-42nd St) Designed by William Van Alen in 1930, the 77-floor Chrysler Building is prime-time architecture: a fusion of moderne and Gothic aesthetics, adorned with steel eagles and topped by a spire that screams *Bride of Frankenstein*. The building was constructed as the headquarters for Walter P Chrysler and his automobile empire; unable to compete on the production line with bigger rivals Ford and General Motors, Chrysler trumped them on the skyline, and with one of Gotham's most beautiful lobbies.

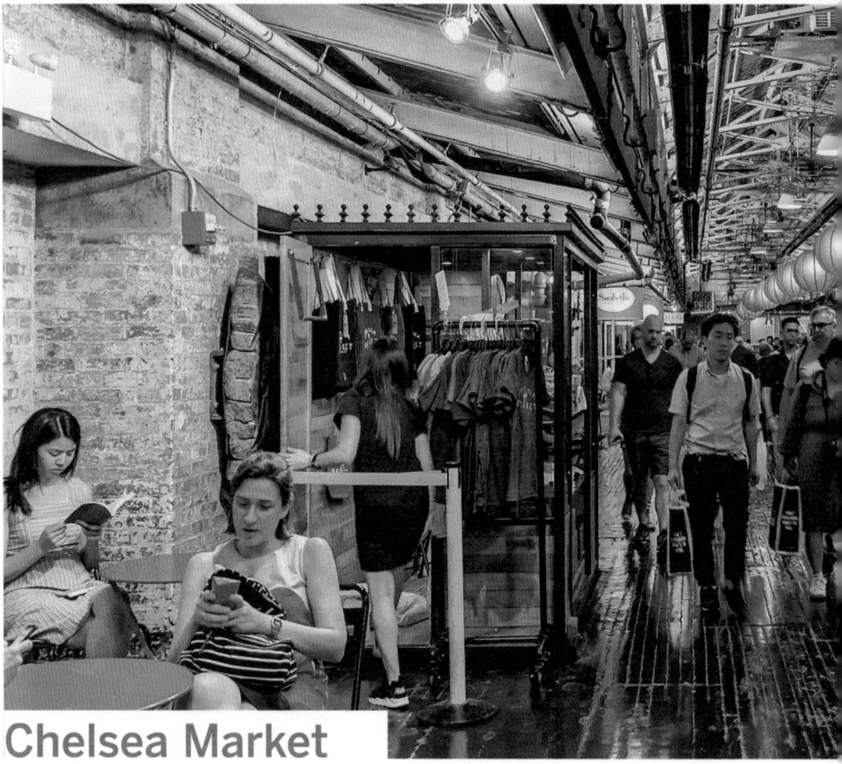

Chelsea Market

In a shining example of redevelopment and preservation, the Chelsea Market has transformed a former factory into a shopping concourse that caters to foodies and fashionistas.

The long brick edifice occupied by Chelsea Market was built in the 1890s to house a massive bakery complex that became the headquarters of the National Biscuit Company (better known as Nabisco, makers of Saltines, Fig Newtons and Oreos). The market, which opened in the 1990s, is now a base camp for gourmet outlets and apparel boutiques.

Foodie Hub

More than two dozen food vendors ply their temptations, including Mokbar (ramen with Korean accents), Takumi tacos (mixing Japanese and Mexican ingredients), Tuck Shop (Aussie-style savory pies), Bar Suzette (crepes), Num Pang (Cambodian sandwiches), Ninth St Espresso (perfect lattes), Doughnuttery (piping hot mini-doughnuts) and L'Arte de Gelato (rich ice cream). Also

Great For...

🍽️ 🛍️ ☕

☑ **Don't Miss**

Fusion tacos from Takumi and a browse through the stalls at Artists and Fleas.

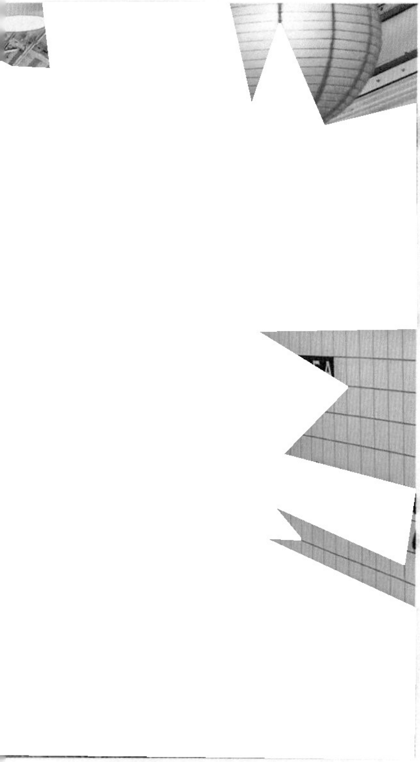

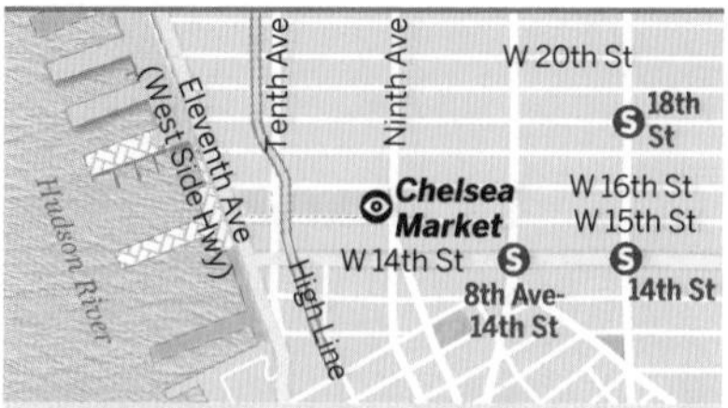

Need to Know

Map p252; ☎212-652-2121; www.chelseamarket.com; 75 Ninth Ave, btwn 15th & 16th Sts; ⏰7am-9pm Mon-Sat, 8am-8pm Sun; [S]A/C/E, L to 8th Ave-14th St

🍴 Take a Break

Hop up to the High Line (p52) from the entrance on 16th St and Tenth Ave to grab some fresh air.

★ Top Tip

Get your food to go – seating is limited at most of the eateries.

worth visiting is one of the market's longtime tenants, The Lobster Place (overstuffed lobster rolls and killer sushi).

If you're after something more indulgent, linger over a meal at the Green Table, which serves farm-fresh organic ingredients; sample the first-rate seafood and raw bar at Cull & Pistol; or stop by Friedman's Lunch for upscale American comfort food.

Or for foodie souvenirs, visit Bowery Kitchen Supply to browse a dizzying array of cooking odds and ends.

Discount Fashion Bonanzas

Those looking for a bargain on high-end fashions should head to the event space near the Ninth Ave entrance. There are frequent pop-up shops and sample sales featuring racks of discounted men's and women's clothing. At the other end of the market near the Tenth Ave entrance is Artists and Fleas, a permanent market for local designers and craftspeople to sell their wares. It's the place to stop for a quirky new wallet, trendy pair of sunglasses or a piece of statement jewelry.

There's also a large Anthropologie at the Ninth Ave entrance. The clothing is located on the basement level, where you'll also find an impressively large discount rack.

Browsing & Business Spaces

Browse the various nonfood offerings at Imports from Marrakesh, which specializes in Moroccan art and design; check out the latest literary hits at Posman Books; or pick up a bottle at the expert-staffed Chelsea Wine Vault.

The market only takes up the lower part of a larger, million-sq-ft space, occupying a full city block, which is the current home of TV channels the Food Network, Oxygen Network and NY1, the local news channel. Cellists and bluegrass players fill the main walkway with music, and the High Line passes right by the rear of the building.

Ruby's, on the Riegelmann Boardwalk

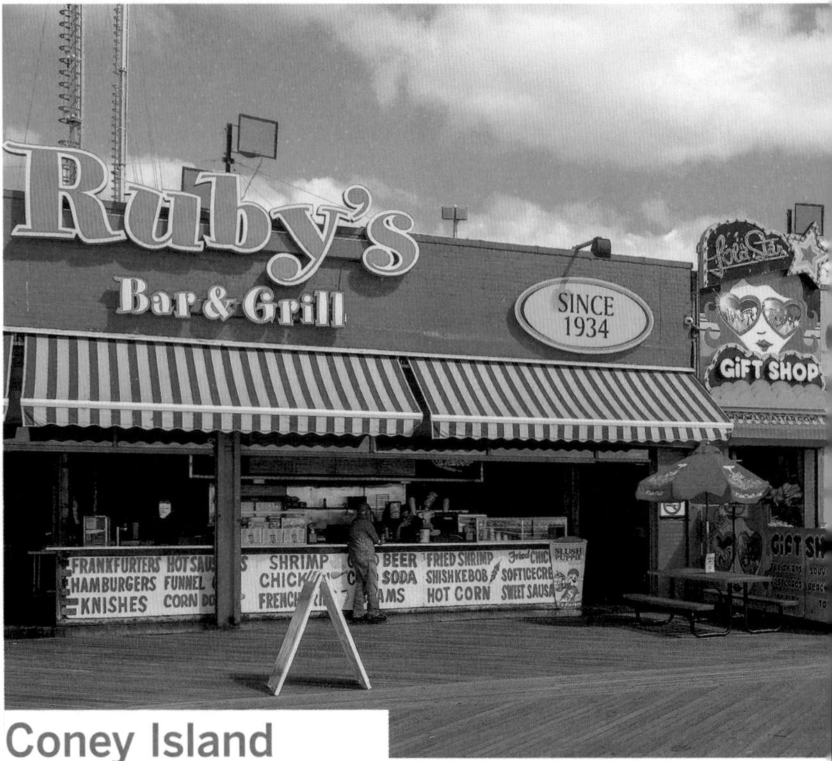

ALESSIO CATELLI/SHUTTERSTOCK ©

Coney Island

One of New York's most popular beachside amusement areas, Coney Island draws summertime crowds for hot dogs, roller coasters, minor-league baseball games and strolls down the boardwalk.

Great For...

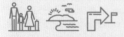

☑ Don't Miss

Ride the Cyclone, then head to the boardwalk for a cold beer.

Seaside Fun By Day

Coney Island – a name synonymous in American culture with seaside fun and frolicking in days of yore – achieved world-wide fame as a working-class amusement park and beach-resort area at the turn of the 20th century. After decades of seedy decline, its kitschy charms have experienced a 21st-century revival. Though it's no longer the booming, peninsula-wide attraction it once was, it still draws crowds of tourists and locals alike for roller-coaster rides, hot dogs and beer on the beachside boardwalk.

Luna Park (☎718-373-5862; www.lunaparknyc.com; Surf Ave, at 10th St; ⏰Apr-Oct; [S]D/F, N/Q to Coney Island-Stillwell Ave) is one of Coney Island's most popular amusement parks and contains one of its most legendary rides: the Cyclone ($10),

Deno's Wonder Wheel

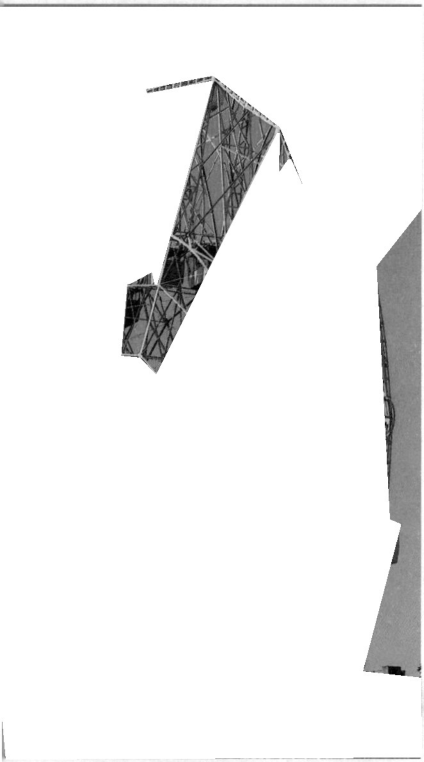

ALESSIO CATELLI/SHUTTERSTOCK ©

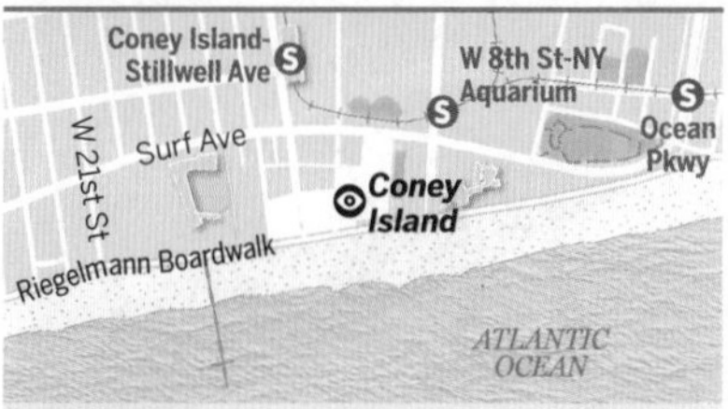

Need to Know

www.coneyisland.com; Surf Ave & Boardwalk, btwn W 15th & W 8th Sts; S D/F, N/Q to Coney Island-Stillwell Ave

Take a Break

Totonno's (☎718-372-8606; www.totonnosconeyisland.com; 1524 Neptune Ave, near W 16th St; pizzas $18-21, toppings $2.50; ⏰noon-8pm Thu-Sun; ✍; S D/F, N/Q to Coney Island-Stillwell Ave) is one of Brooklyn's oldest and most authentic pizza joints.

★ Top Tip

Go weekdays during the daytime to avoid crowds and long lines.

a wooden roller coaster that reaches speeds of 60mph and makes near-vertical drops. The pink-and-mint-green **Deno's Wonder Wheel** (☎718-372-2592; www.denoswonderwheel.com; 1025 Riegelmann Boardwalk, at W 12th St; rides $8; ⏰from noon Jul & Aug, from noon Sat & Sun Apr-Jun & Sep-Oct; 👪; S D/F, N/Q to Coney Island-Stillwell Ave), at its eponymous Amusement Park, has been delighting New Yorkers since 1920. It is the best place to survey Coney Island from up high.

The hot dog was invented in Coney Island in 1867, and there's no better place to eat one than **Nathan's Famous** (☎718-333-2202; www.nathansfamous.com; 1310 Surf Ave, cnr Stillwell Ave; hot dogs from $4; ⏰10am-midnight; 📶; S D/F to Coney Island-Stillwell Ave), established in 1916. When thirst strikes, head to **Ruby's** (☎718-975-7829; www.rubysbar.com; 1213 Riegelmann Boardwalk, btwn Stillwell Ave & 12th St; ⏰11am-10pm Sun-Thu, to 1am Fri & Sat Apr-Sep, weekends only Oct; S D/F, N/Q to Coney Island-Stillwell Ave), a legendary dive bar right on the boardwalk.

...and By Night

Cap off your day with an evening game of minor-league baseball to cheer on the **Brooklyn Cyclones** (☎718-372-5596; www.brooklyncyclones.com; 1904 Surf Ave, at 17th St; tickets $10-20, all tickets on Wed $10; S D/F, N/Q to Coney Island-Stillwell Ave) – especially if they're playing crosstown rivals the Staten Island Yankees – or else just relax with some beer on the boardwalk and watch the sun go down. If you're there on a Friday night in July or August, stick around for the fireworks show at 9:30pm.

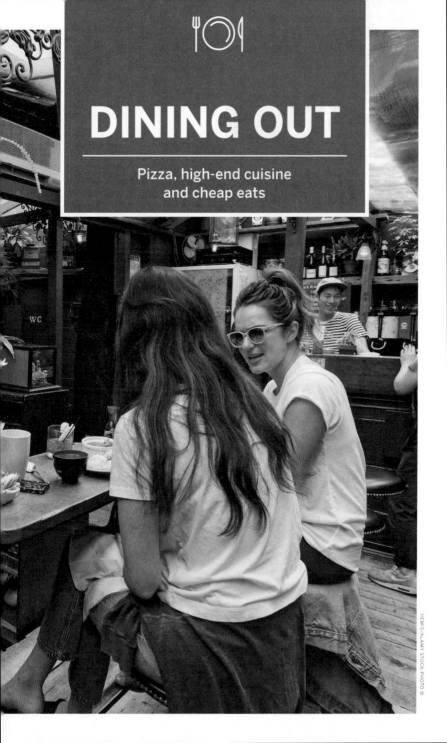

DINING OUT

Pizza, high-end cuisine
and cheap eats

Dining Out

From inspired iterations of world cuisine to quintessentially local nibbles, New York City's dining scene is infinite, all-consuming and a proud testament to its kaleidoscope of citizens. Even if you're not an obsessive foodie hitting ethnic enclaves or the newest cult-chef openings, an outstanding meal is always only a block away.

Unlike California or the South, New York doesn't have one defining cuisine. Food in this multicultural town is global by definition, and just like the city itself, it's a scene that's constantly evolving, driven by insatiable ambition.

In This Section

Price Ranges & Tipping

The following price ranges refer to a main dish, exclusive of tax and tip:

$ under $15

$$ $15–25

$$$ more than $25

New Yorkers tip between 18% and 20% of the final price of the meal. For takeout, it's polite to drop a few dollars in the tip jar.

Harlem & Upper Manhattan
Comfort cuisine meets global flavors (p137)

Upper West Side
A few top eats tucked between
apartment blocks (p137)

Upper East Side
Ladies who lunch meet
cafe culture (p135)

Midtown
Fine dining, cocktail-literate
bistros and old-school delis (p134)

**West Village, Chelsea &
Meatpacking District**
See-and-be-seen brunch spots, wine
bars and New American darlings (p128)

Union Square, Flatiron District & Gramercy
Everything from Michelin-starred
meccas to parkside burgers (p132)

SoHo & Chinatown
Dirt-cheap noodles, hip cafes and
fashionable foodie hangouts (p125)

East Village & Lower East Side
Unpretentious spectrum of eats,
from Asia to the Middle East (p127)

**Financial District &
Lower Manhattan**
Celebrity-chef hot spots and a gourmet
French marketplace (p124)

Brooklyn
Neighborhood pizzerias, Michelin-star
dining and retro–New American fare (p138)

Useful Blogs & Websites

Yelp (www.yelp.com) Comprehensive listings
and reviews.

Open Table (www.opentable.com) Click-and-
book reservation service.

Tasting Table (www.tastingtable.com) Sends
out handy news blasts about the latest and
greatest.

The Infatuation (www.theinfatuation.com/
new-york) Searches reviews and guides to
compile restaurant info.

Grub Street (www.grubstreet.com) In-the-
know articles on NYC dining.

Classic NYC Dishes

Bagel A great start to the day, best
served with cream cheese and lox
(smoked salmon).

Pizza The perfect anytime snack,
served up at ubiquitous pizza parlors.

Hot Dog Served both high- and low-
brow style, best with brown mustard
and caramelized onions.

New York–Style Cheesecake Iconic
dessert with cream cheese and a cookie
crust.

The Best...

Experience New York City's finest eating establishments.

By Budget

$

Taïm (p128) Outstanding falafel sandwiches at downtown locations.

Mamoun's (p127) Famous, spicy shawarma sandwiches at rock-bottom prices.

Le Grainne (p130) Good-value French restaurant in Chelsea.

$$

Upstate (p127) A seafood feast awaits in the East Village.

Jeffrey's Grocery (p132) Much-loved West Village neighborhood spot.

Babu Ji (p129) A celebration of Indian street food in a cheeky Village dining room.

$$$

Eleven Madison Park (p133) Arresting, cutting-edge cuisine laced with unexpected whimsy.

Blue Hill (p132) A West Village classic using ingredients sourced straight from the upstate farm.

Degustation (p128) A tiny East Village eatery where you can watch the chefs create edible works of art.

For Upscale Groceries

Eataly (pictured above; p132) A mecca for lovers of Italian food.

Union Square Greenmarket (p152) Delicious veggies and bakery items from upstate producers.

Le District (p125) A sprawling food emporium on the Hudson packed with Gallic larder essentials.

For Old-School New York

Barney Greengrass (p137) Perfect plates of smoked salmon and sturgeon for over 100 years in the Upper West Side.

Russ & Daughters (pictured above; p150) A celebrated Jewish deli in the Lower East Side.

Zabar's (p157) Upper West Side store selling gourmet, kosher foods since the 1930s.

By Cuisine

Asian

Uncle Boons (p126) Zesty, Michelin-starred Thai with a generous serve of fun in Nolita.

Zenkichi (p139) Candlelit culinary temple of exquisite sushi in Williamsburg.

Lan Larb (p125) Real-deal northeastern Thai in a cheap, cheery hole-in-the-wall on the edge of Chinatown.

Italian

Rosemary's (p129) A beautifully designed West Village spot with memorable cooking.

Barbuto (p129) Serves creative modern Italian fare in a buzzing space in the Meat-packing District.

ViceVersa (p135) Elegant Italian and first-rate brunch spot in the shadow of the Theater District.

Vegetarian & Vegan

Nix (p129) Serving some of the best cruelty-free dishes in the city.

The Butcher's Daughter (pictured above; p126) Inventive vegetarian menu in Nolita.

Modern Love (p139) Comfort-food classics in East Williamsburg with outstanding vegan plates.

Two Boots (p135) Get your pizza fix with vegan and gluten-free options.

COOKSHOP

For Brunch

Locanda Verde (p124) Creative, Italian-inspired dishes in lower Manhattan.

Cookshop (pictured above; p129) Great indoor-outdoor dining spot in west Chelsea.

Cafe Mogador (p127) An icon of the East Village brunch scene.

★ Lonely Planet's Top Choices

Chefs Club (p126) Visiting chefs from around the globe showcase outstanding recipes.

Gramercy Tavern (p133) Prime produce, culinary finesse and the choice of bustling tavern or fine-dining den.

RedFarm (p130) Savvy Sino-fusion dishes boast bold flavors but it doesn't take itself too seriously.

Dovetail (p137) Simplicity is key at this Upper West Side stunner – vegetarians unite on Mondays.

Foragers Table (p130) A triumph of farm-to-table cooking with flavorful sustainable recipes in Chelsea.

🍴 Financial District & Lower Manhattan

Arcade Bakery Bakery $

(Map p248; ☎212-227-7895; www.arcadebakery.com; 220 Church St, btwn Worth & Thomas Sts; pastries from $3, sandwiches $9, pizzas $9-13; 🕒8am-4pm Mon-Fri; [S]1 to Franklin St) It's easy to miss this little treasure in the vaulted lobby of a 1920s office building, with a counter trading in beautiful, just-baked goods. Edibles include artful sandwiches and (between noon and 4pm) a small selection of puff-crust pizzas with combos like mushroom, caramelized onion and goat's cheese. Top of the lot is one of the city's finest almond croissants.

Brookfield Place Food Hall, Market $$

(Map p246; ☎212-978-1698; www.brookfieldplaceny.com; 230 Vesey St, at West St; 📶; [S]E to World Trade Center; 2/3 to Park Pl; R/W to Cortlandt St; 4/5 to Fulton St; A/C to Chambers St) This polished, high-end office and retail complex offers two fabulous food halls. Francophile foodies should hit Le District (p125), a charming and polished marketplace with several stand-alone restaurants and counters selling everything from stinky cheese to steak *frites*. One floor above is **Hudson Eats** (Map p246; ☎212-417-2445; www.brookfieldplaceny.com/directory/food; dishes from $7; 🕒10am-9pm Mon-Sat, noon-7pm Sun; 📶), a fashionable enclave of upmarket fast bites, from sushi and tacos to salads and burgers.

Locanda Verde Italian $$$

(Map p248; ☎212-925-3797; www.locandaverdenyc.com; 377 Greenwich St, at N Moore St; mains lunch $23-34, dinner $25-38; 🕒7am-11pm Mon-Thu, to 11:30pm Fri, 8am-11:30pm Sat, to 11pm Sun; [S]A/C/E to Canal St; 1 to Franklin St) Step through the velvet curtains into a scene of loosened button-downs, black dresses and slick bar staff behind a long, crowded bar. This celebrated brasserie showcases modern, Italo-inspired fare like housemade rigatoni with rabbit *genovese* or grilled swordfish with eggplant caponata. Weekend brunch is no less creative: try scampi and grits or lemon ricotta

Le District

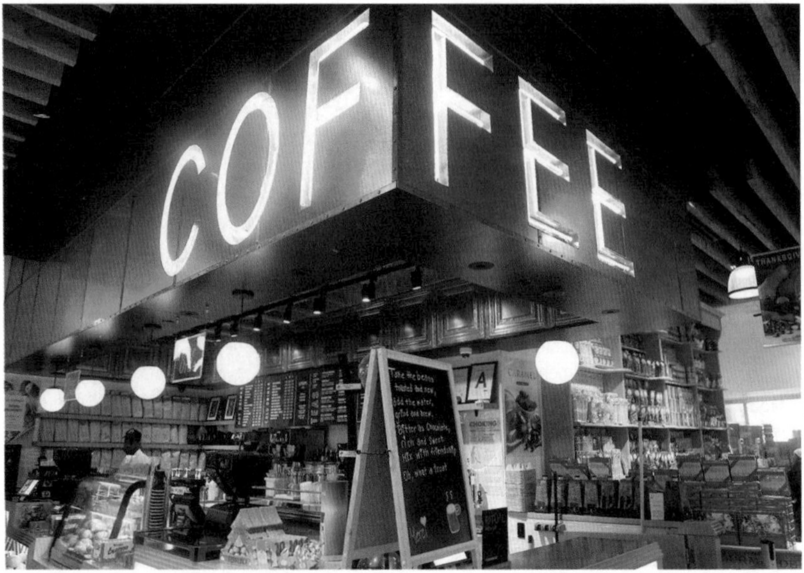

LEONARD ZHUKOVSKY/SHUTTERSTOCK ©

pancakes with blueberries. Bookings recommended.

Le District   French, Food Hall $$$

(Map p246; ☑212-981-8588; www.ledistrict. com; Brookfield Place, 225 Liberty St, at West St; market mains $12-30, Beaubourg dinner mains $25-37; ☺Beaubourg 7:30am-11pm Mon-Fri, from 8am Sat & Sun, other hours vary; ☜; ⓢE to World Trade Center; 2/3 to Park Place; R/W to Cortlandt St; 4/5 to Fulton St; A/C to Chambers St) Paris on the Hudson reigns at this sprawling French food emporium selling everything from high-gloss pastries and pretty *tartines* to stinky cheese and savory steak *frites*. Main restaurant **Beaubourg** has a large bistro menu, but for a quick sit-down feed, head to the **Market District** counter for a burger or the **Cafe District** for a savory crepe.

⊗ SoHo & Chinatown

Prince Street Pizza   Pizza $

(Map p248; ☑212-966-4100; 27 Prince St, btwn Mott & Elizabeth Sts; pizza slices from $2.95; ☺11:45am-11pm Sun-Thu, to 2am Fri & Sat; ⓢN/R to Prince St; 6 to Spring St) It's a miracle the oven door hasn't come off its hinges at this classic slice joint, its brick walls hung with shots of B-list celebrity fans. Ditch the average cheese slice for the exceptional square varieties (the pepperoni will blow your socks off, Tony). The sauces, mozzarella and ricotta are made in-house and while the queues can get long, they usually move fast.

Lan Larb   Thai $

(Map p248; ☑646-895-9264; www.lanlarb. com; 227 Centre St, at Grand St; dishes $9-21; ☺11:30am-10:15pm; ⓢN/Q/R/W, J/Z, 6 to Canal St) Food fiends flock to Lan Larb for cheap, flavor-packed Thai. It specializes in *larb,* a spicy, minced-meat salad from Thailand's northeast Isan region (try the duck version; $12). Other top choices include sucker-punch *som tam* (green papaya salad; $11) and a delicate *kui teiw*

⛛ To Market, To Market

Don't let the concrete streets and buildings fool you – NYC has a thriving greens scene. Top of the list is **Chelsea Market** (p114), which is packed with gourmet goodies of all kinds – both shops (where you can assemble picnics) and food stands (where you can eat on-site). Many other food halls have opened in recent years, including **Gansevoort Market** (p128) in the Meatpacking District and a trio of food halls at **Brookfield Place** (p124), in Lower Manhattan. Also popular are high-end market-cum-grocers like **Eataly** (p132) and **Dean & DeLuca** (Map p248; ☑212-226-6800; www.deananddeluca.com; 560 Broadway, at Prince St, SoHo; pastries from $3, sandwiches $11; ☺7am-9pm Mon-Fri, 8am-9pm Sat & Sun; ⓢN/R to Prince St; 6 to Spring St), where fresh produce and ready-made fare are given the five-star treatment.

Many neighborhoods in NYC have their own greenmarket. One of the biggest is the **Union Square Greenmarket** (p152), open four days a week throughout the year. Check Grow NYC (www.grownyc.org/greenmarket) for a list of the other 50-plus markets around the city.

Union Square Greenmarket
GABRIELI2/SHUTTERSTOCK ©

nam tok nuer (dark noodle soup with beef, morning glory, scallion, cilantro and bean sprouts; $11).

★ Best Bakeries

Four & Twenty Blackbirds (p138)

Dominique Ansel Kitchen (p129)

Arcade Bakery (p124)

From left: Dominique Ansel Kitchen; Peking Duck House; Cafe Mogador

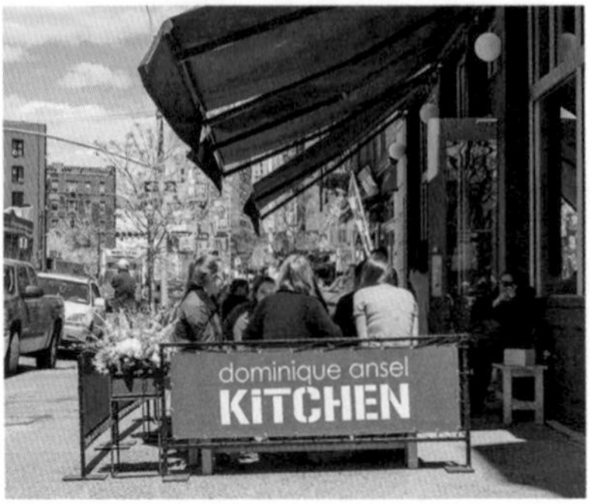

RICHARD LEVINE/ALAMY STOCK PHOTO ©

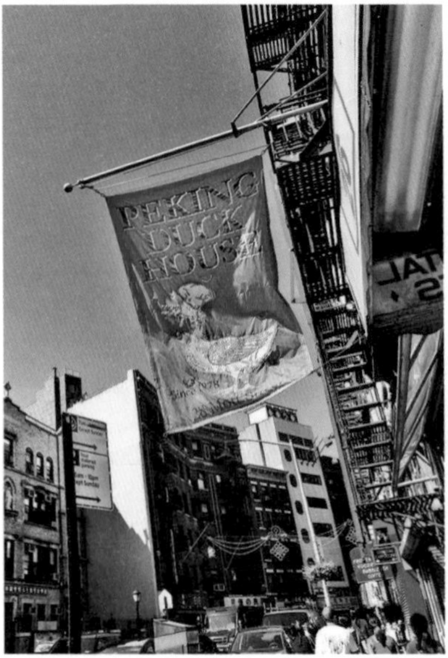

LEN HOLSBORG/ALAMY STOCK PHOTO ©

Uncle Boons Thai **$$**

(Map p248; ☎646-370-6650; www.uncleboons.com; 7 Spring St, btwn Elizabeth St & Bowery; small plates $12-16, large plates $21-29; ⏰5:30-11pm Mon-Thu, to midnight Fri & Sat, to 10pm Sun; 📶; [S]J/Z to Bowery; 6 to Spring St) Michelin-star Thai served up in a fun, tongue-in-cheek combo of retro wood-paneled dining room with Thai film posters and old family snaps. Spanning the old and the new, zesty dishes include fantastically crunchy *mieng kum* (betel-leaf wrap with ginger, lime, coconut, dried shrimp, peanuts and chili; $12), *kao pat puu* (crab fried rice; $26) and banana blossom salad ($15).

The Butcher's Daughter Vegetarian **$$**

(Map p248; ☎212-219-3434; www.thebutchersdaughter.com; 19 Kenmare St, at Elizabeth St; salads & sandwiches $12-14, dinner mains $16-19; ⏰8am-11pm; 🌿; [S]J to Bowery; 6 to Spring St) The butcher's daughter certainly has rebelled, peddling nothing but fresh herbivorous fare in her whitewashed cafe. While healthy it is, boring it's not: everything from the soaked organic muesli to the spicy kale Caesar salad with almond Parmesan or the dinnertime Butcher's burger (vegetable and black-bean patty with cashew cheddar cheese) is devilishly delish.

Chefs Club Fusion **$$$**

(Map p248; ☎212-941-1100; www.chefsclub.com; 275 Mulberry St; mains $19-68; ⏰6-10:30pm Mon-Thu, to 11:30pm Fri & Sat) In a building used in part for the show *Will & Grace*, Chefs Club sounds more like a discount warehouse than the spectacular dining spot it really is: visiting chefs prepare a menu for anywhere from three weeks to three months, offering their finest selections in menus that span the flavors of the globe.

Peking Duck House Chinese **$$$**

(☎212-227-1810; www.pekingduckhousenyc.com; 28a Mott St; Peking duck per person $45; ⏰11:30am-10:30pm Sun-Thu, 11:45am-11pm Fri & Sat; [S]J/Z to Chambers St, 6 to Canal St) Offering arguably the best Peking duck in the region, the eponymous restaurant has a variety of set menus that include the house specialty. The space is fancier than some Chinatown spots, making it great to come with someone special. Do have the duck: perfectly crispy skin and moist meat make

the slices ideal for a pancake, scallion strips and sauce.

Dutch   Modern American $$$

(Map p248; ✆212-677-6200; www.thedutchnyc. com; 131 Sullivan St, at Prince St; mains lunch $18-37, dinner $28-66; ⏱11:30am-11pm Mon-Thu, from 10am Sun, to 11:30pm Fri & Sat; ⓢC/E to Spring St; R/W to Prince St; 1 to Houston St) Whether perched at the bar or dining snugly in the back room, you can always expect smart, farm-to-table comfort grub at this see-and-be-seen stalwart. Flavors traverse the globe, from crispy fish tacos with wasabi and yuzu ($18) to veal schnitzel ($35). Reservations are recommended. Cocktails delight – try the Macadamia Maitai ($16).

❊ East Village & Lower East Side

Mamoun's   Middle Eastern $

(Map p248; ✆646-870-5785; http://mamouns. com; 30 St Marks Pl, btwn Second & Third Aves; sandwiches $4-7, plates $7-12; ⏱11am-2am

Mon-Wed, to 3am Thu, to 5am Fri & Sat, to 1am Sun; ⓢ6 to Astor Pl; L to 3rd Ave) This former grab-and-go outpost of the beloved NYC falafel chain has expanded its iconic St Marks storefront with more seating inside and out. Come late on a weekend to find a line of inebriated bar hoppers ending the night with a juicy shawarma covered in Mamoun's famous hot sauce.

Upstate   Seafood $$

(Map p248; ✆212-460-5293; www.upstatenyc. com; 95 First Ave, btwn E 5th & 6th Sts; mains $15-30; ⏱5-11pm; ⓢF to 2nd Ave) Upstate serves outstanding seafood dishes and craft beers. The small, always-changing menu features the likes of beer-steamed mussels, seafood stew, scallops over mushroom risotto, soft-shell crab and wondrous oyster selections. There's no freezer – seafood comes from the market daily, so you know you'll be getting only the freshest ingredients. Lines can be long, so go early.

Cafe Mogador   Moroccan $$

(Map p248; ✆212-677-2226; www.cafemogador. com; 101 St Marks Pl, btwn 1st St & Ave A; mains lunch $9-18, dinner $16-22; ⏱9am-midnight

⦿ Urban Farm to Table

Whether it's upstate triple-cream Kunik at **Bedford Cheese Shop** (Map p252; ⏹718-599-7588; www.bedfordcheeseshop. com; 67 Irving Pl, btwn E 18th & 19th Sts, Gramercy; ⏰8am-9pm Mon-Sat, to 8pm Sun; ⓢ4/5/6, N/Q/R/W, L to 14th St-Union Sq) or Montauk Pearls oysters at fine-dining **Craft** (p133), New York City's passion for all things local and artisanal continues unabated. The city itself has become an unlikely food bowl, with an ever-growing number of rooftops, back-yards and community gardens finding new purpose as urban farms.

While you can expect to find anything from organic tomatoes atop Upper East Side delis to beehives on East Village tenement rooftops, the current queen of the crop is **Brooklyn Grange** (www.brooklyngrangefarm.com), a 2.5-acre organic farm covering two rooftops in Long Island City and the Brooklyn Navy Yards. The project is the brainchild of young farmer Ben Flanner; obsessed with farm-to-table eating, this former E*Trade marketing manager kick-started NYC's rooftop revolution in 2009 with the opening of its first rooftop soil farm – Eagle Street Rooftop Farm – in nearby Greenpoint. Flanner's collaborators include some of the city's top eateries, among them **Roberta's** (p139) in Brooklyn, and **Dutch** (p127) in Manhattan.

Bedford Cheese Shop
STEVEN GREAVES/GETTY IMAGES ©

Sun-Thu, until 1am Fri & Sat; ⓢ6 to Astor Pl) Family-run Mogador is a long-running NYC classic, serving fluffy piles of couscous, chargrilled lamb and *merguez* (a spicy lamb or beef sausage) over basmati rice, as well as satisfying mixed platters of hummus and baba ganoush. The standouts, however, are the tagines – traditionally spiced, long-simmered chicken or lamb dishes served up five different ways.

Degustation   Modern European **$$$**
(Map p248; ⏹212-979-1012; www.degustation-nyc.com; 239 E 5th St, btwn Second & Third Aves; small plates $12-22, tasting menu $85; ⏰6-11:30pm Tue-Sat; ⓢ6 to Astor Pl) Blending Iberian, French and new-world recipes, Degustation does a beautiful array of tapas-style plates at this narrow, 19-seat eatery. It's an intimate setting, with guests seated around a long wooden counter while chef Oscar Islas Díaz and his team are center stage, firing up mole octopus and oyster tacos, among other inventive dishes.

⊗ West Village, Chelsea & Meatpacking District

Gansevoort Market   Market **$**
(Map p248; www.gansmarket.com; 353 W 14th St, at Ninth Ave; mains $5-20; ⏰8am-8pm; ⓢA/C/E, L to 8th Ave-14th St) Inside a brick building in the heart of the Meatpacking District, this sprawling market is the latest and greatest food emporium to land in NYC. A raw, indus-trial space lit by skylights, it features several dozen gourmet vendors slinging tapas, arepas, tacos, pizzas, meat pies, ice cream, pastries and more.

Taïm   Israeli **$**
(Map p248; ⏹212-691-1287; www.taimfalafel. com; 222 Waverly Pl, btwn Perry & W 11th Sts; sandwiches $7-8; ⏰11am-10pm; ⓢ1/2/3, A/C/E to 14th St; L to 6th Ave-14th St) This tiny joint whips up some of the best falafel in the city. You can order it Green (traditional style), Harissa (with Tunisian spices) or Red (with roasted peppers) – whichever you choose, you'll get it stuffed into pita bread with

creamy tahini sauce and a generous dose of Israeli salad.

Stumptown Coffee Roasters Coffee $

(Map p248; ☎855-711-3385; www.stumptowncoffee.com; 30 W 8th St, at MacDougal St; ⏲7am-8pm; [S]A/C/E, B/D/F/M to W 4th St-Washington Sq) This renowned Portland roaster is helping to reinvent the NYC coffee scene with its exquisitely made brews. It has an elegant interior with coffered ceiling and walnut bar, though its few tables are often overtaken by the laptop-toting crowd.

Dominique Ansel Kitchen Bakery $

(Map p248; ☎212-242-5111; www.dominiqueanselkitchen.com; 137 Seventh Ave, btwn Charles & W 10th Sts; pastries $4-8; ⏲8am-7pm Mon-Sat, 9am-7pm Sun; [S]1 to Christopher St-Sheridan Sq) The famed creator of the cronut owns this small sun-lit bakery in the West Village where you can nibble on raspberry passion-fruit pavlova, blueberry shortcake and many other heavenly treats (but no cronuts). There's also light savory fare, such as turkey pot pie with foie gras gravy and edamame avocado toast.

Rosemary's Italian $$

(Map p248; ☎212-647-1818; www.rosemarysnyc.com; 18 Greenwich Ave, at W 10th St; mains $14-40; ⏲8am-4pm & 5-11pm Mon-Thu, until midnight Fri, from 10am Sat & Sun, until 11pm Sun; [S]1 to Christopher St-Sheridan Sq) One of the West Village's hottest restaurants, Rosemary's serves high-end Italian fare that more than lives up to the hype. In a vaguely farmhouse-like setting, diners tuck into generous portions of housemade pastas, rich salads, and cheese and *salumi* (cured meat) boards. Everything, from the simple walnut herb pesto to the succulent smoked lamb shoulder, is incredible.

Nix Vegetarian $$

(Map p248; ☎212-498-9393; www.nixny.com; 72 University Pl, btwn 10th & 11th Sts; mains $20-28; ⏲11:30am-2:30pm & 5:30-11pm Mon-Fri, from 10:30am Sat & Sun; [S]4/5/6, N/Q/R/W, L to 14th St-Union Sq) At this understated Michelin-starred eatery, head chefs Nicolas Farias and John Fraser transform vegetables into high art in beautifully executed dishes that delight the senses. Start off with tandoor bread and creative dips like spiced eggplant with pine nuts before moving on to richly complex plates of cauliflower tempura with steamed buns, or spicy tofu with chanterelle mushrooms, kale and Szechuan pepper.

Cookshop Modern American $$

(Map p252; ☎212-924-4440; www.cookshopny.com; 156 Tenth Ave, btwn W 19th & 20th Sts; mains brunch $15-22, lunch $17-21, dinner $22-48; ⏲8am-11pm Mon-Fri, from 10am Sat, 10am-10pm Sun; [S]1, C/E to 23rd St) A brilliant brunching pit stop before (or after) tackling the verdant High Line across the street, Cookshop is a lively place that knows its niche and does it oh so well. Excellent service, eye-opening cocktails (good morning, bacon-infused BLT Mary!), a perfectly baked-bread basket and a selection of inventive egg mains make this a Chelsea favorite on a Sunday afternoon.

Barbuto Modern Italian $$

(Map p248; ☎212-924-9700; www.barbutonyc.com; 775 Washington St, at W 12th St; mains $22-28; ⏲noon-3:30pm & 5:30-11pm Mon-Thu, until midnight Fri & Sat, until 10pm Sun; [S]A/C/E, L to 8th Ave-14th St; 1 to Christopher St-Sheridan Sq) Occupying a cavernous garage space with sweeping see-through doors that roll up and into the ceiling during the warmer months, Barbuto slaps together a delightful assortment of nouveau Italian dishes, such as duck breast with plum and crème fraîche, and calamari drizzled with squid ink and chili aioli.

Babu Ji Indian $$

(Map p248; ☎212-951-1082; www.babujinyc.com; 22 E 13th St, btwn University Pl & Fifth Ave; mains $16-26; ⏲5-10:30pm Sun-Thu, to 11:30pm Fri & Sat, also 10:30am-3pm Sat & Sun; [S]4/5/6, N/Q/R/W, L to 14th St-Union Sq) A playful spirit marks this excellent Australian-run Indian restaurant, which recently relocated to Union Sq. You can assemble a meal from street food–style dishes such as *papadi chaat* (chickpeas, pomegranate and yogurt chutney) and potato croquettes stuffed with lobster, or feast on heartier dishes like tandoori lamb chops or scallop coconut curry. A $62 tasting menu is also on offer.

Le Grainne French $$

(Map p252; ☎646-486-3000; www.legrainnecafe.com; 183 Ninth Ave, btwn 21st & 22nd Sts; mains $11-30; ⏰8am-11:30pm; [S]1, C/E to 23rd St) Tap the top of your French onion soup as you dream of ingénue Amélie cracking open her crème brûlée; Le Grainne transports the senses from the busy blocks of Chelsea to the backstreets of Paris. The tin-topped eatery excels at lunchtime, when baguette sandwiches and savory crepes are scarfed down amid cramped quarters.

Foragers Table Modern American $$$

(Map p252; ☎212-243-8888; www.foragersmarket.com/restaurant; 300 W 22nd St, at Eighth Ave; mains $17-32; ⏰8am-4pm & 5:30-10pm Mon-Fri, 10am-2pm & 5:30-10pm Sat, to 9:30pm Sun; ✎; [S]1, C/E to 23rd St) Owners of this outstanding restaurant run a 28-acre farm in the Hudson Valley, from which much of their seasonal menu is sourced. It changes frequently, but recent temptations include Long Island duck breast with roasted acorn squash, apples, chanterelle mushrooms and figs, grilled skate with red quinoa, creamed kale and *cippolini* onion and deviled farm eggs with Dijon mustard.

RedFarm Fusion $$$

(Map p248; ☎212-792-9700; www.redfarmnyc.com; 529 Hudson St, btwn W 10th & Charles Sts; mains $19-57, dumplings $14-20; ⏰5-11:45pm, plus 11am-2:30pm Sat & Sun, closes 11pm Sun; [S]A/C/E, B/D/F/M to W 4th St-Washington Sq; 1 to Christopher St-Sheridan Sq) RedFarm transforms Chinese cooking into pure, delectable artistry at this small, buzzing space on Hudson St. Fresh crab and eggplant bruschetta, juicy rib steak (marinated overnight in papaya, ginger and soy) and pastrami egg rolls are among the many creative dishes that brilliantly blend cuisines. Other hits include spicy crispy

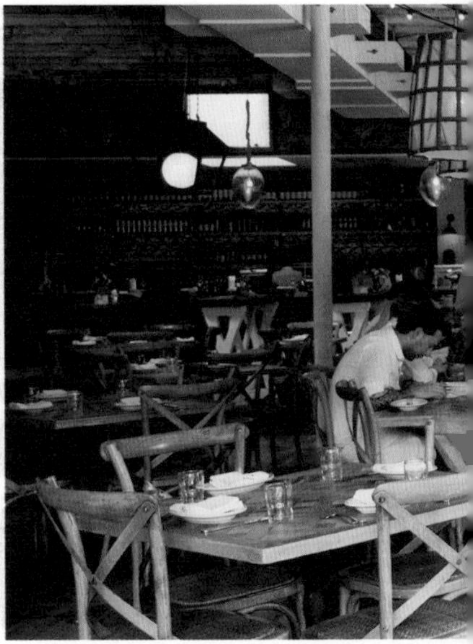

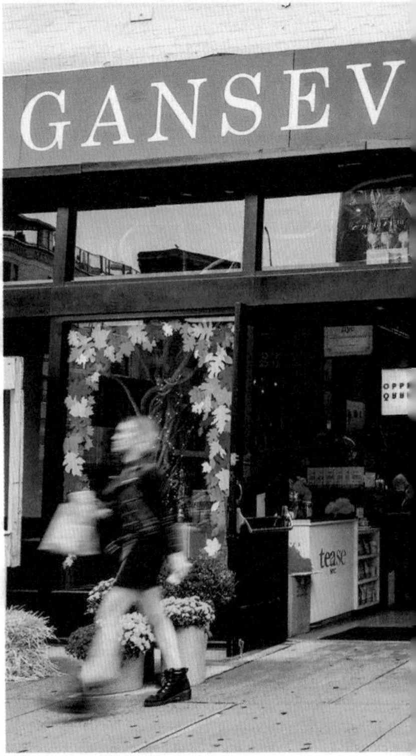

Clockwise from top: Rosemary's (p129); Jeffrey's Grocery (p132); Gansevoort Market (p128)

👍 Meat-Free Metropolis

A slew of new meat-free eateries have enticed skeptics by injecting big doses of cool ambience – and top-notch wine and dessert options – into the mix. Topping the list is **Nix** (p129), a brilliantly creative vegetarian restaurant that's earned rave reviews and a Michelin star. Even the most meat-heavy four-star restaurants are figuring out the lure of legumes; the market-inspired *le potager* section on the menu at **Café Boulud** (p137) offers highbrow veggie dishes, while on Monday night **Dovetail** (p137) hosts a decadent prix-fixe vegetarian feast.

Vegans have much to celebrate with the arrival of excellent eateries serving up guilt-free goodness all around town. Top choices include **Modern Love** (p139), which serves up comfort fare out in Williamsburg, and elegant **Blossom** (Map p252; ☏212-627-1144; www. blossomnyc.com; 187 Ninth Ave, btwn 21st & 22nd Sts, Chelsea; mains lunch $15-20, dinner $22-24; ⊙noon-2:45pm daily & 5-9:30pm Mon-Thu, to 10pm Sat & Sun, to 9pm Sun; 🖉; 🚇1, C/E to 23rd St), with locations in Chelsea and elsewhere. Other icons include **Candle Cafe** (p135), which has several locations around the city, and the soul food gem **Seasoned Vegan** (p137) up in Harlem.

beef, pan-fried lamb dumplings and grilled jumbo-shrimp red curry.

Jeffrey's Grocery   Modern American $$$
(Map p248; ☏646-398-7630; www.jeffreys grocery.com; 172 Waverly Pl, at Christopher St; mains $23-30; ⊙8am-11pm Mon-Wed, to 1am Thu-Fri, 9:30am-1am Sat, to 11pm Sun; 🚇1 to Christopher St-Sheridan Sq) This West Village classic is a lively eating and drinking spot that hits all the right notes. Seafood is the focus: there's an oyster bar and beautifully

executed selections, such as mussels with crème fraîche, tuna steak tartine and sharing platters. Meat dishes include hanger steak with roasted veggies in a *romesco* (nut and red pepper) sauce.

Blue Hill   American $$$
(Map p248; ☏212-539-1776; www.bluehillfarm. com; 75 Washington Pl, btwn Sixth Ave & Washington Sq W; prix-fixe menu $95-108; ⊙5-11pm Mon-Sat, to 10pm Sun; 🚇A/C/E, B/D/F/M to W 4th St-Washington Sq) A place for slow-food junkies with deep pockets, Blue Hill was an early crusader in the 'Local is Better' movement. Gifted chef Dan Barber, who hails from a farm family in the Berkshires, MA, uses harvests from that land and from farms in upstate New York to create his widely praised fare.

Chumley's   Modern American $$$
(Map p248; ☏212-675-2081; http://chumleys newyork.com; 86 Bedford St, btwn Grove & Barrow Sts; mains $18-34; ⊙5:30-10:15pm Mon-Thu, to 10:30pm Fri & Sat; 🚇1 to Christopher St-Sheridan Sq) Occupying the same space as the legendary West Village speakeasy, this new incarnation maintains its historic air while upgrading everything else. The ambitious, seasonal menu includes aged rib-eye and arctic char, but the highlight might be the burger – constructed from two 4oz patties. Walls are lined with portraits and book jackets of Prohibition-era writers, many of whom were once bar patrons.

⊗ Union Square, Flatiron District & Gramercy

Eataly   Food Hall $$
(Map p252; ☏212-229-2560; www.eataly.com; 200 Fifth Ave, at W 23rd St; ⊙7am-11pm; 🖉; 🚇R/W, F/M, 6 to 23rd St) Mario Batali's sleek, sprawling temple to Italian gastronomy is a veritable wonderland. Feast on everything from vibrant *crudo* (raw fish) and *fritto misto* (tempura-style vegetables) to steamy pasta and pizza at the emporium's string of sit-down eateries. Alternatively, guzzle espresso at the bar and scour the

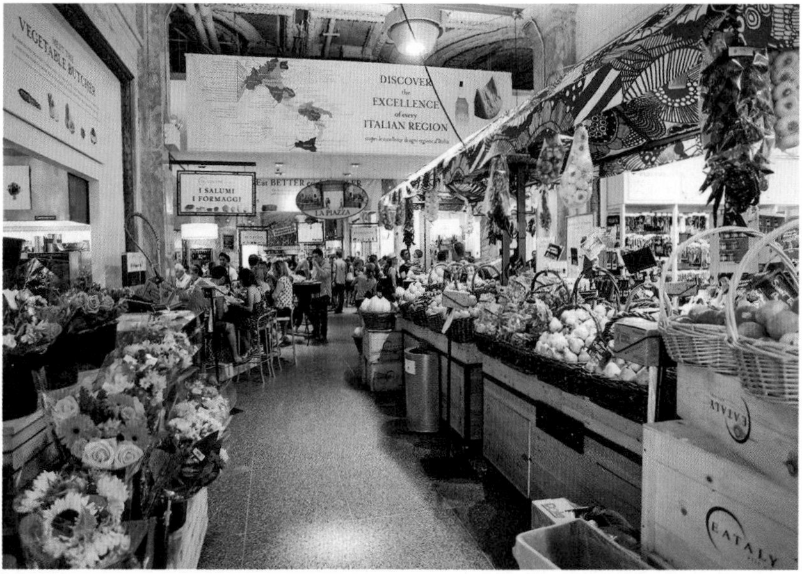

Eataly

countless counters and shelves for a DIY picnic hamper *nonna* would approve of.

Eleven Madison Park Modern American **$$$**

(Map p252; ☎212-889-0905; www.elevenmadisonpark.com; 11 Madison Ave, btwn 24th & 25th Sts; tasting menu $295; 🕒5:30-10pm Mon-Wed, to 10:30pm Thu-Sun, also noon-1pm Fri-Sun; [S]R/W, 6 to 23rd St) Fine-dining Eleven Madison Park came in at number one in the 2017 San Pellegrino World's 50 Best Restaurants list. Frankly, we're not surprised: this revamped poster child of modern, sustainable American cooking is also one of only six NYC restaurants sporting three Michelin stars.

Gramercy Tavern Modern American **$$$**

(Map p252; ☎212-477-0777; www.gramercytavern.com; 42 E 20th St, btwn Broadway & Park Ave S; tavern mains $29-36, dining room 3-course menu $125, tasting menus $149-179; 🕒tavern noon-11pm Sun-Thu, to midnight Fri & Sat, dining room noon-2pm & 5:30-10pm Mon-Thu, to 11pm Fri, noon-1:30pm & 5:30-11pm Sat, 5:30-10pm Sun; 📶✎; [S]R/W, 6 to 23rd St) 🍃 Seasonal, local ingredients drive this perennial favorite, a vibrant, country-chic institution aglow with copper sconces, murals and dramatic floral arrangements. Choose from two spaces: the walk-in-only tavern and its à la carte menu, or the swankier dining room and its fancier prix-fixe and degustation feasts. Tavern highlights include a showstopping duck meatloaf with mushrooms, chestnuts and brussels sprouts.

Craft Modern American **$$$**

(Map p252; ☎212-780-0880; www.craftrestaurant.com; 43 E 19th St, btwn Broadway & Park Ave S; lunch $29-36, dinner mains $24-55; 🕒noon-2:30pm & 5:30-10pm Mon-Thu, to 11pm Fri, 5:30-11pm Sat, to 9pm Sun; 📶; [S]4/5/6, N/Q/R/W, L to 14th St-Union Sq) 🍃 Humming, high-end Craft flies the flag for small, family-owned farms and food producers, their bounty transformed into pure, polished dishes. Whether nibbling on flawlessly charred braised octopus, pillowy scallops or pumpkin mezzaluna pasta with sage, brown butter and Parmesan, expect every ingredient to sing with flavor. Book ahead

Wednesday to Saturday or head in by 6pm or after 9:30pm.

🍴 Midtown

Totto Ramen Japanese $
(Map p254; ☎212-582-0052; www.tottoramen.com; 366 W 52nd St, btwn Eighth & Ninth Aves; ramen $11-18; 🕒noon-4:30pm & 5:30pm-midnight Mon-Sat, 4-11pm Sun; [S]C/E to 50th St) There might be another two branches in Midtown, but purists know that neither beats the tiny 20-seat original. Write your name and number of guests on the clipboard and wait your turn. Your reward: extraordinary ramen. Go for the pork, which sings in dishes like miso ramen (with fermented soybean paste, egg, scallion, bean sprouts, onion and homemade chili paste).

Burger Joint Burgers $
(Map p254; ☎212-708-7414; www.burgerjointny.com; Le Parker Meridien, 119 W 56th St, btwn Sixth & Seventh Aves; burgers $9-16; 🕒11am-11:30pm Sun-Thu, to midnight Fri & Sat; [S]F to 57th St) With only a small neon burger as your clue, this speakeasy-style burger hut lurks behind the lobby curtain in the Le Parker Meridien hotel. Though it might not be as 'hip' or as 'secret' as it once was, it still delivers the same winning formula of graffiti-strewn walls, retro booths and attitude-loaded staff slapping up beef 'n' patty brilliance.

Le Bernardin Seafood $$$
(Map p254; ☎212-554-1515; www.le-bernardin.com; 155 W 51st St, btwn Sixth & Seventh Aves; prix-fixe lunch/dinner $88/157, tasting menus $185-225; 🕒noon-2:30pm & 5:15-10:30pm Mon-Thu, to 11pm Fri, 5:15-11pm Sat; [S]1 to 50th St; B/D, E to 7th Ave) The interiors may have been subtly sexed-up for a 'younger clientele' (the stunning storm-themed triptych is by Brooklyn artist Ran Ortner), but triple-Michelin-starred Le Bernardin remains a luxe, fine-dining holy grail. At the helm is French-born celebrity chef Éric Ripert, whose deceptively simple-looking seafood often borders on the transcendental. Life is short, and you only live (er, eat!) once.

ViceVersa

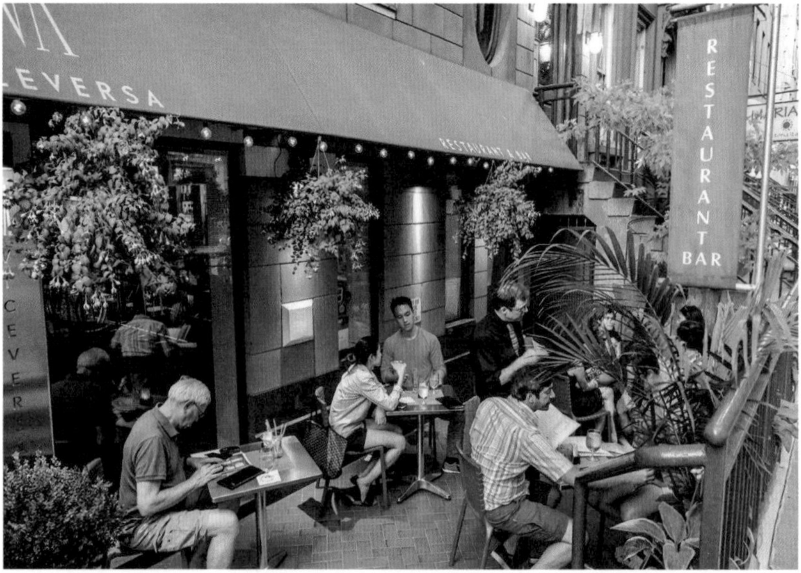

ROSAIRENEBETANCOURT 10/ALAMY STOCK PHOTO ©

ViceVersa Italian $$$

(Map p254; ☎212-399-9291; www.viceversanyc.com; 325 W 51st St, btwn Eighth & Ninth Aves; 3-course lunch $29, dinner mains $24-33; ⏰noon-2:30pm & 5-11pm Mon-Fri, 4:30-11pm Sat, 11:30am-3pm & 5-10pm Sun; [S]C/E to 50th St) ViceVersa is quintessential Italian: suave and sophisticated, affable and scrumptious. The menu features refined, cross-regional dishes like arancini with black truffle and fontina cheese. For a celebrated classic, order the *casoncelli alla bergamasca* (ravioli-like pasta filled with minced veal, raisins and amaretto cookies and seasoned with sage, butter, pancetta and Grana Padano), a nod to chef Stefano Terzi's Lombard heritage.

Grand Central Oyster Bar & Restaurant Seafood $$$

(Map p254; ☎212-490-6650; www.oysterbarny.com; Grand Central Terminal, 42nd St, at Park Ave; mains $15-39; ⏰11:30am-9:30pm Mon-Sat; [S]S, 4/5/6, 7 to Grand Central-42nd St) This buzzing bar and restaurant within Grand Central is hugely atmospheric, with a vaulted tiled ceiling by Catalan-born engineer Rafael Guastavino. While the extensive menu covers everything from clam chowder and seafood stews to pan-fried soft-shell crab, the real reason to head here is for the two-dozen oyster varieties. Get slurping.

O-ya Sushi $$$

(Map p252; ☎212-204-0200; https://o-ya.restaurant/o-ya-nyc; 120 E 28th St; nigiri $16-38; ⏰11am-10pm Mon-Sat; [S]4/6 to 28th St) With the cheapest nigiri pairs at close to $20 each, this is not a spot you'll come to every day. But if you're looking for a special night out and sushi's in the game plan, come here for exquisite flavors, fish so tender it melts like butter on the tongue, and preparations so artful you almost apologize for eating them.

🍴 Upper East Side

Two Boots Pizza $

(Map p254; ☎212-734-0317; www.twoboots.com; 1617 Second Ave, cnr E 84th St; pizza slices $3.50-4.25; ⏰11:30am-11pm Sun-Tue, to midnight Wed, to 2am Thu, to 4am Fri & Sat; 🥕; [S]Q, 4/5/6 to 86th St) With the two 'boots' of Italy and Louisiana as inspiration, this quirky, pioneering NYC chain has over 40 original, eclectic pizza flavors in all (with plenty of vegetarian and vegan options) – all named after comedians, scientists, musicians, local sports teams and even fictional characters. Our favorite? The Tony Clifton (shiitake mushrooms, Vidalia onions, mozzarella and red-pepper pesto).

Café Sabarsky Austrian $$

(Map p254; ☎212-288-0665; www.neuegalerie.org/cafes/sabarsky; 1048 Fifth Ave, cnr E 86th St; mains $18-30; ⏰9am-6pm Mon & Wed, to 9pm Thu-Sun; 🥕; [S]4/5/6 to 86th St) The lines can get long at this popular cafe evoking an opulent, turn-of-the-century Vienna coffeehouse. But the well-rendered Austrian specialties make it worth the wait. Expect crepes with smoked trout, goulash soup and roasted bratwurst. There's also a mouth-watering list of specialty sweets, including a divine Sacher torte (dark chocolate cake with apricot confiture).

Candle Cafe Vegan $$

(Map p254; ☎212-472-0970; www.candlecafe.com; 1307 Third Ave, btwn E 74th & 75th Sts; mains $15-22; ⏰11:30am-10:30pm Mon-Sat, to 9:30pm Sun; 🥕; [S]Q to 72nd St-2nd Ave) The moneyed yoga set piles into this attractive vegan cafe serving a long list of sandwiches, salads, comfort food and market-driven specials. The specialty here is the housemade seitan. There is a juice bar and a gluten-free menu.

Tanoshi Sushi $$$

(☎917-265-8254; www.tanoshisushinyc.com; 1372 York Ave, btwn E 73rd & 74th Sts; chef's sushi selection $80-100; ⏰seatings 6pm, 7:30pm & 9pm Mon-Sat; [S]Q to 72nd St) It's not easy to snag one of the 20 stools at Tanoshi, a wildly popular, pocket-sized sushi spot. The setting may be humble, but the flavors are simply magnificent. Only sushi is on offer and only *omakase* (chef's selection) – which might include Hokkaido scallops, king salmon or mouthwatering *uni* (sea urchin). BYO beer, sake or whatnot. Reserve well in advance.

New York City on a Plate

The dough base is hand-tossed and baked into a thin crust.

The tomato sauce must perfectly balance acidity and sweetness.

Typical toppings include pepperoni, green peppers, onions and mushrooms. (Never pineapple!)

Grated mozzarella cheese is used (ricotta is added for a 'white pie').

The proper way to hold a NY slice is folded lengthwise.

The Best Pizza Slice

★ Top Places for Pizza

Juliana's (p139)

Roberta's (p139)

Prince Street Pizza (p125)

Two Boots (p135)

Totonno's (p117)

A Slice of Heaven

Whether grabbed on the go as a slice or eaten whole at a sit-down restaurant, pizza is one of New York's most ubiquitous and beloved foods. The light, springy crunch of the thin NY-style crust combines with the slightly sweet tomato sauce and thick, melted mozzarella cheese to create a symphony in your mouth. Add on some meat or vegetable toppings for a classic New York meal.

Juliana's

Café Boulud
French $$$

(Map p254; ✆212-772-2600; www.cafeboulud. com/nyc; 20 E 76th St, btwn Fifth & Madison Aves; mains around $45; ⏱7-10:30am, noon-2:30pm & 5:45-10:30pm Mon-Fri, from 8am Sat & Sun; ✉; Ⓢ6 to 77th St) This Michelin-starred bistro – part of Daniel Boulud's gastronomic empire – attracts a rather staid crowd with its globe-trotting French cuisine. Seasonal menus include classic dish coq au vin, as well as more inventive fare such as scallop *crudo* (raw) with white miso. Foodies on a budget will be interested in the three-course prix-fixe lunch ($45; two courses for $39).

⊗ Upper West Side

Irving Farm Roasters
Coffee $

(Map p254; ✆212-874-7979; www.irvingfarm.com; 224 W 79th St, btwn Broadway & Amsterdam Ave; ⏱7am-10pm Mon-Fri, 8am-10pm Sat & Sun; Ⓢ1 to 79th St) Tucked into a little ground-floor shop, the Upper West Side branch of this popular local coffee chain is bigger on the inside – beyond the coffee counter the space opens up into a backroom with a sunny skylight. Enjoy a menu of light meals along with your fresh-pulled espresso. No wi-fi.

Barney Greengrass
Deli $$

(Map p254; ✆212-724-4707; www.barneygreen grass.com; 541 Amsterdam Ave, at 86th St; mains $12-26; ⏱8:30am-4pm Tue-Fri, to 5pm Sat & Sun; Ⓢ1 to 86th St) The self-proclaimed 'King of Sturgeon', Barney Greengrass serves up the same heaping dishes of eggs and salty lox, luxuriant caviar and melt-in-your-mouth chocolate babkas that first made it famous when it opened over a century ago. Pop in to fuel up in the morning or for a quick lunch (there are rickety tables set amid the crowded produce aisles).

Boulud Sud
Mediterranean $$$

(Map p254; ✆212-595-1313; www.bouludsud. com; 20 W 64th St, btwn Broadway & Central Park W; 3-course prix fixe 5-7pm Mon-Sat $63, mains lunch $24-34, dinner $32-58; ⏱11:30am-2:30pm & 5-11pm Mon-Fri, 11am-3pm & 5-11pm Sat, 11am-3pm & 5-10pm Sun; Ⓢ) Pear-wood

paneling and a yellow-gray palette lend a 1960s *Mad Men* feel to Daniel Boulud's take on cuisines from around the entire Mediterranean region: Catalan lobster paella, Marseille-style *soupe de poisson* (fish soup), Moroccan spiced pumpkin soup, Lebanese braised lamb with smoked-eggplant tahini, Greek taramosalata with smoked cod roe and many more, with an emphasis on fish, vegetables and regional spices.

Dovetail
Modern American $$$

(Map p254; ✆212-362-3800; www.dovetailnyc. com; 103 W 77th St, cnr Columbus Ave; prix fixe $68-88, tasting menu $145; ⏱5:30-10pm Mon-Thu, to 10:30pm Fri & Sat, 5-10pm Sun; ✉; ⒮B, C to 81st St-Museum of Natural History; 1 to 79th St) This Michelin-starred restaurant showcases its Zen-like beauty in both its decor (exposed brick, bare tables) and its delectable, seasonal menus – think striped bass with sunchokes and burgundy truffle, and venison with bacon, golden beets and foraged greens. Each evening there are two seven-course tasting menus: one for omnivores ($145) and one for vegetarians ($125).

⊗ Harlem & Upper Manhattan

Seasoned Vegan
Vegan $

(✆212-222-0092; www.seasonedvegan.com; 55 St Nicholas Ave, at 113th St, Harlem; mains $11-17; ⏱5-10pm Tue-Thu, to 2am Fri, 11am-2am Sat, 11am-9pm Sun; ✉; Ⓢ2/3, 5 to 110th St) Run by a mother-and-son team, the Seasoned Vegan has earned a loyal following for its delicious twist on soul food. Everything here is organic and made entirely without animal products. You'll find creative takes on barbecued ribs (made with lotus root and fermented soy), po'boys (featuring yams) and mac 'n' cheese (made with cashew milk).

Red Rooster
Modern American $$$

(✆212-792-9001; www.redroosterharlem.com; 310 Malcolm X Blvd, btwn W 125th & 126th Sts, Harlem; mains lunch $18-32, dinner $24-38; ⏱11:30am-10:30pm Mon-Thu, to 11:30pm Fri, 10am-11:30pm Sat, to 10pm Sun; Ⓢ2/3 to

125th St) Transatlantic superchef Marcus Samuelsson laces upscale comfort food with a world of flavors at his effortlessly cool, vibrant brasserie. Like the work of the New York–based contemporary artists displayed on the walls, dishes are up to date: mac 'n' cheese joins forces with lobster, blackened catfish pairs with pickled mango, and spectacular Swedish meatballs salute Samuelsson's home country.

❸ Brooklyn

Smorgasburg   Market $
(www.smorgasburg.com; ☺11am-6pm Sat & Sun Apr-Oct) The largest foodie event in Brooklyn brings together more than 100 vendors selling an incredible array of goodness: Italian street snacks, duck confit, Indian flatbread tacos, roasted-mushroom burgers, vegan Ethiopian comfort food, sea-salt caramel ice cream, passion-fruit doughnuts, craft beer and much more. Smorgasburg locations tend to change from season to season, so check the website for the latest.

DeKalb Market Hall   Food Hall $
(Map p256; www.dekalbmarkethall.com; City Point, 445 Albee Sq W, at DeKalb Ave, Downtown Brooklyn; ☺7am-9pm Sun-Wed, to 10pm Thu-Sat; 🖥; Ⓢ B, Q/R to DeKalb Ave; 2/3 to Hoyt St; A/C, G to Hoyt-Schermerhorn) One of Downtown Brooklyn's best options for a quick feed is this popular basement food hall in the City Point retail center. Choose from 40 different vendors with offerings across the culinary spectrum. Finish up with an ice-cream cone from **Ample Hills** (📞929-368-2762; www.amplehills.com; cones $4-7; ☺noon-10pm Mon-Fri, 11am-10pm Sat-Sun, shorter hours in winter).

Four & Twenty
Blackbirds   Bakery $
(Map p256; 📞718-499-2917; www.birdsblack. com; 439 Third Ave, cnr 8th St, Gowanus; pie slices $5.75; ☺8am-8pm Mon-Fri, from 9am Sat, 10am-7pm Sun; 🖥; Ⓢ R to 9th St) Sisters Emily and Melissa Elsen use flaky, buttery crusts and seasonal, regionally sourced fruits to create NYC's best pies, hands down. Any time is just right to drop in to their shop

Smorgasburg

ALLEN.G/SHUTTERSTOCK ©

for a slice – the plum-strawberry streusel is *divine* – and a cup of Irving Farm coffee. Add a dollop of fresh whipped cream and you'll be in pie heaven.

Olmsted   Modern American **$$**

(Map p256; ☎718-552-2610; www.olmstednyc. com; 659 Vanderbilt Ave, btwn Prospect & Park Pls, Prospect Heights; small plates $13-16, large plates $22-24; ☺5-10:30pm; ⓢB, Q to 7th Ave) ☛ Chef-owner Greg Baxtrom creates seasonally inspired dishes so skillfully done that even Manhattanites cross the river for this extremely popular restaurant. Olmsted's locavore credentials are evident: much of the menu comes from the restaurant's own backyard garden – which makes a lovely place for cocktails or dessert (try the DIY s'mores) while you wait. Reservations recommended (Mondays are walk-ins only).

Zenkichi   Japanese **$$**

(Map p257; ☎718-388-8985; www.zenkichi. com; 77 N 6th St, at Wythe Ave, Williamsburg; tasting menus vegetarian/regular $65/75; ☺6pm-midnight Mon-Sat, 5:30-11:30pm Sun; ☒; ⓢL to Bedford Ave) A temple of refined Japanese cuisine, Zenkichi presents beautifully prepared dishes in an atmospheric setting that has wowed foodies from far and wide. The recommendation here is the *omakase*, a seasonal eight-course tasting menu featuring highlights like salmon marinated and cured with *shiso* and basil and topped with caviar, or roasted Hudson Valley duck breast with seasonal vegetables.

Juliana's   Pizza **$$**

(Map p256; ☎718-596-6700; www.julianaspizza. com; 19 Old Fulton St, btwn Water & Front Sts, Brooklyn Heights; pizzas $18-32; ☺11:30am-10pm, closed 3:15-4pm; ☒; ⓢA/C to High St) Legendary pizza maestro Patsy Grimaldi has returned to Brooklyn, with delicious, thin-crust perfection in both classic and creative combos – like the No 1, with mozzarella, *scamorza affumicata* (an Italian smoked cow's cheese), pancetta, scallions and white truffles in olive oil. It's in Brooklyn Heights, close to the continually developing Brooklyn waterfront.

Modern Love   Vegan, American **$$**

(Map p257; ☎929-298-0626; www.modern lovebrooklyn.com; 317 Union St, at S 1st St, East Williamsburg; mains brunch $16, dinner $19-24; ☺6-10:30pm Wed & Thu, to 11pm Fri, 5:30-11pm Sat, 11am-3pm & 5-10:30pm Sun, closed Mon & Tue; ☒; ⓢL to Lorimer St; G to Metropolitan Ave) This new restaurant from celebrated chef Isa Chandra Moskowitz serving 'swanky vegan comfort food' is a welcome addition to the scene, with delicious, plant-based versions of classics like mac 'n' shews (with creamy cashew cheese and pecan-cornmeal crusted tofu), Manhattan glam chowder, seitan Philly cheesesteak and truffle poutine. It's always buzzing, so bookings are a good idea (though not required).

Roberta's   Pizza **$$**

(Map p257; ☎718-417-1118; www.robertaspizza. com; 261 Moore St, near Bogart St, East Williamsburg; pizzas $12-19; ☺11am-midnight Mon-Fri, from 10am Sat & Sun; ☒; ⓢL to Morgan Ave) This hipster-saturated warehouse restaurant consistently produces some of the best pizza in NYC. Service can be lackadaisical and the waits long (lunch is best), but the brick-oven pies are the right combination of chewy and fresh. The classic margherita is sublimely simple; more adventurous palates can opt for the seasonal hits like 'speckenwolf' (mozzarella, *speck*, crimini and onion).

Cheryl's Global Soul   Fusion **$$**

(Map p256; ☎347-529-2855; www.cheryls globalsoul.com; 236 Underhill Ave, btwn Eastern Pkwy & St Johns Pl, Prospect Heights; sandwiches $8-14, dinner mains $14-21; ☺8am-4pm Mon, to 10pm Tue-Thu & Sun, to 11pm Fri & Sat; ☒☷; ⓢ2/3 to Eastern Pkwy-Brooklyn Museum) Around the corner from the Brooklyn Museum (p105) and the Brooklyn Botanic Garden (p105), this homey brick-and-wood favorite serves up fresh, unpretentious cooking that draws on a world of influences: from sake-glazed salmon with jasmine rice to exceptional homemade quiche to a long list of tasty sandwiches. There are veggie options and a separate kids' menu. Expect long waits for weekend brunch.

TREASURE HUNT

Begin your shopping adventure

Treasure Hunt

Not surprisingly for a capital of commercialism, creativity and fashion, New York City is one of the best shopping destinations on the planet. From indie designer boutiques to landmark department stores, thrift shops to haute couture, record stores to the Apple store, antiques to gourmet groceries, it's quite easy to blow one's budget.

Shopping lets you experience the city's stunning variety: classic LPs, avant-garde sample sales, handmade jewelry, antiquarian books, vegan clothing, home decorations, vintage prints, gently used designer clothing – no matter what you're looking for, NYC has it.

In This Section

Useful Websites

Time Out (www.timeout.com/newyork/shopping) The latest info on store openings, sales and pop-up shops.

New York Magazine (www.nymag.com) Trustworthy opinions on the Big Apple's best places to swipe your plastic.

The Glamourai (www.theglamourai.com) Glossy downtown fashion blog that's packed with cutting-edge style ideas.

Harlem & Upper Manhattan
Tend to be locally minded, with shops
catering to a neighborhood crowd (p158)

Upper West Side
Home to some great bookstores (new and used),
along with some little boutiques (p157)

Upper East Side
The country's most expensive boutiques
are found along Madison Ave (p155)

Midtown
Epic department stores, global chains
and the odd in-the-know treasure –
window shoppers unite! (p153)

**West Village, Chelsea &
Meatpacking District**
Bleecker St, running off Abingdon Sq, is lined with
boutiques, with a handful on nearby W 4th St (p151)

Union Square, Flatiron District & Gramercy
This big block of neighborhoods
harbors its own retail gems (p152)

SoHo & Chinatown
West Broadway is a veritable outdoor mall of
encyclopedic proportions. It's like the UN of retail (p147)

East Village & Lower East Side
Hipster treasure trove of vintage wares
and design goods (p149)

Financial District & Lower Manhattan
While not a shopping hot spot per se, Lower
Manhattan serves up a trickle of gems (p146)

Brooklyn
A healthy mix of independent
boutiques and thrift stores (p148)

Opening Hours

In general, most businesses are open
from 10am to around 7pm on weekdays
and 11am to around 8pm Saturdays.
Sundays can be variable – some stores
stay closed while others keep weekday
hours. Stores tend to stay open later in
the neighborhoods downtown. Small
boutiques often have variable hours –
many open at noon.

Sales

Clothing sales happen throughout the
year, usually at the end of each season,
when old stock needs to be moved out.
There are also other big sales during the
holidays, particularly for long weekends
(Memorial Day, Labor Day etc) and over
the weeks leading up to Christmas.

The Best...

Shop till you drop in New York City's best stores.

For Women

Shishi (p157) Get a new wardrobe without breaking the bank at this Upper West Side gem.

Verameat (p151) Exquisite jewelry that treads between beauty and whimsy.

Beacon's Closet (p159) Valhalla for vintage lovers at multiple locations.

MiN New York (p147) Unique perfumes in an apothecary-like setting.

For Children

Dinosaur Hill (p150) Fun, creative toys, books and music to inspire young minds.

Mary Arnold Toys (p155) A treasure trove of games and toys on the Upper East Side.

Books of Wonder (p153) Great gift ideas for kids at this shop near Union Square.

Flying Tiger Copenhagen (pictured above; p157) Loads of inexpensive supplies to keep kids happily occupied.

Vintage

Beacon's Closet (p159) Get a new outfit without breaking the bank.

Housing Works Thrift Shop (p152) Always fun to browse, with locations around the city.

Screaming Mimi's (p151) Lots of appealing clothes from decades past.

Resurrection (pictured above; p149) Mint-condition pieces from couture labels.

For Men

By Robert James (p150) Rugged menswear by a celebrated new local designer.

Nepenthes New York (p154) Japanese collective selling covetable, in-the-know labels.

Odin (p148) Tiny downtown men's boutique for one-of-a-kind pieces.

Bookstores

Strand Book Store (pictured above; p149)
Hands-down NYC's best indie bookstore.
McNally Jackson (p148) Great SoHo spot
for book browsing and author readings.
Housing Works Bookstore (p149) Used
books and a cafe in an atmospheric setting
in Nolita.

Fashion Boutiques

Steven Alan (p147) Stylish, heritage-inspired
fashion, with branches around NYC.
Marc by Marc Jacobs (p151) A downtown
and uptown favorite, in the West Village.
Rag & Bone (p148) Beautifully tailored
clothes for men and women in SoHo.
John Varvatos (p150) Rugged but worldly
wearables in a former downtown rock club.
Opening Ceremony (pictured above; p148)
Head-turning threads and kicks for the
avant-garde in SoHo.

Homewares & Design

Shinola (p146) Unusual accessories from a
cutting-edge Detroit design house.
A&G Merch (p159) Clever decorating ideas
from this artful Williamsburg shop.
Magpie (p157) Ecofriendly curios to feather
your nest, on the Upper West Side.

★ Lonely Planet's Top Choices

Barneys (p153) Serious fashionistas
shop at Barneys, well known for its
spot-on collections of in-the-know labels.

Brooklyn Flea (p158) Brooklyn's
collection of flea markets offers plenty
of vintage furnishings, retro clothing and
bric-a-brac.

ABC Carpet & Home (p152) Spread
over six floors like a museum, ABC is
packed with treasures large and small.

MoMA Design & Book Store (p153)
The perfect one-stop shop for coffee-
table tomes, art prints and 'Where-did-
you-get?' that homewares.

Idlewild Books (p151) An inspiring
place for travelers and daydreamers
with titles spanning the globe.

Financial District & Lower Manhattan

Century 21 Fashion & Accessories
(Map p246; ☎212-227-9092; www.c21stores.com; 22 Cortlandt St, btwn Church St & Broadway; 🕒7:45am-9pm Mon-Wed, to 9:30pm Thu & Fri, 10am-9pm Sat, 11am-8pm Sun; [S]A/C, J/Z, 2/3, 4/5 to Fulton St; R/W to Cortlandt St) For penny-pinching fashionistas, this giant cut-price department store is dangerously addictive. Physically dangerous as well, considering the elbows you might have to throw to ward off the competition beelining for the same rack. Not everything is a knockout or a bargain, but persistence pays off. You'll also find accessories, shoes, cosmetics, homewares and toys.

Pearl River Mart Department Store
(Map p248; ☎212-431-4770; www.pearlriver.com; 395 Broadway, at Walker St; 🕒10am-7:20pm; [S]N/Q/R/W, J/M/Z, 6 to Canal St) Pearl River has been a downtown shopping staple for 40 years, chock-full of a dizzying array of Asian gifts, housewares, clothing and accessories: silk men's pajamas, cheongsam dresses, blue-and-white Japanese ceramic tableware, clever kitchen gadgets, paper lanterns, origami and calligraphy kits, bamboo plants and more lucky-cat figurines than you can wave a paw at. A great place for gifts.

Shinola Fashion & Accessories
(Map p248; ☎917-728-3000; www.shinola.com; 177 Franklin St, btwn Greenwich & Hudson Sts; 🕒11am-7pm Mon-Sat, noon-6pm Sun; [S]1 to Franklin St) Well known for its coveted wristwatches, Detroit-based Shinola branches out with a super-cool selection of Made-in-USA life props. Bag anything from leather iPad cases and journal covers to grooming products, jewelry and limited-edition bicycles with customized bags. Added bonuses include complimentary monogramming of leather goods and stationery, and an in-house espresso bar, **Smile Newstand** (Map p248; ☎917-728-3023; www.thesmilenyc.com; 177 Franklin St, btwn Greenwich & Hudson Sts; 🕒7am-7pm Mon-Fri, 8am-7pm Sat, 8am-6pm Sun; 📶; [S]1 to Franklin St).

Century 21

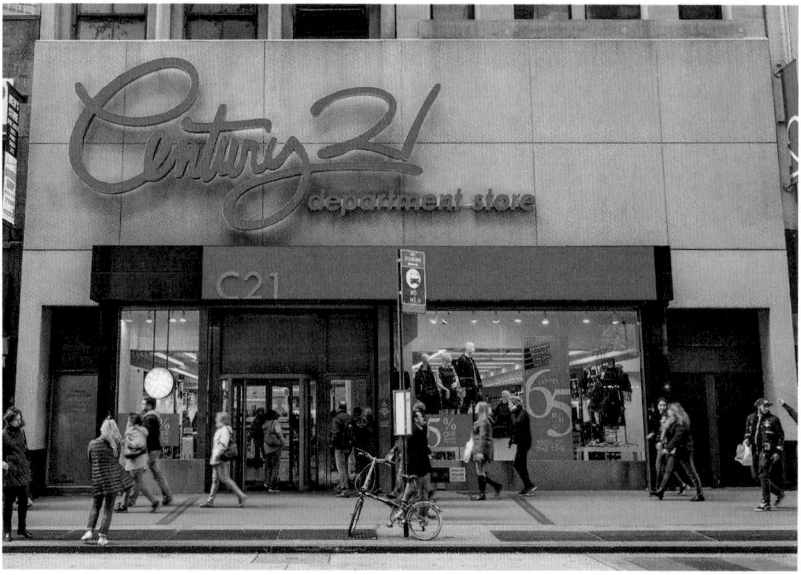

TOOYKRUB/SHUTTERSTOCK ©

Steven Alan Fashion & Accessories

(Map p248; ☎212-343-0692; www.stevenalan.com; 103 Franklin St, btwn Church St & W Broadway; 🕒11am-7pm Mon-Sat, noon-6pm Sun; [S]A/C/E to Canal St; 1 to Franklin St) New York designer Steven Alan mixes his hip, heritage-inspired threads for men and women with a beautiful edit of clothes from indie-chic labels like France's Arpenteur and Scandinavia's Acne and Norse Projects. Accessories include hard-to-find fragrances, bags, jewelry and a selection of shoes by cognoscenti brands such as Common Projects and Isabel Marant Étoile.

Bowne Stationers & Co Gifts & Souvenirs

(Map p246; ☎646-628-2707; 211 Water St, btwn Beekman & Fulton Sts; 🕒11am-7pm; [S]2/3, 4/5, A/C, J/Z to Fulton St) Suitably set in cobbled South Street Seaport and affiliated with the attached **South Street Seaport Museum** (Map p246; www.southstreetseaportmuseum.org; 12 Fulton St; printing press & shop free; [S]2/3, 4/5, A/C, J/Z to Fulton St), this 18th-century veteran stocks reproduction vintage New York posters and NYC-themed notepads, pencil cases, cards, stamps and even wrapping paper. At the **printing workshop** you can order customized business cards or hone your printing skills in monthly classes (see the museum website's Events page).

CityStore Gifts & Souvenirs

(Map p246; ☎212-386-0007; www.nyc.gov/citystore; North Plaza, Municipal Bldg, 1 Centre St, at Chambers St; 🕒10am-5pm Mon-Fri; [S]4/5/6 to Brooklyn Bridge-City Hall; R/W to City Hall; J/Z to Chambers St) Score all manner of officially produced New York City memorabilia here, from authentic-looking taxi medallions, sewerhole-cover coasters and borough-themed T-shirts to NYPD baseball caps, subway station signs and books about NYC. (Curious, though less relevant for the average visitor, are the municipal building codes and other regulatory guides for sale.)

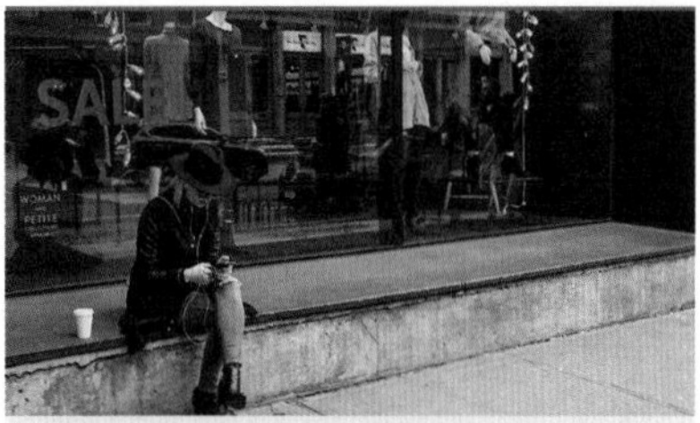

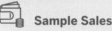

Sample Sales

While clothing sales happen year-round – usually when seasons change and old stock must be moved out – sample sales are held frequently, mostly in the huge warehouses in the Fashion District of Midtown or in SoHo. While the original sample sale was a way for designers to get rid of one-of-a-kind prototypes that weren't quite up to snuff, most sample sales these days are for high-end labels to get rid of overstock at wonderfully deep discounts. For the latest sample sales, check out NY Racked (http://ny.racked.com/sales). Consignment stores are another fine place to look for top (gently used) fashions at reduced prices; label hunters find the Upper East Side prime territory with standouts like Michael's (p157).

A SoHo sale

ZAZDRAVNAYA/SHUTTERSTOCK ©

SoHo & Chinatown

MiN New York Cosmetics

(Map p248; ☎212-206-6366; www.min.com; 117 Crosby St, btwn Jersey & Prince Sts; 🕒11am-7pm Tue-Sat, noon-6pm Mon & Sun; [S]B/D/F/M to Broadway-Lafayette St; N/R to Prince St) This super-friendly, chic, library-like fragrance apothecary has exclusive perfumes, bath and grooming products, and scented candles. Look out for artisanal fragrance 'stories' from MiN's own line. Prices span affordable to astronomical, and the scents are divine. Unlike many places, here there's no pressure to buy.

Odin Fashion & Accessories
(Map p248; ☎212-966-0026; www.odinnewyork.com; 161 Grand St, btwn Lafayette & Centre Sts; 🕒11am-8pm Mon-Sat, noon-7pm Sun; [S]6 to Spring St; N/R to Prince St) Odin's flagship men's boutique carries hip downtown labels, and a select edit of imports, among them Nordic labels Acne. Other in-store tempters include fragrances, jewelry from Brooklyn creatives such as Naval Yard and Uhuru, and street-smart footwear from cult labels like Common Projects.

You'll find another branch in the **West Village** (Map p248; ☎212-243-4724; 106 Greenwich Ave, near Jane St; 🕒noon-8pm Mon-Sat, to 7pm Sun; [S]A/C/E, L to 8th Ave-14th St; 1/2/3 to 14th St).

McNally Jackson Books
(Map p248; ☎212-274-1160; www.mcnallyjackson.com; 52 Prince St, btwn Lafayette & Mulberry Sts; 🕒store 10am-10pm Mon-Fri, to 9pm Sun, cafe 9am-9pm Mon-Fri, from 10am Sat, 10am-8pm Sun; [S]N/R to Prince St; 6 to Spring St) Bustling indie MJ stocks an excellent selection of magazines and books, covering contemporary fiction, food writing, architecture and design, art and history. If you can score a seat, the in-store cafe is a fine spot to settle in with some reading material or to catch one of the frequent readings and book signings held here.

Opening Ceremony Fashion & Accessories
(Map p248; ☎212-219-2688; www.openingceremony.com; 35 Howard St, btwn Broadway & Lafayette St; 🕒11am-8pm Mon-Sat, noon-7pm Sun; [S]N/Q/R/W, J/Z, 6 to Canal St) Unisex Opening Ceremony is famed for its never-boring edit of A-list indie labels. It showcases a changing roster of names from across the globe, both established and emerging; complementing them are Opening Ceremony's own avant-garde creations. No matter who's hanging on the racks, you can always expect showstopping, 'where-did-you-get-that?!' threads that are street smart, bold and refreshingly unexpected.

Rag & Bone Fashion & Accessories
(Map p248; ☎212-219-2204; www.rag-bone.com; 117-119 Mercer St, btwn Prince & Spring Sts; 🕒11am-9pm Mon-Sat, 11am-7pm Sun; [S]N/R to Prince St) Downtown label Rag & Bone

From left: Opening Ceremony; Rag & Bone; Housing Works Bookstore

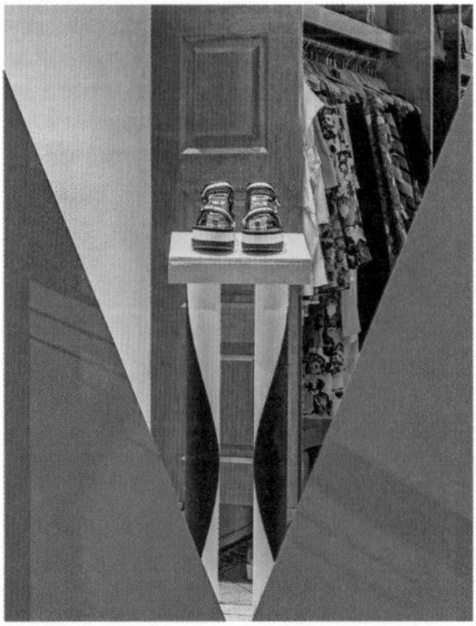
EUGENE GOLOGURSKY/STRINGER/GETTY IMAGES ©

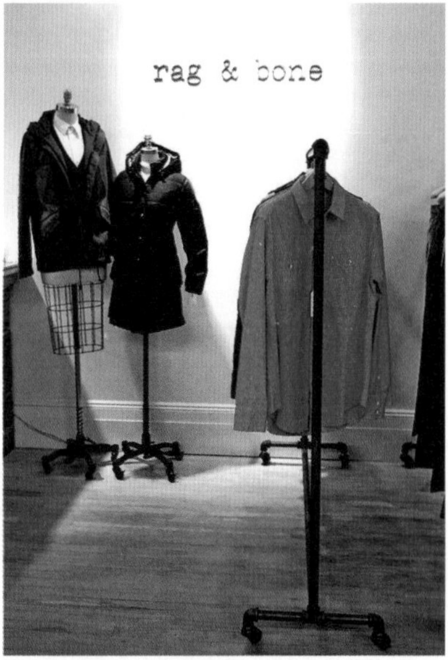

ROB LOUD/STRINGER/GETTY IMAGES ©

is a hit with many of New York's coolest, sharpest dressers – both men and women. Detail-oriented pieces range from clean-cut shirts and blazers and graphic tees to monochromatic sweaters, feather-light strappy dresses, leather goods and Rag & Bone's highly prized jeans. The tailoring is generally impeccable, with accessories including shoes, hats, bags and wallets.

Resurrection Vintage

(Map p248; ☎212-625-1374; www.resurrectionvintage.com; 45 Great Jones Rd, btwn Lafayette & Bowery Sts; 🕒11am-7pm Mon-Sat; [S]6 to Spring St; N/R to Prince St) Resurrection gives new life to cutting-edge designs from past decades. Striking, mint-condition pieces cover the eras of mod, glam-rock and new-wave design, and design deities such as Marc Jacobs have dropped by for inspiration. Top picks include Halston dresses and Courrèges coats and jackets.

Housing Works Bookstore Books

(Map p248; ☎212-334-3324; www.housingworks.org/locations/bookstore-cafe; 126 Crosby St, btwn E Houston & Prince Sts; 🕒9am-9pm Mon-Fri, 10am-5pm Sat & Sun; [S]B/D/F/M to Broadway-Lafayette St; N/R to Prince St) Relaxed, earthy and featuring a great selection of secondhand books, vinyl, CDs and DVDs you can buy for a good cause (proceeds go to the city's HIV-positive and AIDS-infected homeless population), this creaky hideaway is a very local place to while away a few quiet afternoon hours browsing or sitting in the on-site cafe.

East Village & Lower East Side

Strand Book Store Books

(Map p248; ☎212-473-1452; www.strandbooks.com; 828 Broadway, at E 12th St; 🕒9:30am-10:30pm Mon-Sat, from 11am Sun; [S]L, N/Q/R/W, 4/5/6 to 14th St-Union Sq) Beloved and legendary, the iconic Strand embodies downtown NYC's intellectual bona fides – a bibliophile's Oz, where generations of book lovers carrying the store's trademark tote bags happily lose themselves for hours. In operation since 1927, the Strand sells new, used and rare titles, spreading an incredible 18 miles of books (over 2.5 million of them) among three labyrinthine floors.

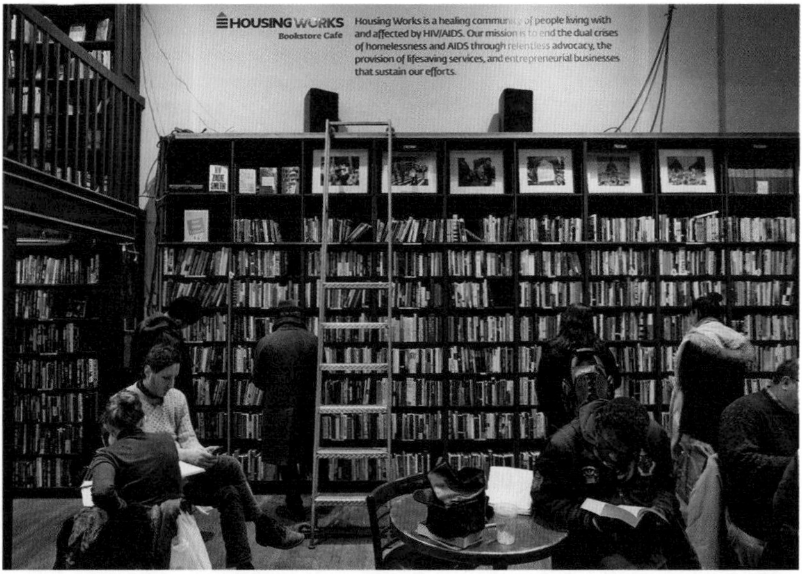

BRUCE YUANYUE BI/ALAMY STOCK PHOTO ©

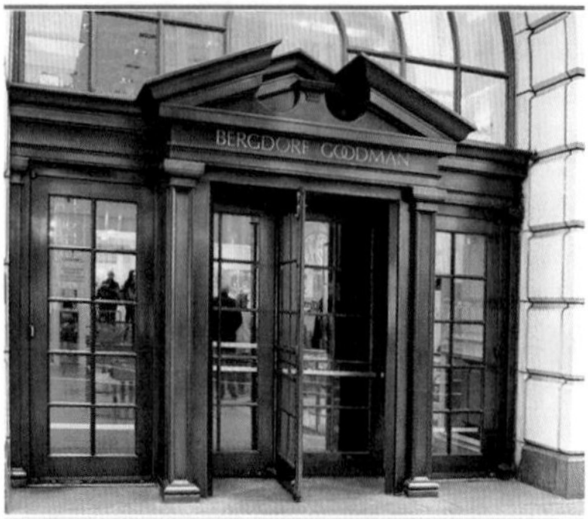

Bergdorf Goodman
JAMES R. MARTIN/SHUTTERSTOCK ©

Luxury Fashion

One of the world's fashion capitals, NYC is ever setting trends for the rest of the country to follow. For checking out the latest designs hitting the streets, it's worth browsing some of the best-loved boutiques around town – regardless of whether you intend to spend. A few favorites include Opening Ceremony, Issey Miyake, Marc Jacobs, Steven Alan, Rag & Bone, John Varvatos, By Robert James and Piperlime.

If time is limited, or you simply want to browse a plethora of labels in one go, then head to those heady conglomerations known worldwide as department stores. New York has a special blend of alluring draws – in particular don't miss **Barneys** (p153), **Bergdorf Goodman** (p154), **Macy's** (p154) and **Bloomingdale's** (p154).

Russ & Daughters Food
(Map p248; ☎212-475-4800; www.russanddaughters.com; 179 E Houston St, btwn Orchard & Allen Sts; 🕒8am-7pm Mon-Wed, to 7pm Thu, to 6pm Fri-Sun; [S]F to 2nd Ave) In business since 1914, this landmark establishment serves up Eastern European Jewish delicacies, such as caviar, herring and lox, and, of course, smear by the pound. It's a great place to load up for a picnic or stock your fridge with breakfast goodies.

Kiehl's Cosmetics
(Map p248; ☎212-677-3171; 109 Third Ave, btwn 13th & 14th Sts; 🕒10am-9pm Mon-Sat, 11am-7pm Sun; [S]L to 3rd Ave) Making and selling skincare products since it opened in NYC as an apothecary in 1851, this Kiehl's flagship store has doubled its shop size and expanded into an international chain, but its personal touch remains – as do the coveted, generous sample sizes.

By Robert James Fashion & Accessories
(Map p248; ☎212-253-2121; www.byrobertjames.com; 74 Orchard St, btwn Broome & Grand Sts; 🕒noon-8pm Mon-Sat, to 6pm Sun; [S]F to Delancey St; J/M/Z to Essex St) Rugged, beautifully tailored menswear is the mantra of Robert James, who sources and manufactures right in NYC (the design studio is just upstairs). The racks are lined with slim-fitting denim, handsome button-downs and classic-looking sports coats. Lola, James' black lab, sometimes roams the store. He also has a store in Williamsburg.

John Varvatos Fashion & Accessories
(Map p248; ☎212-358-0315; www.johnvarvatos.com; 315 Bowery, btwn E 1st & 2nd Sts; 🕒noon-8pm Mon-Fri, from 8pm Sat, noon-6pm Sun; [S]F/M to 2nd Ave; 6 to Bleecker St) Set in the hallowed halls of former punk club CBGB, this John Varvatos store goes to great lengths to tie fashion to rock and roll, with records, '70s audio equipment and even electric guitars for sale alongside JV's denim, leather boots, belts and graphic tees. Sales associates dressed in Varvatos' downtown cool seem far removed from the Bowery's gritty past.

Dinosaur Hill Toys
(Map p248; ☎212-473-5850; www.dinosaurhill.com; 306 E 9th St, btwn First & Second Aves; 🕒11am-7pm; [S]6 to Astor Pl) A small, old-fashioned toy store that's inspired more by imagination than Disney movies, this shop has loads of great gift ideas: Czech marionettes, shadow puppets, micro building blocks, calligraphy sets, toy pianos, art and science kits, kids' music CDs from around

the globe, and wooden blocks in half-a-dozen different languages, plus natural-fiber clothing for infants.

Verameat Jewelry

(Map p248; ☎212-388-9045; www.verameat.com; 315 E 9th St, btwn First & Second Aves; 🕙10am-8pm; [S]6 to Astor Pl; F/M to 2nd Ave) Designer Vera Balyura creates exquisite little pieces with a dark sense of humor in this delightful small shop on 9th St. Tiny, artfully wrought pendants, rings, earrings and bracelets appear almost too precious…until a closer inspection reveals zombies, Godzilla robots, animal heads, dinosaurs and encircling claws – bringing a whole new level of miniaturized complexity to the realm of jewelry.

🔒 West Village, Chelsea & Meatpacking District

Screaming Mimi's Vintage

(Map p248; ☎212-677-6464; www.screamingmimis.com; 240 W 14th St, btwn Seventh & Eighth Aves; 🕙noon-8pm Mon-Sat, 1-7pm Sun; [S]A/C/E, L to 8th Ave-14th St) If you dig vintage threads, you may just scream, too. This funtastic shop carries an excellent selection of yesteryear pieces, organized – ingeniously – by decade, from the '50s to the '90s. (Ask to see the small, stashed-away collection of clothing from the 1920s through '40s.)

Idlewild Books Books

(Map p248; ☎212-414-8888; www.idlewildbooks.com; 170 Seventh Ave S, at Perry St; 🕙noon-8pm Mon-Thu, to 6pm Fri-Sun; [S]1 to Christopher St-Sheridan Sq; 1/2/3 to 14th St; A/C/E, L to 8th Ave-14th St) Named after JFK airport's original moniker, this indie travel bookstore gets feet seriously itchy. Divided by region, books include guidebooks, fiction, travelogues, history, cookbooks and other stimulating fare for delving into different corners of the world. The store also runs popular language classes in French, Italian, Spanish and German; see the website for details.

Marc by Marc Jacobs Fashion & Accessories

(Map p248; ☎212-924-0026; www.marcjacobs.com; 403 Bleecker St, btwn Bank & W 11th Sts; 🕙11am-7pm Mon-Sat, noon-6pm Sun; [S]A/C/E,

Russ & Daughters

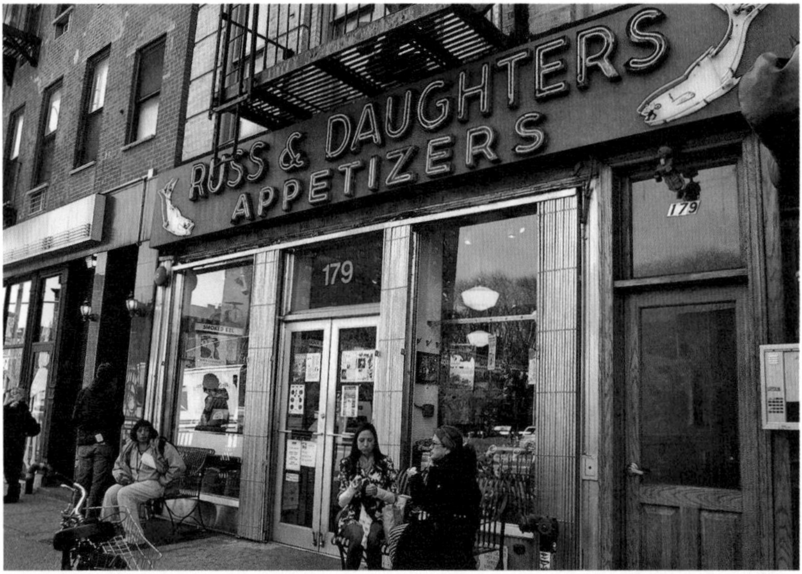

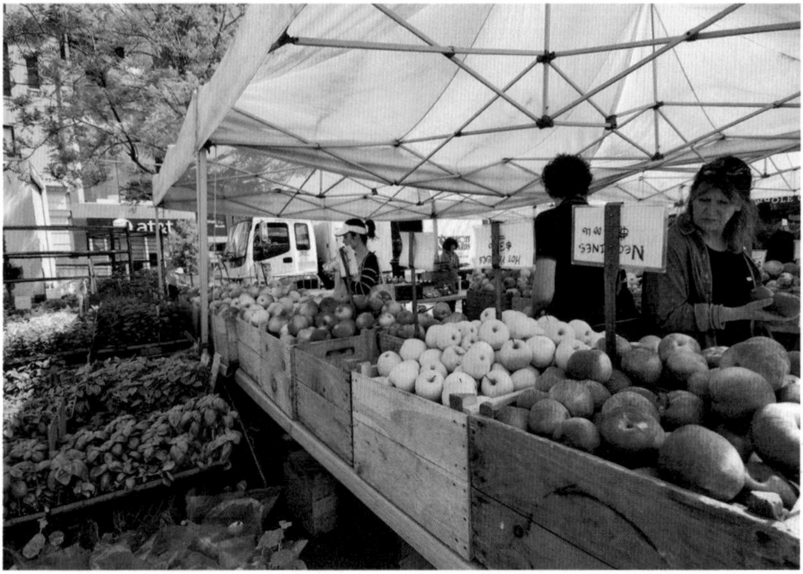

LITTLENYSTOCK/SHUTTERSTOCK ©

Union Square Greenmarket

L to 8th Ave-14th St) At home in this well-heeled neighborhood, this Marc Jacobs outpost sells the designer's women's line. The store's large front windows allow easy peeking – assuming there's not a sale, during which you'll only see hordes of fawning shoppers. There's also **BookMarc** (for books, stationery and knickknacks) at No 400.

Housing Works Thrift Shop Vintage

(Map p252; ☎718-838-5050; www.housingworks.org; 143 W 17th St, btwn Sixth & Seventh Aves; 🕒10am-7pm Mon-Sat, 11am-5pm Sun; [S]1 to 18th St) With its swank window displays, this shop looks more boutique than thrift, but its selections of clothes, accessories, furniture, books and records are great value. It's the place to go to find discarded designer clothes for a bargain. All proceeds benefit the charity serving the city's HIV-positive and AIDS homeless communities. There are 13 other branches around town.

Union Square, Flatiron District & Gramercy

Union Square Greenmarket Market

(Map p252; www.grownyc.org; Union Sq, 17th St, btwn Broadway & Park Ave S; 🕒8am-6pm Mon, Wed, Fri & Sat; [S]4/5/6, N/Q/R, L to 14th St-Union Sq) Don't be surprised if you spot some of New York's top chefs prodding the produce here: Union Square's Greenmarket is arguably the city's most famous. Whet your appetite trawling the stalls, which peddle anything and everything from upstate fruit and vegetables to artisanal breads, cheeses and cider.

ABC Carpet & Home Homewares

(Map p252; ☎212-473-3000; www.abchome.com; 888 Broadway, at E 19th St; 🕒10am-7pm Mon-Wed, Fri & Sat, to 8pm Thu, 11am-6:30pm Sun; [S]4/5/6, N/Q/R/W, L to 14th St-Union Sq) A mecca for home designers and decorators brainstorming ideas, this beautifully curated, seven-level temple to good taste heaves with all sorts of furnishings, small and large. Shop for easy-to-pack knickknacks, textiles and jewelry, as well as statement furniture, designer lighting, ceramics and antique carpets. Come Christmas season the shop is a joy to behold.

Fishs Eddy Homewares

(Map p252; ☎212-420-9020; www.fishseddy.com; 889 Broadway, at E 19th St; 🕒9am-9pm Mon-Thu, to 10pm Fri & Sat, 10am-8pm Sun; [S]R/W, 6 to 23rd St) High-quality and irreverent design has made Fishs Eddy a staple in the homes of hip New Yorkers for years. Its store is a veritable landslide of cups, saucers, butter dishes, carafes and anything else that belongs in a cupboard. Styles range from tasteful color blocking to delightfully outrageous patterns.

Books of Wonder Books

(Map p252; ☎212-989-3270; www.booksofwonder.com; 18 W 18th St, btwn Fifth & Sixth Aves; 🕒10am-7pm Mon-Sat, 11am-6pm Sun; 👪; [S]F/M to 14th St, L to 6th Ave) Devoted to children's and young-adult titles, this wonderful bookstore is a great place to take little ones on a rainy day, especially when a kids' author is giving a reading or a storyteller is on hand. There's an impressive range of NYC-themed picture books, plus a section dedicated to rare and vintage children's books and limited-edition children's-book artwork.

Midtown

MoMA Design & Book Store Gifts, Books

(Map p254; ☎212-708-9700; www.momastore.org; 11 W 53rd St, btwn Fifth & Sixth Aves; 🕒9:30am-6:30pm Sat-Thu, to 9pm Fri; [S]E, M to 5th Ave-53rd St) The flagship store at the Museum of Modern Art (p48) is a fab spot for souvenir shopping. Besides gorgeous books (from art and architecture tomes to pop-culture readers and kids' picture books), you'll find art prints and posters and one-of-a-kind knickknacks. For furniture, lighting, homewares, jewelry, bags and MUJI merchandise, head to the **MoMA Design Store** across the street.

Barneys Department Store

(Map p254; ☎212-826-8900; www.barneys.com; 660 Madison Ave, at E 61st St; 🕒10am-8pm Mon-Fri, to 7pm Sat, 11am-7pm Sun; [S]N/R/W to 5th Ave-59th St) Serious fashionistas swipe their plastic at Barneys, respected for its collections of top-tier labels like Isabel Marant Étoile, Mr & Mrs Italy and Lanvin. For (slightly) less expensive deals geared to a younger market, shop street-chic brands on the 8th floor. Other highlights include a basement cosmetics department and Genes, a futuristic cafe with touch-screen communal tables for online shopping.

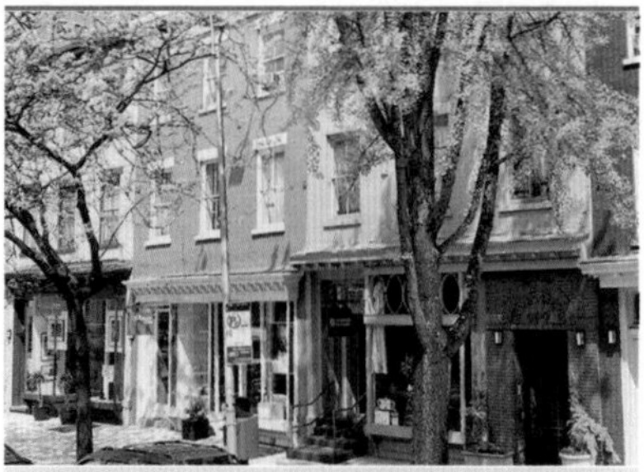

Shopping in Brooklyn

Whatever your preferred flavor of retail therapy, Brooklyn's got it. Williamsburg and Greenpoint are full of home-design shops, vintage furniture and clothing stores, and indie boutiques, bookstores and record shops. In southern Brooklyn, you'll find some satisfying browsing (and good consignment) in the vicinity of Boerum and Cobble Hills. Atlantic Ave, running east to west near Brooklyn Heights, is sprinkled with antique stores, while Park Slope features a good selection of laid-back clothing shops.

Atlantic Avenue

CATE_89/SHUTTERSTOCK ©

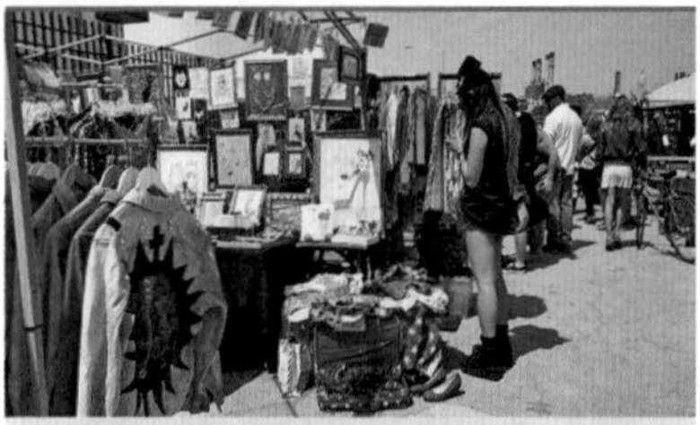

Flea Markets & Vintage Adventures

As much as New Yorkers gravitate toward all that's shiny and new, it can be infinitely fun to riffle through closets of unwanted wares and threads. The most popular flea market is the **Brooklyn Flea** (p158), housed in all sorts of spaces throughout the year. Another gem is **Artists & Fleas** (p158), with scores of vendors. The East Village is the city's de facto neighborhood for secondhand and vintage stores – the uniform of the unwavering legion of hipsters.

Brooklyn Flea
LITTLENYSTOCK/SHUTTERSTOCK ©

Bergdorf Goodman Department Store

(Map p254; ☎888-774-2424, 212-753-7300; www.bergdorfgoodman.com; 754 Fifth Ave, btwn W 57th & 58th Sts; ⏰10am-8pm Mon-Sat, 11am-7pm Sun; [S]N/Q/R/W to 5th Ave-59th St, F to 57th St) Not merely loved for its Christmas windows (the city's best), plush BG – at this location since 1928 – leads the fashion race, headed by its industry-leading fashion director Linda Fargo. A mainstay of ladies who lunch, its drawcards include exclusive collections of Tom Ford and Chanel shoes and a coveted women's shoe department. The men's store is across the street.

Bloomingdale's Department Store

(Map p254; ☎212-705-2000; www.bloomingdales.com; 1000 Third Ave, at E 59th St; ⏰10am-8:30pm Mon-Sat, 11am-7pm Sun; 📶; [S]4/5/6 to 59th St; N/R/W to Lexington Ave-59th St) Blockbuster Bloomie's is something like the Metropolitan Museum of Art of the shopping world – historic, sprawling, overwhelming and packed with bodies, but you'd be sorry to miss it. Raid the racks for clothes and shoes from a who's who of US and global designers, including many 'new-blood' collections. Refueling pit stops include a branch of cupcake heaven **Magnolia Bakery**.

Macy's Department Store

(Map p252; ☎212-695-4400; www.macys.com; 151 W 34th St, at Broadway; ⏰10am-10pm Mon-Sat, 11am-9pm Sun; [S]B/D/F/M, N/Q/R/W to 34th St-Herald Sq; A/C/E to Penn Station) Occupying most of an entire city block, the country's largest department store covers most bases, with fashion, furnishings, kitchenware, sheets, cafes, hair salons and even a branch of the Metropolitan Museum of Art gift store – more 'mid-priced' than 'exclusive,' with mainstream labels and big-name cosmetics. The store also houses a NYC Information Center (p234) with information desk and free city maps.

Nepenthes New York Fashion & Accessories

(Map p252; ☎212-643-9540; www.nepenthesny.com; 307 W 38th St, btwn Eighth & Ninth Aves; ⏰noon-7pm Mon-Sat, to 5pm Sun; [S]A/C/E to 42nd St-Port Authority Bus Terminal) Occupying an old sewing machine shop in the **Garment District**, this cult Japanese collective stocks edgy menswear from the likes of Engineered Garments and Needles, known for their quirky detailing and artisanal production value, with a vintage-inspired Americana workwear type feel. Accessories include bags and satchels, gloves, eyewear and footwear.

B&H Photo Video Electronics

(Map p252; ☎212-444-6600; www.bhphotovideo.com; 420 Ninth Ave, btwn W 33rd & 34th Sts; ⏰9am-7pm Mon-Thu, to 1pm Fri, 10am-6pm Sun, closed Sat; [S]A/C/E to 34th St-Penn Station) Visiting NYC's most popular camera shop is an experience in itself – it's massive and crowded, and bustling with black-clad (and tech-savvy) Hasidic Jewish salesmen.

Your chosen item is dropped into a bucket, which then moves up and across the ceiling to the purchase area (which requires waiting in another line).

🅞 Upper East Side

Diptyque
Perfume

(Map p254; ☏212-879-3330; www.diptyque paris.com; 971 Madison Ave, cnr E 76th St; ⊗10am-7pm Mon-Sat, noon-6pm Sun; ⓢ6 to 77th St) Come out smelling like a rose – or wisteria, jasmine, cypress or sandalwood – at this olfactory oasis. Parisian company Diptyque has been creating signature scents since 1961, using innovative combinations of plants, woods and flowers. Besides perfumes and other personal fragrances (our favorite is the woodsy Tam Dao), it also has a large range of candles, lotions and soaps.

La Maison du Chocolat
Chocolate

(Map p254; ☏212-744-7118; www.lamaisondu chocolat.us; 1018 Madison Ave, btwn E 78th & 79th Sts; ⊗10am-7pm Mon-Sat, 11am-6pm Sun;

ⓢ6 to 77th St) The US flagship store of the famed Parisian chocolatier is a dangerous place for chocoholics. Dark, sweet decadence comes in many forms here, from cocoa-dusted truffles to intensely rich bars made from the world's finest beans. There's a small cafe where you can sink your teeth into creamy chocolate éclairs or crisp macarons, and sip a cup of hot chocolate.

Mary Arnold Toys
Toys

(Map p254; ☏212-744-8510; www.maryarnold toys.com; 1178 Lexington Ave, btwn E 80th & 81st Sts; ⊗9am-6pm Mon-Fri, from 10am Sat, 10am-5pm Sun; ⚹; ⓢ4/5/6 to 86th St) Several generations of Upper East Siders have spent large chunks of their childhood browsing the stuffed shelves of this personable local toy store, opened in 1931. Its range is extensive – stuffed animals, action figures, science kits, board games, arts and crafts, educational toys, you name it. Check the website for free monthly events, such as scavenger hunts or Lego-making sessions.

Macy's

New York City Souvenirs

MoMA Skyline Mug

Both beautiful and functional, this mug from the MoMA Design & Book Store (p153) features some of NYC's most iconic buildings.

Sports Merch

Show your love for New York teams with a classic baseball cap or vintage jersey found at No Relation Vintage (p159).

Local Wears

Add something NYC-made to your wardrobe, like some rugged outerwear from By Robert James (p150).

Strand Books Totes & Tees

Stop into NYC's largest independent bookstore (p149) to get their iconic logo on a canvas tote bag or T-shirt.

Old Prints & Photographs

Frame a piece of old New York with a reproduction of an old lithograph or photo, available at Bowne Stationers & Co (p147).

Michael's
Clothing

(Map p254; ☑212-737-7273; www.michaels consignment.com; 1041 Madison Ave, btwn E 79th & 80th Sts, 2nd fl; ⊙10am-6pm Mon-Sat, to 8pm Thu; ⓢ6 to 77th St) In operation since the 1950s, this vaunted Upper East Side resale store features high-end labels, including Chanel, Gucci and Prada – and an entire shelf dedicated to Jimmy Choo heels. Almost everything on display is less than two years old. It's pricey but cheaper than shopping the flagship boutiques on Madison Ave.

Jacadi
Children's Clothing

(Map p254; ☑212-717-9292; www.jacadi.us; 1260 3rd Ave, btwn E 72nd & 73rd Sts; ⊙10am-6pm Mon-Sat, 11:30am-5:30pm Sun; ⓪; ⓢQ to 72nd St; 6 to 68th St-Hunter College) Fashionistas aren't born: they're made. And where better to start than with some on-trend duds from this Parisian purveyor of effortlessly chic kids' clothes and shoes? With a range of seasonal choices for girls and boys (newborns to tweens) – scalloped-collar cardigans, shearling-cuff boots – your kids will be the best-dressed in their class.

ⓞ Upper West Side

Shishi
Fashion & Accessories

(Map p254; ☑646-692-4510; www.shishi boutique.com; 2488 Broadway, btwn 92nd & 93rd Sts; ⊙11am-8pm Mon-Sat, to 7pm Sun; ⓢ1/2/3 to 96th St) A welcome addition to a fashion-challenged 'hood, Shishi is a delightful boutique stocking an ever-changing selection of stylish but affordable apparel: elegant sweaters, sleeveless shift dresses and eye-catching jewelry, among others. (All its clothes are wash-and-dry friendly too.) It's fun for browsing, and with the enthusiastic staff kitting you out, you'll feel like you have your own personal stylist.

Zabar's
Food

(Map p254; ☑212-787-2000; www.zabars.com; 2245 Broadway, at W 80th St; ⊙8am-7:30pm Mon-Fri, to 8pm Sat, 9am-6pm Sun; ⓢ1 to 79th St) A bastion of gourmet kosher foodie-ism,

this sprawling local market has been a neighborhood fixture since the 1930s. And what a fixture it is! It features a heavenly array of cheeses, meats, olives, caviar, smoked fish, pickles, dried fruits, nuts and baked goods, including pillowy, fresh-out-of-the-oven knishes (Eastern European–style potato dumplings wrapped in dough).

Icon Style
Vintage, Jewelry

(Map p254; ☑212-799-0029; www.iconstyle.net; 104 W 70th St, near Columbus Ave; ⊙noon-8pm Tue-Fri, 11am-7pm Sat, noon-6pm Sun; ⓢ1/2/3 to 72nd St) This tiny gem of a vintage shop, tucked away on a side street, specializes in carefully curated dresses, gloves, bags, hats and other accessories, as well as antique fine and costume jewelry. Half of the shop is covered in a strikingly restored apothecary's wall, with the goods displayed in open drawers. Stop by and indulge your inner Grace Kelly.

Magpie
Arts & Crafts

(Map p254; ☑212-579-3003; www.magpie newyork.com; 488 Amsterdam Ave, btwn 83rd & 84th Sts; ⊙11am-7pm Mon-Sat, to 6pm Sun; ⓢ1 to 86th St) ✿ This charming little outpost carries a wide range of ecofriendly objects: elegant stationery, beeswax candles, hand-painted mugs, organic-cotton scarves, recycled resin necklaces, hand-dyed felt journals and wooden earth puzzles are a few things that may catch your eye. Most products are fair-trade, made of sustainable materials or locally designed and made.

Flying Tiger Copenhagen
Homewares

(Map p254; ☑646-998-4755; www.flyingtiger. com; 424 Columbus Ave, btwn 80th & 81st Sts; ⊙10am-8pm Mon-Sun; ⓪; ⓢB, C to 81st St-Museum of Natural History) In the market for well-designed, quirky and inexpensive doo-dads and tchotchkes? This Danish import will scratch that itch. Something of a miniature Ikea, with items grouped thematically (kitchen, kids, arts and crafts etc) – you could never have imagined the things you didn't know you needed. Remove the price tag and friends will think you've spent too much on a gift.

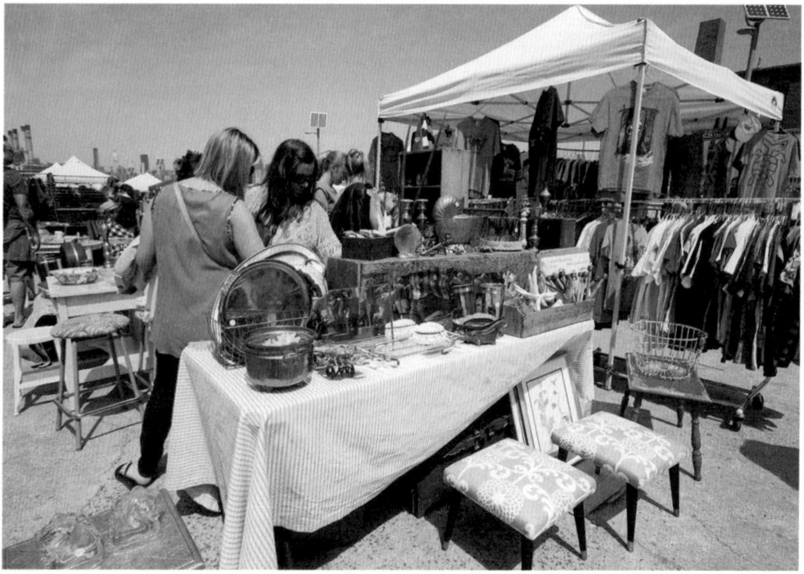

LITTLENYSTOCK/SHUTTERSTOCK ©

Brooklyn Flea

Harlem & Upper Manhattan

Harlem Haberdashery Fashion & Accessories
(☎646-707-0070; www.harlemhaberdashery.com; 245 Malcolm X Blvd, btwn 122nd & 123rd Sts; 🕐noon-8pm Mon-Sat; [S]2/3 to 125th St) Keep your wardrobe fresh at this uber-hip uptown boutique, which has covetable apparel in all shapes and sizes. Lovely T-shirts, high-end sneakers, dapper woven hats, bespoke denim jackets and perfectly fitting button-downs are among the ever-changing collections on display.

Flamekeepers Hat Club Fashion & Accessories
(☎212-531-3542; 273 W 121st St, at St Nicholas Ave; 🕐noon-7pm Tue & Wed, to 8pm Thu-Sat, to 6pm Sun; [S]A/C, B/D to 125th St) Polish your look at this sassy little hat shop owned by affable Harlem local Marc Williamson. His carefully curated stock is a hat-lover's dream: soft Barbisio fedoras from Italy, Selentino top hats from the Czech Republic, and woolen patchwork caps from Ireland's Hanna Hats of Donegal. Prices range from $90 to $350, with optional customization for true individualists.

Brooklyn

Brooklyn Flea Market
(Map p256; www.brooklynflea.com; 80 Pearl St, Manhattan Bridge Archway, Anchorage Pl at Water St, Dumbo; 🕐10am-6pm Sun Apr-Oct; 👪; 🚌B67 to York/Jay Sts, [S]F to York St) Every Sunday from spring through early fall, several dozen vendors sell their wares inside a giant archway under the Manhattan Bridge, ranging from antiques, records and vintage clothes to craft items, housewares and furniture. A slightly smaller indoor version, with around 60 vendors, runs every Saturday and Sunday (10am to 6pm) in SoHo (Sixth Ave at Watt St).

Artists & Fleas Market
(Map p257; www.artistsandfleas.com; 70 N 7th St, btwn Wythe & Kent Aves, Williamsburg; 🕐10am-7pm Sat & Sun; [S]L to Bedford Ave)

In operation for over a decade, this popular Williamsburg flea market has an excellent selection of crafty goodness. Over a hundred artists, designers and vintage vendors sell their wares: clothing, records, paintings, photographs, hats, handmade jewelry, one-of-a-kind T-shirts, canvas bags and more. Two locations in Manhattan are smaller but open daily: one in SoHo, the other inside the Chelsea Market (p114).

Catbird Jewelry

(Map p257; ☎718-599-3457; www.catbirdnyc.com; 219 Bedford Ave, btwn N 4th & 5th Sts, Williamsburg; 🕐noon-8pm Mon-Fri, 11am-7pm Sat, noon-6pm Sun; [S]L to Bedford Ave) 🌿 Still going strong in Williamsburg after 14 years, this jewelry shop stocks both its own pieces – made in a studio a few blocks away – and jewelry from independent makers around the world. Everything is either sterling silver or solid gold, and uses conflict-free, authentic gems. Catbird specializes in rings, especially stacking sets and engagement rings (hey, no pressure).

A&G Merch Homewares

(Map p257; ☎718-388-1779; www.aandgmerch.com; 111 N 6th St, btwn Berry & Wythe Sts, Williamsburg; 🕐11am-7pm; [S]L to Bedford Ave) With its mix of whimsy and elegance, A&G Merch is a fun little shop to explore. Check out antique plates adorned with animal heads, rustic wicker baskets, cast-iron whale bookends, silver tree-branch-like candleholders, brassy industrial table lamps and other goods to give your nest that artfully rustic Brooklyn look.

No Relation Vintage Vintage

(Map p256; ☎718-858-4906; http://ltrainvintage.com; 654 Sackett St, near Fourth Ave, Gowanus; 🕐noon-8pm; [S]R to Union St) Looking for a sports jersey? What about a piece of vintage designer clothing? There are many thrift stores in NYC, but few have quite this range. This gigantic vintage shop in the Gowanus area has a staggering inventory (you'll need to spend some time here), with great deals for bargain hunters. No Relation has five other shops around Brooklyn.

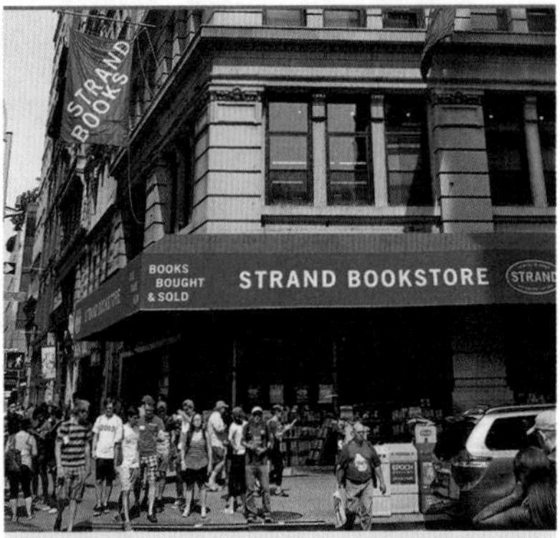

New York Icons

A few stores have cemented their status as NYC legends. This city just wouldn't quite be the same without them. For label hunters, **Century 21** (p146) is a Big Apple institution, with wears by D&G, Prada, Marc Jacobs and many others at low prices. Book lovers of the world unite at the **Strand** (p149), the city's biggest and best bookseller. Run by Hassidic Jews and employing mechanized whimsy, **B&H Photo Video** (p154) is a mecca for digital and audio geeks. For secondhand clothing, home furnishings and books, good-hearted **Housing Works** (p152), with many locations around town, is a perennial favorite.

Strand Book Store

MATTHEW DICKER/SHUTTERSTOCK ©

Beacon's Closet Vintage

(Map p257; ☎718-486-0816; www.beaconscloset.com; 74 Guernsey St, btwn Nassau & Norman Aves, Greenpoint; 🕐11am-8pm; [S]L to Bedford Ave; G to Nassau Ave) Twenty-something groovers find this massive 5500-sq-ft warehouse of vintage clothing part goldmine, part grit. Lots of coats, polyester tops and '90s-era T-shirts are displayed by color, but the sheer mass can take time to conquer. You'll also find shoes of all sorts, flannels, hats, handbags, chunky jewelry and brightly hued sunglasses.

BAR OPEN

Thirst-quenching venues, craft-beer
culture and beyond

Bar Open

You'll find all manner of thirst-quenching venues here, from terminally hip cocktail lounges and historic dive bars to specialty taprooms and 'third wave' coffee shops. Here in the land where the term 'cocktail' was born, mixed drinks are stirred with the utmost gravitas. The city's craft beer culture is equally dynamic, with an ever-expanding bounty of breweries, bars and shops showcasing local artisanal brews. Then there's the legendary club scene, spanning everything from celebrity staples to gritty, indie hangouts. Head downtown or to Brooklyn for the parts of the city that, as they say, truly never sleep.

In This Section

Opening Hours

Opening times vary. While some dive bars open as early as 8am, most drinking establishments get rolling around 5pm. Numerous bars stay open until 4am, while others close around 1am early in the week and 2am from Thursday to Saturday. Clubs generally operate from 10pm to 4am or 5pm.

Harlem & Upper Manhattan
A burgeoning mix of fabulous live
music spots, speakeasy-style bars
and old-school dives (p177)

Upper West Side
Not party central, but there are some beer halls
and wine bars worth checking out (p177)

Upper East Side
Traditionally the home of pricey,
luxe lounge bars, but downtown-cool
gastropubs are arriving (p175)

Midtown
Rooftop bars with skyline views, historic
cocktail salons and rough-n-ready
dive bars: welcome to Midtown (p173)

**West Village, Chelsea &
Meatpacking District**
Jet-setters flock here, with wine bars,
backdoor lounges and gay hangouts (p170)

Union Square, Flatiron District & Gramercy
Vintage drinking dens, swinging cocktail bars and
fun student hangouts – this trio spans all tastes (p171)

SoHo & Chinatown
Stylish cocktail lounges, a sprinkling of dives
and a few speakeasy-style bars (p167)

East Village & Lower East Side
Proud home of the original-flavor dive bar,
the East Village is brimming with options (p168)

**Financial District &
Lower Manhattan**
FiDi office slaves loosen their ties in
everything from specialist beer and brandy
bars to revered cocktail hot spots (p166)

Brooklyn
Offers everything on the nightlife
spectrum with Williamsburg as its heart (p178)

Tipping

If you grab a beer at the bar, bartenders
will expect at least a $1 tip *per drink;* tip
$2 to $3 for fancier cocktails. Sit-down
bars with waitstaff may expect more of
a standard restaurant-style 18% to 20%
tip, particularly if you snacked along
with your boozing.

Useful Websites

New York Magazine (www.nymag.com/
nightlife) Brilliantly curated nightlife options.

Thrillist (www.thrillist.com) An on-the-ball
roundup of what's hot on the NYC bar scene.

Urbandaddy (www.urbandaddy.com) Up-to-
the-minute info and a 'hot right now' list.

Time Out (www.timeout.com/newyork/
nightlife) Reviews of where to drink and
dance.

The Best...

Drinking and nightlife spots to sip the night away.

For Beer

Spuyten Duyvil (p179) A much-loved Williamsburg spot serving unique, high-quality crafts.

Bier International (p177) Some of Europe's finest beers on draft at this Harlem hall.

Proletariat (p170) Tiny East Village bar serving up extremely uncommon brews.

Birreria (p172) Unfiltered, unpasteurized Manhattan ales on a Flatiron rooftop.

For Wine

Terroir Tribeca (p166) An enlightened, encyclopedic wine list in trendy Tribeca.

La Compagnie des Vins Surnaturels (p168) A love letter to Gallic wines steps away from Little Italy.

Buvette (p171) A buzzing, candlelit wine bar on a tree-lined West Village street.

Immigrant (p170) Wonderful wines and service in a skinny East Village setting.

For Spirits

Ghost Donkey (p167) Eclectic downtown space that specializes in mezcal and tequila.

Brandy Library (p166) Blue-blooded cognacs, brandies and more for Tribeca connoisseurs.

Rum House (p173) Unique, coveted rums and a pianist to boot in Midtown.

Dead Rabbit (p166) NYC's finest collection of rare Irish whiskeys in the Financial District.

Dive Bars

Spring Lounge (p167) Soaks, ties and cool kids unite at this veteran Nolita rebel.

Malachy's (p177) The perfect place for a 1pm pick-me-up in the Upper West Side.

Cowgirl SeaHorse (pictured above; p167) Always a good time at this nautically themed drinkery in Lower Manhattan.

In Brooklyn

Maison Premiere (p178) Absinthe, juleps and oysters shine bright at this Big Easy tribute in Williamsburg.

Lavender Lake (p179) A hidden gem serving seasonal cocktails by the Gowanus.

Rookery (p179) An airy, chilled-out spot for cocktails and local craft brews.

Dance Clubs & House DJs

Cielo (pictured above; p171) A thumping, modern classic in the Meatpacking District.

Le Bain (p171) Well-dressed crowds still pack this favorite near the High Line.

Berlin (p170) Yesteryear's free-spirited days live on at this East Village bolt-hole.

Classic Date Bars

Manhattan Cricket Club (p177) Intimate, handsomely designed cocktail spot in the Upper West Side.

Pegu Club (p168) Made-from-scratch concoctions in a Burma-inspired SoHo hideaway.

Little Branch (p171) Speakeasy-chic is all the craze, but no one does it quite like this West Village hideout.

★ Lonely Planet's Top Choices

Silvana (p177) Hidden basement bar in Harlem with great live music every night of the week.

House of Yes (p178) Unrivaled destination for a wild night out at this Bushwick warehouse space.

Apothéke (p168) An atmospheric lounge and former opium den with great cocktails hidden away in Chinatown.

Rue B (p168) An appealing little East Village den with live jazz and a fun crowd.

Financial District & Lower Manhattan

Dead Rabbit Cocktail Bar

(Map p246; ☎646-422-7906; www.deadrabbitnyc.com; 30 Water St, btwn Broad St & Coenties Slip; 🕒taproom 11am-4am, parlor 5pm-2am Mon-Sat, to midnight Sun; [S]R/W to Whitehall St; 1 to South Ferry) Named in honor of a dreaded Irish-American gang, this most-wanted rabbit is regularly voted one of the world's best bars. Hit the sawdust-sprinkled Taproom for specialty beers, historic punches and pop-inns (lightly soured ale spiked with different flavors). Come evening, scurry upstairs to the cozy Parlor for meticulously researched cocktails. The Wall St crowd packs the place after work.

Brandy Library Cocktail Bar

(Map p248; ☎212-226-5545; www.brandylibrary.com; 25 N Moore St, near Varick St; 🕒5pm-1am Sun-Wed, 4pm-2am Thu, 4pm-4am Fri & Sat; [S]1 to Franklin St) When sipping means serious business, settle in at this uber-luxe 'library'; its handsome club chairs facing floor-to-ceiling, bottle-lined shelves. Go for top-shelf cognac, malt Scotch or vintage brandies, expertly paired with nibbles such as Gruyère-cheese puffs and a wonderful tartare made to order. Saturday nights are generally quieter than weeknights, making it a civilized spot for a weekend tête-à-tête.

Terroir Tribeca Wine Bar

(Map p248; ☎212-625-9463; www.wineisterroir.com; 24 Harrison St, at Greenwich St; 🕒4pm-midnight Mon & Tue, to 1am Wed-Sat, to 11pm Sun; [S]1 to Franklin St) Award-winning Terroir gratifies oenophiles with its well-versed, well-priced wine list (the offbeat, entertaining menu book is a must-read). Drops span the Old World and the New, among them natural wines and inspired offerings from smaller producers. A generous selection of wines by the glass makes your global wine tour a whole lot easier. Offers early *and* late happy hours, too.

Weather Up Cocktail Bar

(Map p248; ☎212-766-3202; www.weatherupnyc.com; 159 Duane St, btwn Hudson St & W Broadway; 🕒5pm-1am Mon-Wed, to 2am Thu-Sat,

Shark mural by Antony Zito at Spring Lounge

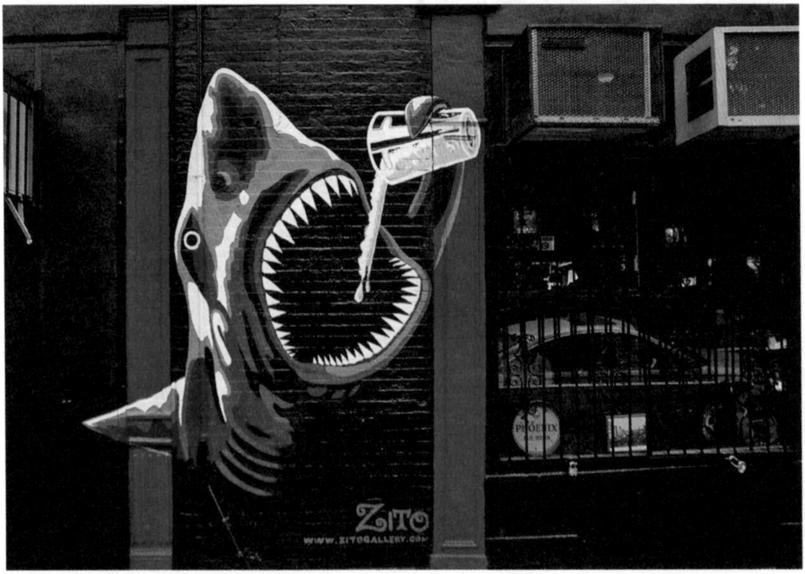

TED PINK/ALAMY STOCK PHOTO ©

to 10pm Sun; §1/2/3 to Chambers St) Simultaneously cool and classy: softly lit subway tiles, amiable and attractive barkeeps and seductive cocktails make for a bewitching trio at Weather Up. Sweet-talk the staff over a Fancy Free (bourbon, maraschino, orange and Angostura Bitters). Failing that, comfort yourself with some satisfying bites like oysters and steak tartare. There's a Brooklyn branch in **Prospect Heights** (Map p256; 589 Vanderbilt Ave, at Dean St; ⊘5:30pm-midnight Sun-Thu, to 2am Fri & Sat).

Cowgirl SeaHorse　　　　Bar

(Map p246; ☏212-608-7873; www.cowgirl seahorse.com; 259 Front St, at Dover St; ⊘11am-11pm Mon-Thu, 11am-late Fri, 10am-late Sat, 10am-11pm Sun; §A/C, J/Z, 2/3, 4/5 to Fulton St) In a sea of very serious bars and restaurants, Cowgirl SeaHorse is a party ship. Its nautical theme and perfect bar fare – giant plates of nachos piled with steaming meat, and frozen margaritas so sweet and tangy you won't be able to say no to a second round – make this dive a can't-miss for those looking to let loose.

❽ SoHo & Chinatown

Genuine Liquorette　　Cocktail Bar

(Map p248; ☏212-726-4633; www.genuine liquorette.com; 191 Grand St, at Mulberry St, Little Italy; ⊘6pm-midnight Sun, Tue & Wed, to 2am Thu-Sat, from 5pm Fri; §J/Z, N/Q/R/W, 6 to Canal St; B/D to Grand St) What's not to love about a jamming basement bar with canned cocktails and a Farrah Fawcett–themed restroom? You're even free to grab bottles and mixers and make your own drinks. At the helm is Ashlee, the beverage director, who regularly invites New York's finest barkeeps to create cocktails using less-celebrated hooch.

Ghost Donkey　　　　　　Bar

(Map p248; ☏212-254-0350; www.ghostdonkey. com; 4 Bleecker St, NoHo; ⊘5pm-2am; §6 to Bleecker St; B/D/F/M to Broadway-Lafayette St) Laid-back meets trippy meets craft at this one-of-a-kind, classy mezcal house

🏙 Clubbing in NYC

New Yorkers are always looking for the next big thing, so the city's club scene changes faster than a New York minute. Promoters drag revelers around the city for weekly events held at all of the finest addresses, and when there's nothing on, it's time to hit the dancefloor stalwarts.

When clubbing it never hurts to plan ahead; having your name on a guest list can relieve unnecessary frustration and disappointment. If you're an uninitiated partier, dress the part. If you're fed the 'private party' line, try to bluff – chances are high that you've been bounced. Also, don't forget a wad of cash as many nightspots (even the swankiest ones) often refuse credit cards, and in-house ATMs scam a fortune in fees.

that gives vibes of Mexico, the Middle East and the Wild West. If the moon had a saloon, this place would fit right in. Dark, dim, yet pink, with low-cushioned couches encircling lower coffee tables, this bar also serves excellent craft cocktails. (Try the frozen house margarita! Tasty, right?)

Spring Lounge　　　　　Bar

(Map p248; ☏212-965-1774; www.thespring lounge.com; 48 Spring St, at Mulberry St, Nolita; ⊘8am-4am Mon-Fri, from noon Sat & Sun; §6 to Spring St; R/W to Prince St) This neon-red rebel has never let anything get in the way of a good time. In Prohibition days, it peddled buckets of beer. In the '60s its basement was a gambling den. These days,

Happy hour beers typically start from $4; expect to pay about $7 or $8 for a regular draft, and more for imported bottles. Glasses of wine start at around $9. Specialty cocktails run from $14 to well over $20. Expect to pay between $5 and $30 to get into clubs.

it's best known for its kooky stuffed sharks, early-start regulars and come-one, come-all late-night revelry. Perfect last stop on a bar-hopping tour of the neighborhood.

Apothéke   Cocktail Bar

(Map p248; ☏212-406-0400; www.apothekenyc.com; 9 Doyers St, Chinatown; ⊗6:30pm-2am Mon-Sat, from 8pm Sun; Ⓢ J/Z to Chambers St; 4/5/6 to Brooklyn Bridge-City Hall) It takes a little effort to track down this former opium-den-turned-apothecary bar on Doyers St. Inside, skilled barkeeps work like careful chemists, using local, seasonal produce from Greenmarkets to produce intense, flavorful 'prescriptions.' Their cocktail ingredient ratio is always on point, such as the pineapple-cilantro blend in the Sitting Buddha, one of the best drinks on the menu.

Pegu Club   Cocktail Bar

(Map p248; ☏212-473-7348; www.peguclub.com; 77 W Houston St, btwn W Broadway & Wooster St, SoHo; ⊗5pm-2am Sun-Wed, to 4am Thu-Sat; Ⓢ B/D/F/M to Broadway-Lafayette St; C/E to Spring St) Dark, elegant Pegu Club (named after a legendary gentleman's club in colonial-era Rangoon) is an obligatory stop for cocktail connoisseurs. Sink into a velvet lounge and savor seamless libations such as the silky-smooth Earl Grey MarTEAni (tea-infused gin, lemon juice and raw egg white). Grazing options are suitably Asianesque, among them duck wontons and Mandalay coconut shrimp.

La Compagnie des Vins Surnaturels   Wine Bar

(Map p248; ☏212-343-3660; www.compagnienyc.com; 249 Centre St, btwn Broome & Grand Sts, Nolita; wines by the glass $11-22; ⊗5pm-1am Mon-Wed, to 2am Thu & Fri, 3pm-2am Sat, to 1am Sun; Ⓢ6 to Spring St; R/W to Prince St) A snug melange of Gallic-themed wallpaper, svelte armchairs and tea lights, La Compagnie des Vins Surnaturels is an offshoot of a Paris bar by the same name. Head sommelier Theo Lieberman steers an impressive, French-heavy wine list, with some 600 drops and no shortage of arresting labels by the glass. A short, sophisticated menu includes housemade charcuterie and chicken rillettes.

⊕ East Village & Lower East Side

Rue B   Bar

(Map p248; ☏212-358-1700; www.ruebnyc188.com; 188 Ave B, btwn E 11th & 12th Sts, East Village; ⊗5pm-4am; Ⓢ L to 1st Ave) There's live jazz (and the odd rockabilly group) every night from 9pm to midnight at this tiny, amber-lit drinking den on a bar-dappled stretch of Ave B. A young, celebratory crowd packs the small space – so mind the tight corners, lest the trombonist end up in your lap. B&W photos of jazz greats and other NYC icons enhance the ambience.

Bar Goto   Bar

(Map p248; ☏212-475-4411; www.bargoto.com; 245 Eldridge St, btwn E Houston & Stanton Sts, Lower East Side; ⊗5pm-midnight Tue-Thu & Sun, to 2am Fri & Sat; Ⓢ F to 2nd Ave) Maverick mixologist Kenta Goto has cocktail connoisseurs spellbound at his eponymous hot spot. Expect meticulous, elegant drinks that revel in Koto's Japanese heritage (the sake-spiked Sakura Martini is utterly smashing), paired with authentic, Japanese comfort bites, such as *okonomiyaki* (savory pancakes).

★ **Top Five Cocktail Bars**

Bar Goto (p168)

Dead Rabbit (p166)

Employees Only (p170)

Lantern's Keep (p174)

Genuine Liquorette (p167)

Clockwise from top: Genuine Liquorette; Dead Rabbit; 'Deal Closer' cocktail at Apothéke

Signature Manhattan cocktail at Employees Only

Berlin   Club
(Map p248; ☑646-827-3689; 25 Ave A, btwn
First & Second Aves, East Village; ⊙8pm-4am;
Ⓢ F to 2nd Ave) Like a secret bunker hidden
beneath the ever-gentrifying streets of
the East Village, Berlin is a throwback to
the neighborhood's more riotous days of
wildness and dancing. Once you find the
unmarked entrance, head downstairs to the
grotto-like space with vaulted brick ceilings,
a long bar and tiny dancefloor, with funk
and rare grooves spilling all around.

Immigrant   Bar
(Map p248; ☑646-308-1724; www.theimmi
grantnyc.com; 341 E 9th St, btwn First & Second
Aves, East Village; ⊙5pm-2am; Ⓢ L to 1st Ave; 6
to Astor Pl) Wholly unpretentious, these twin
boxcar-sized bars could easily become
your neighborhood local if you decide to
stick around town. The staff are knowl-
edgeable and kind, mingling with faithful
regulars while dishing out tangy olives and
topping up glasses with imported snifters.
    Enter the right side for the wine bar,
with an excellent assortment of glasses

and bottles on the menu. The left entrance
takes you into the taproom, where the
focus is on unique microbrews. Both have
a similar design – chandeliers, exposed
brick, vintage charm.

Proletariat   Bar
(Map p248; www.proletariatny.com; 102 St Marks
Pl, btwn Ave A & First Ave, East Village; ⊙5pm-
2am; Ⓢ L to 1st Ave) The cognoscenti of NYC's
beer world pack this tiny, 10-stool bar just
west of Tompkins Square Park. Promising
'rare, new and unusual beers,' Proletariat
delivers the goods with a changing lineup of
brews you won't find elsewhere. Recent hits
have included Brooklyn and New Jersey
drafts from artisanal brewers.

❷ West Village, Chelsea & Meatpacking District

Employees Only   Bar
(Map p248; ☑212-242-3021; www.employees
onlynyc.com; 510 Hudson St, btwn W 10th &
Christopher Sts, West Village; ⊙6pm-4am; Ⓢ 1

to Christopher St-Sheridan Sq) Duck behind the neon 'Psychic' sign to find this hidden hangout. Bartenders are ace mixologists, fizzing up crazy, addictive libations like the Ginger Smash and an upscale Bellini. Great for late-night drinking and eating, courtesy of the on-site restaurant that serves till 3:30am – housemade chicken soup is ladled out to stragglers. The bar gets busier as the night wears on.

Buvette   Wine Bar

(Map p248; ☎212-255-3590; www.ilovebuvette. com; 42 Grove St, btwn Bedford & Bleecker Sts, West Village; ☺7am-2am Mon-Fri, from 8am Sat & Sun; ⑤1 to Christopher St-Sheridan Sq; A/C/E, B/D/F/M to W 4th St-Washington Sq) The rustic-chic decor here (think delicate tin tiles and a swooshing marble counter) makes it the perfect place for a glass of wine – no matter the time of day. For the full experience at this self-proclaimed *gastrothèque,* grab a seat at one of the surrounding tables and nibble on small plates while enjoying old-world wines (mostly from France and Italy).

Cubbyhole   Gay & Lesbian

(Map p248; ☎212-243-9041; www.cubbyholebar. com; 281 W 12th St, at W 4th St, West Village; ☺4pm-4am Mon-Fri, from 2pm Sat & Sun; ⑤A/C/E, L to 8th Ave-14th St) This West Village dive bills itself as 'lesbian, gay and straight friendly since 1994.' While the crowd is mostly ladies, as its motto suggests it's a welcoming place for anyone looking for a cheap drink. It's got a great jukebox, friendly bartenders and plenty of regulars who prefer to hang and chat rather than hook up and leave.

Happy hour is until 7pm Monday to Saturday. There are also daily drink specials, so make sure to check the website.

Cielo   Club

(Map p248; ☎212-645-5700; www.cieloclub. com; 18 Little W 12th St, btwn Ninth Ave & Washington St, Meatpacking District; cover $15-25; ⑤A/C/E, L to 8th Ave-14th St) This long-running club boasts a largely attitude-free crowd and an excellent sound system. Join dance lovers on TOCA Tuesdays, when DJ Tony Touch spins classic hip-hop, soul and funk. Other nights feature various DJs from Europe, who mix entrancing, seductive sounds that pull everyone to their feet.

Le Bain   Club

(Map p248; ☎212-645-7600; www.standard hotels.com; 444 W 13th St, btwn Washington St & Tenth Ave, Meatpacking District; ☺4pm-3am Mon, to 4am Tue-Thu, 2pm-4am Fri & Sat, to 3am Sun; ⑤A/C/E, L to 8th Ave-14th St) The sweeping rooftop venue at the tragically hip Standard Hotel, Le Bain sees a garish parade of party promoters who do their thing on any day of the week. Brace yourself for skyline views, a dancefloor with a giant Jacuzzi built right into it and an eclectic crowd getting wasted on pricey snifters.

Little Branch   Cocktail Bar

(Map p248; ☎212-929-4360; 20 Seventh Ave S, at Leroy St, West Village; ☺7pm-3am Mon-Sat, to 2am Sun; ⑤1 to Houston St; A/C/E, B/D/F/M to W 4th St-Washington Sq) If it weren't for lines later in the evening, you'd never guess that a charming drinking den lurked beyond the plain metal door positioned at this triangular intersection – walk downstairs to find a basement bar that feels like a kickback to Prohibition times. Locals clink glasses and sip inventive, artfully prepared cocktails, with live jazz performances Sunday through Thursday nights.

❷ Union Square, Flatiron District & Gramercy

Flatiron Lounge   Cocktail Bar

(Map p252; ☎212-727-7741; www.flatironlounge. com; 37 W 19th St, btwn Fifth & Sixth Aves, Flatiron District; ☺4pm-2am Mon-Wed, to 3am Thu, to 4am Fri, 5pm-4am Sat; ☎; ⑤F/M, R/W, 6 to 23rd St) Head through a dramatic archway and into a dark, swinging, art-deco–inspired fantasy of lipstick-red booths, racy jazz tunes and sassy grown-ups downing

👍 Brooklyn Brews

Beer brewing was once a thriving industry in the city – by the 1870s, Brooklyn boasted a belly-swelling 48 breweries. Most of these were based in Williamsburg, Bushwick and Greenpoint, neighborhoods packed with German immigrants with extensive brewing know-how. By the eve of Prohibition in 1919, the borough was one of the country's leading beer peddlers, but by the end of Prohibition in 1933, most breweries had shut shop. Though the industry rose from the ashes in WWII, local flavor gave in to big-gun Midwestern brands.

Today Brooklyn is once more a catchword for good beer as a handful of craft breweries put integrity back on tap. Head of the pack is Williamsburg's **Brooklyn Brewery** (www.brooklyn brewery.com), whose seasonal offerings include a nutmeg-spiked Post Road Pumpkin Ale (available August to November) and a luscious Black Chocolate Stout (a take on Imperial Stout, available October to March). The brewery's comrades-in-craft include **SixPoint Craft Ales** (www. sixpoint.com), **Threes Brewing** (www. threesbrewing.com) and **Other Half Brewing Co** (www.otherhalf brewing.com). Justifiably famed for its piney, hoppy Imperial IPA Green Diamonds, Other Half Brewing Co gathers its hops and malts from local farms.

Brooklyn Brewery
JOSE OTERO/500PX ©

seasonal drinks. Cocktails run $14 a pop, but happy-hour cocktails are only $10 (4pm to 6pm weekdays).

Birreria   Beer Hall
(Map p252; 📞212-937-8910; www.eataly.com; 200 Fifth Ave, at W 23rd St, Flatiron District; ☺11:30am-11pm; Ⓢ F/M, R/W, 6 to 23rd St) The crown jewel of Italian food emporium Eataly (p132) is this rooftop beer garden tucked betwixt the Flatiron's corporate towers. An encyclopedic beer menu offers drinkers some of the best suds on the planet. If you're hungry, the signature beer-braised pork shoulder will pair nicely, or check out the seasonally changing menu of the on-site pop-up restaurant (mains $17 to $37).

Raines Law Room   Cocktail Bar
(Map p252; www.raineslawroom.com; 48 W 17th St, btwn Fifth & Sixth Aves, Flatiron District; ☺5pm-2am Mon-Wed, to 3am Thu-Sat, 7pm-1am Sun; Ⓢ F/M to 14th St, L to 6th Ave, 1 to 18th St) A sea of velvet drapes and overstuffed leather lounge chairs, the perfect amount of exposed brick, expertly crafted cocktails using meticulously aged spirits – these folks are as serious as a mortgage payment when it comes to amplified atmosphere. Reservations (recommended) are only accepted Sunday to Tuesday. Whatever the night, style up for a taste of a far more sumptuous era.

Old Town Bar & Restaurant   Bar
(Map p252; 📞212-529-6732; www.oldtownbar. com; 45 E 18th St, btwn Broadway & Park Ave S, Union Sq; ☺11:30am-11:30pm Mon-Fri, noon-11:30pm Sat, to 10pm Sun; Ⓢ 4/5/6, N/Q/R/W, L to 14th St-Union Sq) It still looks like 1892 in here, with the mahogany bar, original tile floors and tin ceilings – the Old Town is an old-world drinking-man's classic (and -woman's: Madonna lit up at the bar here – when lighting up in bars was still legal – in her 'Bad Girl' video). There are cocktails around, but most come for beers and a burger (from $11.50).

Midtown

The Campbell
Cocktail Bar

(Map p254; ☎212-297-1781; www.thecampbell
nyc.com; Grand Central Terminal; ⊙noon-2am)
As swanky as swank can be, the only thing
missing at the Campbell is elevation – you
don't get the sweeping skyline view that
some NYC bars have. Instead, you can sip
top-shelf signature cocktails beneath a
stunning hand-painted ceiling, restored
along with the room with touches that
make it seem Rockefeller or Carnegie
might just join you.

Rum House
Cocktail Bar

(Map p254; ☎646-490-6924; www.therum
housenyc.com; 228 W 47th St, btwn Broadway &
Eighth Ave; ⊙noon-4am; ⓢN/R/W to 49th St)
This sultry slice of old New York is revered
for its rums and whiskeys. Savor them
straight up or mixed in impeccable cocktails like 'The Escape,' a potent piña colada.
Adding to the magic is nightly live music,
spanning solo piano tunes to jaunty jazz
trios and sentimental divas. Bartenders

here are careful with their craft; don't
expect them to rush.

Bar SixtyFive
Cocktail Bar

(Map p254; ☎212-632-5000; www.rainbowroom.
com/bar-sixty-five; 30 Rockefeller Plaza, entrance
on W 49th St; ⊙5pm-midnight Mon-Fri, 4-9pm
Sun; ⓢB/D/F/M to 47th-50th Sts-Rockefeller
Center) Not to be missed, sophisticated
SixtyFive sits on level 65 of the GE Building
at Rockefeller Center (p84). Dress well (no
sportswear or guests under 21) and arrive
by 5pm for a seat with a multi-million-dollar
view. Even if you don't score a table on the
balcony or by the window, head outside to
soak up that sweeping New York panorama.

Industry
Gay

(Map p254; ☎646-476-2747; www.industry-bar.
com; 355 W 52nd St, btwn Eighth & Ninth Aves;
⊙5pm-4am; ⓢC/E, 1 to 50th St) What was
once a parking garage is now one of the
hottest gay bars in Hell's Kitchen – a slick,
4000-sq-ft watering hole with handsome
lounge areas, a pool table and a stage for
top-notch drag divas. Head in between 4pm
and 9pm for the two-for-one drinks special

The Campbell

SIVAN ASKAYO/LONELY PLANET ©

or squeeze in later to party with the eye-candy party hordes. Cash only.

Lantern's Keep Cocktail Bar

(Map p254; ☎212-453-4287; www.iroquoisny.com; Iroquois Hotel, 49 W 44th St, btwn Fifth & Sixth Aves; ⏰5-11pm Mon, to midnight Tue-Fri, 7pm-1am Sat; [S]B/D/F/M to 42nd St-Bryant Park) Cross the lobby of the **Iroquois Hotel** (☎212-840-3080) to slip into this dark, intimate cocktail salon. Its specialty is classic drinks, shaken and stirred by passionate, personable mixologists. If you're feeling spicy, request a Gordon's Breakfast (not on the menu!), a fiery melange of gin, Worcestershire sauce, hot sauce, muddled lime and cucumber, salt and pepper. Reservations are recommended.

Robert Cocktail Bar

(Map p254; ☎212-299-7730; www.robertnyc.com; Museum of Arts & Design, 2 Columbus Circle, btwn Eighth Ave & Broadway; ⏰11:30am-10pm Mon-Fri, from 10:30am Sat & Sun; [S]A/C, B/D, 1 to 59th St-Columbus Circle) Perched on the 9th floor of the Museum of Arts & Design (p65), '60s-inspired Robert is technically a high-end, Modern American restaurant. While the food is satisfactory, we say visit late afternoon or post-dinner, find a sofa and gaze out over Central Park with a MAD Manhattan (bourbon, blood orange vermouth and liquored cherries). Check the website for live jazz sessions.

Top of the Strand Cocktail Bar

(Map p252; ☎646-368-6426; www.topofthestrand.com; Marriott Vacation Club Pulse, 33 W 37th St, btwn Fifth & Sixth Aves, Midtown East; ⏰5pm-midnight Mon & Sun, to 1am Tue-Sat; [S]B/D/F/M, N/Q/R to 34th St) For that 'Oh my God, I'm in New York' feeling, head to the Marriott Vacation Club Pulse (formerly the Strand Hotel) hotel's rooftop bar, order a martini (extra dirty) and drop your jaw (discreetly). Sporting comfy cabana-style seating, a refreshingly mixed-age crowd and a sliding glass roof, its view of the Empire State Building is simply unforgettable.

Therapy Gay

(Map p254; ☎212-397-1700; www.therapy-nyc.com; 348 W 52nd St, btwn Eighth & Ninth Aves, Midtown West; ⏰5pm-2am Sun-Thu, to 4am Fri & Sat; [S]C/E, 1 to 50th St) Multilevel Therapy

From left: Iroquois Hotel; Top of the Strand; Bemelmans Bar

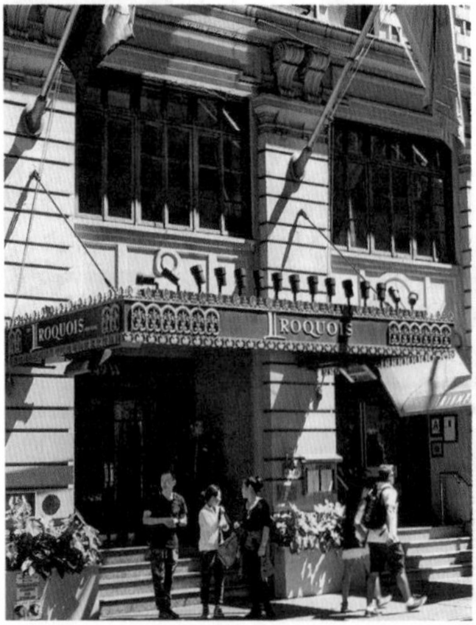

PATTI MCCONVILLE/ALAMY STOCK PHOTO ©

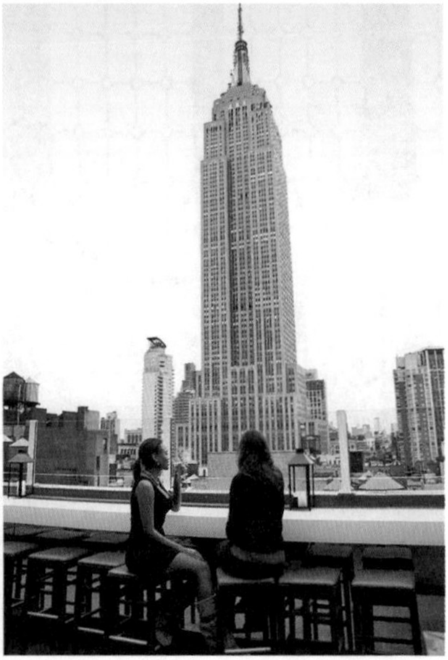

DAN HALLMAN/LONELY PLANET ©

was the first gay men's lounge/club to draw throngs to Hell's Kitchen, and it still pulls a crowd with its nightly shows (from live music to interviews with Broadway stars) and decent grub served Sunday to Friday (the quesadillas are especially popular). Drink monikers match the theme: 'oral fixation' and 'size queen', to name a few.

Upper East Side

Caledonia Bar

(Map p254; ☎212-734-4300; www.caledonia bar.com; 1609 Second Ave, btwn E 83rd & 84th Sts; [S]Q, 4/5/6 to 86th St) The name of this dimly lit, dark-wood bar is a dead giveaway: it's devoted to Scottish whisky, with over a hundred single malts to choose from (be they Highlands, Islands, Islay, Lowlands or Speyside), as well as some blends and even a few from the US, Ireland and Japan. The bartenders know their stuff and will be happy to make recommendations.

Cantor Roof Garden Bar Rooftop Bar

(Map p254; ☎212-570-3711; Metropolitan Museum, 1000 Fifth Ave, 5th fl, cnr E 82nd St; 🕐11am-4:30pm Sun-Thu, to 8:15pm Fri & Sat mid-Apr–Oct; [S]4/5/6 to 86th St) The sort of setting you can't get enough of (even if you are a jaded local). Located atop the Met, this rooftop bar sits right above Central Park's tree canopy, allowing for splendid views of the park and the city skyline all around. Sunset is when you'll find fools in love... then again, it could all be those martinis.

Bemelmans Bar Lounge

(Map p254; ☎212-744-1600; www.thecarlyle.com; Carlyle Hotel, 35 E 76th St, cnr Madison Ave; 🕐noon-1am; [S]6 to 77th St) Sink into a chocolate-leather banquette and take in the glorious, old-school elegance of this fabled bar – the sort of place where the waiters wear white jackets, a pianist tinkles away on a baby grand and the ceiling is 24-carat gold leaf. The walls are covered in charming murals by the bar's namesake Ludwig Bemelman, famed creator of the *Madeline* books.

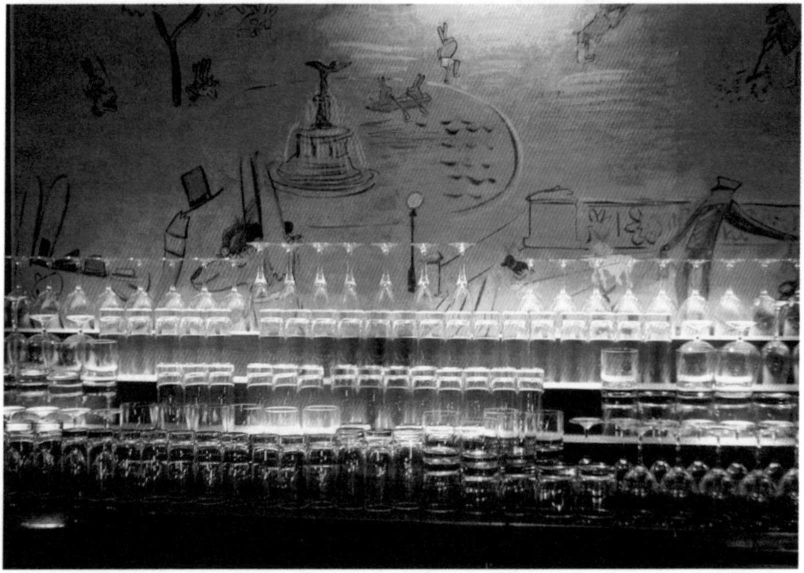

New York City in a Glass

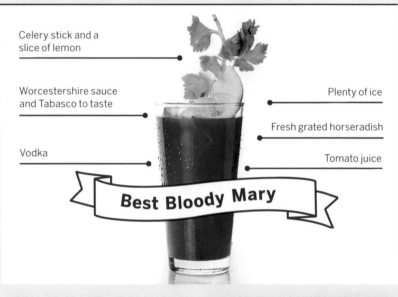

Celery stick and a slice of lemon

Worcestershire sauce and Tabasco to taste

Vodka

Plenty of ice

Fresh grated horseradish

Tomato juice

Best Bloody Mary

History of a Classic

The classic Bloody Mary – considered a true hangover remedy by many – is a staple of weekend brunches in NYC. The modern version of this drink was invented at the St Regis Hotel's King Cole Bar in 1934 (it's still their signature drink). Garnishes range from vegetables like pickles, olives, chili peppers, lemon and celery to outrageous sculptures teetering with bacon, salami or even shrimp.

Elaborate Bloody Marys

★ NYC's Top Places for a Bloody Mary

Cookshop (p129)

Buttermilk Channel (Map p256; ☏718-852-8490; www.buttermilkchannelnyc.com; 524 Court St, at Huntington St, Carroll Gardens; mains lunch $11-27, brunch $12-24, dinner $16-32; ⏱lunch 11:30am-3pm Mon-Fri, brunch 10am-3pm Sat & Sun, dinner 5-10pm Sun-Thu, to 11:30pm Fri & Sat; **S**F, G to Smith-9th Sts)

Pine Box Rock Shop (p179)

Prune (Map p248; ☏212-677-6221; www.prunerestaurant.com; 54 E 1st St, btwn First & Second Aves, East Village; dinner $24-33, mains brunch $14-24; ⏱5:30-11pm, also 10am-3:30pm Sat & Sun; **S**F to 2nd Ave)

Drunken Munkey   Lounge

(Map p254; ☑646-998-4600; www.drunken
munkeynyc.com; 338 E 92nd St, btwn First &
Second Aves; ☺4:30pm-2am Mon-Thu, to 3am
Fri, 11am-3am Sat, to 2am Sun; Ⓢ Q, 6 to 96th St)
This playful lounge channels colonial-era
Bombay with vintage wallpaper, cricket-
ball door handles and jauntily attired
waitstaff. The monkey chandeliers may be
pure whimsy, but the craft cocktails and
tasty curries (small, meant for sharing)
are serious business. Gin, not surprisingly,
is the drink of choice. Try the Bramble:
Bombay gin, blackberry liqueur and fresh
lemon juice and blackberries.

❸ Upper West Side

Manhattan Cricket Club   Lounge

(Map p254; ☑646-823-9252; www.mccnewyork.
com; 226 W 79th St, btwn Amsterdam Ave &
Broadway; ☺6pm-late; Ⓢ 1 to 79th St) Above
an Australian **bistro** (Map p254; ☑646-823-
9251; www.burkeandwillsny.com; mains lunch
$19-32, dinner $19-39; ☺lunch noon-3pm Mon-
Fri, dinner 5:30-11:30pm daily, brunch 11am-4pm
Sat & Sun) – ask its host for access – this
elegant drinking lounge is modeled on the
classy Anglo-Aussie cricket clubs of the
early 1900s. Sepia-toned photos of bats-
men adorn the gold brocaded walls, while
mahogany bookshelves and chesterfield
sofas create a fine setting for quaffing
well-made (but pricey) cocktails. It's a
guaranteed date-pleaser.

Dead Poet   Bar

(Map p254; ☑212-595-5670; www.thedeadpoet.
com; 450 Amsterdam Ave, btwn 81st & 82nd
Sts; ☺noon-4am; Ⓢ 1 to 79th St) This narrow,
mahogany-paneled pub is a neighborhood favorite. It takes its Guinness pours
seriously, and features cocktails named
after deceased masters of verse, including
a Walt Whitman Long Island Iced Tea ($13)
and a Pablo Neruda spiced-rum sangria
($12). Feeling adventurous? Order the
signature cocktail ($15), a secret recipe

of seven alcohols – you even get to keep
the glass.

Malachy's   Pub

(Map p254; ☑212-874-4268; www.malachysnyc.
com; 103 W 72nd St, at Columbus Ave; ☺noon-
4am; Ⓢ B/C, 1/2/3 to 72nd St) Giving new
meaning to the word 'dive,' this crusty local
holdout has a long wooden bar, classic
rock on the speakers, a lineup of regulars
and a bartender with a sense of humor. In
other words: the perfect place for daytime
drinking. There's also a cheap menu of
classic bar food.

❸ Harlem & Upper Manhattan

Silvana   Bar

(www.silvana-nyc.com; 300 W 116th St; ☺8am-
4am; Ⓢ 2/3 to 116th St) This appealing
Middle Eastern cafe and shop whips up
tasty hummus and falafel plates; the real
draw, though, is the hidden downstairs
club, which draws a friendly, easygoing
local crowd with good cocktails and live
bands (kicking off around 6pm) followed
by DJs. The lineup is eclectic, with jazz,
Cuban *son*, reggae and Balkan gypsy punk
all in the rotation.

Bier International   Beer Hall

(☑212-280-0944; www.bierinternational.
com; 2099 Frederick Douglass Blvd, at 113th
St, Harlem; ☺4pm-1am Mon-Wed, to 2am Thu
& Fri, noon-2am Sat, noon-1am Sun; Ⓢ B, C, 1 to
110th St-Cathedral Pkwy; 2/3 to 110th St-Central
Park North) A fun, buzzing beer garden that
peddles some 18 different drafts from
Germany, Belgium and the UK, plus local
brews from the Bronx Brewery and Brooklyn's Sixpoint. The extensive menu makes
it worthwhile to stick around. Think catfish
tacos, truffle fries with shaved Parmesan
and Vienna-style schnitzel. Cash only.

Shrine   Bar

(www.shrinenyc.com; 2271 Adam Clayton
Powell Jr Blvd, btwn 133rd & 134th Sts, Harlem;
☺4pm-4am; Ⓢ 2/3 to 135th St) To see what's

House of Yes

happening on the global music scene, the friendly, unpretentious Shrine (run by the talented team behind Silvana; p177) is a great place to start. Here you'll find live bands taking the small stage every day of the week. Blues, reggae, Afro-beat, funk, soca, Ethiopian grooves and indie rock are among the sounds you'll hear, with no cover charge.

Ginny's Supper Club Cocktail Bar

(☎212-421-3821; www.ginnyssupperclub.com; 310 Malcolm X Blvd, btwn W 125th & 126th Sts, Harlem; ⏰6pm-midnight Thu, to 3am Fri & Sat, brunch 10:30am-2pm Sun; [S]2/3 to 125th St) Looking straight out of the TV series *Boardwalk Empire,* this roaring basement supper club is rarely short of styled-up regulars sipping cocktails, nibbling on soul and global bites (from Red Rooster's kitchen upstairs; p137) and grooving to live jazz from 7:30pm Thursday to Saturday and DJ-spun beats from 11pm Friday and Saturday. Don't miss the weekly Sunday gospel brunch (reservations recommended).

🍷 Brooklyn

House of Yes Club

(www.houseofyes.org; 2 Wyckoff Ave, at Jefferson St, Bushwick; tickets free-$40; ⏰hours vary by event, Tue-Sat; [S]L to Jefferson St) Anything goes at this highly regarded warehouse venue, with two stages, three bars and a covered outdoor area, which offers some of the most creative themed performance and dance nights in Brooklyn. You might see aerial-silk acrobats, punk bands, burlesque shows, drag queens or performance artists, with DJs spinning house and other deep beats for an artsy, inclusive crowd.

Leave the baseball caps and sneakers at home – costumes or other funky outfits will get you priority admission most nights, and on Fridays and Saturdays, they're required for entry (an on-site pop-up costume shop will let you throw something together if you've arrived unprepared).

Maison Premiere Cocktail Bar

(Map p257; ☎347-335-0446; www.maison premiere.com; 298 Bedford Ave, btwn S 1st &

Grand Sts, Williamsburg; ⊙2pm-2am Mon-Wed, to 4am Thu & Fri, 11am-4am Sat, to 2am Sun; ⓢL to Bedford Ave) We kept expecting to see Dorothy Parker stagger into this old-timey place, which features an elegant bar full of syrups and essences, suspender-wearing bartenders and a jazzy soundtrack to further channel the French Quarter New Orleans vibe. The cocktails are serious business: the epic list includes more than a dozen absinthe drinks, various juleps and an array of specialty cocktails.

Spuyten Duyvil   Bar

(Map p257; ☎718-963-4140; www.spuyten duyvilnyc.com; 359 Metropolitan Ave, btwn Havemeyer & Roebling Sts, Williamsburg; ⊙5pm-2am Mon-Fri, noon-3am Sat, to 2am Sun; ⓢL to Lorimer St; G to Metropolitan Ave) This low-key Williamsburg bar looks like it was pieced together from a rummage sale, with red-painted ceilings, vintage maps on the walls and what looks like thrift-store furniture. But the selection of beer and wine is staggering, the locals from various eras are chatty and there's a large backyard with leafy trees that's open in good weather.

Lavender Lake   Pub

(Map p256; ☎347-799-2154; www.lavenderlake. com; 383 Carroll St, btwn Bond Sts & Gowanus Canal, Gowanus; ⊙4pm-midnight Mon-Wed, to 1am Thu, to 2am Fri, noon-2am Sat, to midnight Sun; ⓢF, G to Carroll St; R to Union St) This little gem of a bar – named after the old local nickname for the colorfully polluted Gowanus Canal – is set in a former horse stable and serves carefully selected craft beers and a few seasonal cocktails, which include ingredients such as jalapeño-infused tequila. The light-strewn garden is a brilliant summery spot. There's good food, too (mains $11 to $23).

Toby's Estate   Coffee

(Map p257; ☎347-457-6155; www.tobysestate. com; 125 N 6th St, btwn Bedford Ave & Berry St, Williamsburg; ⊙7am-7pm; 🛜; ⓢL to Bedford Ave) This small-batch roaster brings serious flavor to the streets of Billyburg with bold,

aromatic pour-overs, creamy flat whites and smooth *cortados* (espresso with a dash of milk). There are a few couches and several communal tables generally crowded with MacBook users.

Radegast Hall
& Biergarten   Beer Hall

(Map p257; ☎718-963-3973; www.radegasthall. com; 113 N 3rd St, at Berry St, Williamsburg; ⊙noon-3am Mon-Fri, from 11am Sat & Sun; ⓢL to Bedford Ave) An Austro-Hungarian beer hall in Williamsburg offers up a huge selection of Bavarian brews, and a kitchen full of munchable meats. You can hover in the dark, woody bar area or sit in the adjacent hall, which has a retractable roof and communal tables to feast at – perfect for pretzels, sausages and burgers. Live music every night; no cover.

Rookery   Bar

(www.therookerybar.com; 425 Troutman St, btwn St Nicholas & Wyckoff Aves, Bushwick; ⊙noon-4am Mon-Fri, from 11am Sat & Sun; ⓢL to Jefferson St) A mainstay of the Bushwick scene is the industrial-esque Rookery on street-art-lined Troutman Ave. Come for cocktails, craft brews, fusion pub fare (curried-goat shepherd's pies, oxtail sloppy joes), obscure electro-pop and a relaxed vibe. High ceilings give the space an airy feel and the back patio is a great spot, afternoon or evening, in warm weather.

Pine Box Rock Shop   Bar

(Map p257; ☎718-366-6311; www.pinebox rockshop.com; 12 Grattan St, btwn Morgan Ave & Bogart St, East Williamsburg; ⊙4pm-2am Mon & Tue, to 4am Wed-Fri, 2pm-4am Sat, noon-2am Sun; ⓢL to Morgan Ave) The cavernous Pine Box Rock Shop – a former casket factory – has 17 drafts to choose from, as well as widely heralded, spicy, pint-sized Bloody Marys. It's run by a friendly vegan musician couple, so everything served here uses no animal products, including the empanadas and other bar snacks. Local artwork graces the walls, and a performance back room hosts regular gigs.

SHOWTIME

Music, theater, dance and more

Showtime

Dramatically lit stages, basement jazz joints, high-ceilinged dance halls, and opera houses set for melodramatic tales – for more than a century, New York City has been America's capital of cultural production. It's perhaps best known for its Broadway musicals, presented in lavish early-20th-century theaters that surround Times Square, but beyond Broadway you'll find experimental downtown playhouses, the hallowed concert halls of the Met, and live music joints scattered in all corners of the city. The biggest challenge is deciding where to begin.

In This Section

Ticket Information

To purchase tickets for shows, you can either head directly to the venue's box office, or use one of several ticket agencies such as **Telecharge** (www.telecharge.com) or **Ticketmaster** (www.ticketmaster.com). For discount same-day Broadway tickets, visit a **TKTS Booth** (www.tdf.org). For other entertainment (comedy, cabaret, performance art, music, dance and downtown theater), check out **SmartTix** (www.smarttix.com).

Lincoln Center (p76)

The Best...

Broadway Shows

Book of Mormon (p59) Brilliantly funny, award-winning show by the creators of *South Park*.

Chicago (p60) One of the most scintillating shows on Broadway.

Kinky Boots (p60) Book well ahead to score seats for this over-the-top musical.

Hamilton (p59) If you can't get tickets, try standing in the cancellation line outside the theater.

For Jazz

Jazz at Lincoln Center (p188) Innovative fare under the guidance of jazz luminary Wynton Marsalis.

Village Vanguard (p185) Legendary West Village jazz club.

Smalls (p186) Tiny West Village basement joint that evokes the feel of decades past.

Birdland (p188) Sleek Midtown space that hosts big-band sounds, Afro-Cuban jazz and more.

Financial District & Lower Manhattan

Flea Theater Theater

(Map p248; ☎tickets 212-226-0051; www.theflea.org; 20 Thomas St, btwn Church St & Broadway; 👪; [S]A/C, 1/2/3 to Chambers St; R/W to City Hall) One of NYC's top off-off-Broadway companies, Flea is famous for staging innovative and timely new works. A brand-new location offers three performance spaces, including one named for devoted alum Sigourney Weaver. The year-round program also includes music and dance productions, as well as shows for young audiences (aged five and up) and a rollicking late-night competition series of 10-minute plays.

Soho Rep Theater

(Soho Repertory Theatre; Map p248; ☎212-941-8632; www.sohorep.org; 46 Walker St, btwn Church St & Broadway; [S]A/C/E, 1 to Canal St) This is one of New York's finest off-Broadway companies, wowing theater fans and critics with its annual trio of sharp, innovative new works. Allison Janney, Ed O'Neill and John C Reilly all made their professional debuts here, and the company's productions have garnered more than a dozen Obie (Off-Broadway Theater) Awards.

SoHo & Chinatown

Joe's Pub Live Music

(Map p248; ☎212-539-8778, tickets 212-967-7555; www.joespub.com; Public Theater, 425 Lafayette St, btwn Astor Pl & 4th St, NoHo; [S]6 to Astor Pl; R/W to 8th St-NYU) Part bar, part cabaret and performance venue, intimate Joe's serves up emerging acts and top-shelf performers. Past entertainers have included Patti LuPone, Amy Schumer, the late Leonard Cohen and British songstress Adele (in fact, it was right here that Adele gave her very first American performance, back in 2008).

Film Forum Cinema

(Map p248; ☎212-727-8110; www.filmforum.com; 209 W Houston St, btwn Varick St & Sixth Ave, SoHo; 🕐noon-midnight; [S]1 to Houston St) Plans are in the works to expand to four screens, but for now Film Forum is still a three-screen nonprofit cinema with an astounding array of independent films, revivals and career retrospectives from greats such as Orson Welles. Theaters are small, so get there early for a good viewing spot. Showings often include director talks or other film-themed discussions for hardcore cinephiles.

East Village & Lower East Side

Metrograph Cinema

(Map p248; ☎212-660-0312; www.metrograph.com; 7 Ludlow St, btwn Canal & Hester Sts, Lower East Side; tickets $15; [S]F to East Broadway, B/D to Grand St) The newest movie mecca for downtown movie fans, this two-screen theater with red velvet seats shows curated art-house flicks. Most you'll never find at any multiplex, though the odd mainstream pic like *Magic Mike* is occasionally screened. In addition to movie geeks browsing the bookstore, you'll find a stylish and glamorous set at the bar or in the upstairs restaurant.

Performance Space New York Theater

(Map p248; ☎212-477-5829; www.performancespacenewyork.org; 150 First Ave, at E 9th St, East Village; [S]L to 1st Ave; 6 to Astor Pl) Formerly PS 122, this cutting-edge theater reopened in January 2018 with an entirely new facade, state-of-the-art performance spaces, artist studios, a new lobby and roof deck. The bones of the former schoolhouse remain, as does its experimental theater bonafides: Eric Bogosian, Meredith Monk, the late Spalding Gray and Elevator Repair Service have all performed here.

Bowery Ballroom Live Music

(Map p248; ☎212-533-2111, 800-745-3000; www.boweryballroom.com; 6 Delancey St, at Bowery St, Lower East Side; [S]J/Z to Bowery; B/D to Grand St) This terrific, medium-sized venue has the perfect sound and feel for well-known indie-rock acts such as The Shins, Stephen Malkmus and Patti Smith.

Nuyorican Poets Café Live Performance

(Map p248; ☎212-780-9386; www.nuyorican.org; 236 E 3rd St, btwn Aves B & C, East Village; tickets $8-25; [S]F to 2nd Ave) Still going strong after 40-plus years, the legendary Nuyorican is home to poetry slams, hip-hop performances, plays, and film and video events. It's a piece of East Village history, but also a vibrant and still-relevant nonprofit arts organization. Check the website for the events calendar and buy tickets online for the more popular weekend shows.

✪ West Village, Chelsea & Meatpacking District

Sleep No More Theater

(Map p252; ☎866-811-4111; www.sleepnomorenyc.com; 530 W 27th St, btwn Tenth & Eleventh Aves, Chelsea; tickets from $105; 🕐7pm-midnight Mon-Sat; [S]1, C/E to 23rd St) One of the most immersive theater experiences ever conceived, *Sleep No More* is a loosely based retelling of *Macbeth* set inside a series of Chelsea warehouses that have been redesigned to look like the 1930s-era McKittrick Hotel and its hopping jazz bar.

It's a choose-your-own-adventure kind of experience, where audience members wander the elaborate rooms (ballroom, graveyard, taxidermy shop, lunatic asylum) and follow or interact with the actors, who perform a variety of scenes that can run from the bizarre to the risqué. Be prepared: you must check in *everything* when you arrive (jackets, bag, cell phone), and you must wear a mask, à la *Eyes Wide Shut*.

Village Vanguard Jazz

(Map p248; ☎212-255-4037; www.villagevanguard.com; 178 Seventh Ave S, at W 11th St, West Village; cover around $33; 🕐7:30pm-12:30am; [S]A/C/E, L to 8th Ave-14th St; 1/2/3 to 14th St) Possibly the city's most prestigious jazz club, the Vanguard has hosted literally every major star of the past 50 years. It started as a home to spoken-word performances and occasionally returns to its roots, but most of the time it's just big, bold jazz all night long.

Village Vanguard
KRIS DAVIDSON/LONELY PLANET ©

Musical Metropolis

This is the city where jazz players such as Ornette Coleman, Miles Davis and John Coltrane pushed the limits of improvisation in the '50s. It's where various Latin sounds – from cha-cha-cha to rumba to mambo – came together to form the hybrid we now call salsa, where folks singers such as Bob Dylan and Joan Baez crooned protest songs in coffeehouses, and where bands such as the New York Dolls and the Ramones tore up the stage in Manhattan's gritty downtown. It was the ground zero of disco. And it was the cultural crucible where hip-hop was nurtured and grew – then exploded.

The city remains a magnet for musicians to this day. The local indie-rock scene is especially vibrant: groups including the Yeah Yeah Yeahs, LCD Soundsystem and Animal Collective all emerged out of NYC. Williamsburg is at the heart of the action, packed with clubs and bars, as well as indie record labels and internet radio stations. The best venues for rock include the **Music Hall of Williamsburg** (p193) and the **Brooklyn Bowl** (Map p257; ☎718-963-3369; www.brooklynbowl.com; 61 Wythe Ave, btwn N 11th & N 12th Sts, Williamsburg; 🕐6pm-midnight Mon-Wed, to 2am Thu & Fri, 11am-2am Sat, to midnight Sun; [S]L to Bedford Ave; G to Nassau Ave), as well as Manhattan's **Bowery Ballroom** (p184).

★ Best for Laughs

Upright Citizens Brigade Theatre (p188)

Comedy Cellar (p187)

Magnet Theater (p189)

From left: Kiefer Sutherland performs at the Bowery Ballroom; Blue Note; Joyce Theater

DEBBY WONG/SHUTTERSTOCK ©

ZOLTAN TARLACZ/SHUTTERSTOCK ©

IFC Center Cinema

(Map p248; ☎212-924-7771; www.ifccenter.com; 323 Sixth Ave, at W 3rd St, West Village; tickets $15; 📶; [S]A/C/E, B/D/F/M to W 4th St-Washington Sq) This art-house cinema in NYU-land has a solidly curated lineup of new indies, cult classics and foreign films. Catch shorts, documentaries, '80s revivals, director-focused series, weekend classics and frequent special series, such as cult favorites *(The Shining, Taxi Driver, Aliens)* at midnight.

Blue Note Jazz

(Map p248; ☎212-475-8592; www.bluenote.net; 131 W 3rd St, btwn Sixth Ave & MacDougal St, West Village; [S]A/C/E, B/D/F/M to W 4th St-Washington Sq) This is by far the most famous (and expensive) of the city's jazz clubs. Most shows are $15 to $30 at the bar or $25 to $45 at a table, but can rise for the biggest stars. Go on an off night, and don't talk – all attention is on the stage!

Smalls Jazz

(Map p248; ☎646-476-4346; www.smallslive.com; 183 W 10th St, btwn W 4th St & Seventh Ave S, West Village; cover $20; 🕒7:05pm-3:30am Mon-Fri, from 4pm Sat & Sun; [S]1 to Christopher St-Sheridan Sq; A/C/E, B/D/F/M W 4th St-Washington Sq) Living up to its name, this cramped but appealing basement offers a grab-bag collection of jazz acts who take the stage nightly. Admission includes a come-and-go policy if you need to duck out for a bite. There is an afternoon jam session on Saturday and Sunday that's not to be missed.

Joyce Theater Dance

(Map p252; ☎212-691-9740; www.joyce.org; 175 Eighth Ave, at W 19th St, Chelsea; [S]1 to 18th St; 1, C/E to 23rd St; A/C/E, L to 8th Ave-14th St) A favorite among dance junkies thanks to its excellent sight lines and offbeat offerings, this is an intimate venue, seating 472 in a renovated cinema. Its focus is on traditional modern companies, such as Martha Graham, Stephen Petronio Company and Parsons Dance, as well as global stars.

Cherry Lane Theater Theater

(Map p248; ☎212-989-2020; www.cherrylanetheater.org; 38 Commerce St, off Bedford St, West Village; [S]1 to Christopher St-Sheridan Sq) A theater with a distinctive charm hidden in the West Village, Cherry Lane has a long and distinguished history. Started by poet

MARK WAUGH/ALAMY STOCK PHOTO ©

Edna St Vincent Millay, it has given a voice to numerous playwrights and actors over the years, remaining true to its mission of creating 'live' theater that's accessible to the public. Readings, plays and spoken-word performances rotate frequently.

Le Poisson Rouge — Live Music

(Map p248; ☏212-505-3474; www.lepoisson rouge.com; 158 Bleecker St, btwn Sullivan & Thompson Sts, West Village; ⓢA/C/E, B/D/F/M to W 4th St-Washington Sq) This high-concept art space hosts a highly eclectic lineup of live music, with the likes of Deerhunter, Marc Ribot and Yo La Tengo performing in past years. There's a lot of experimentation and cross-genre pollination between classical, folk music, opera and more.

Comedy Cellar — Comedy

(Map p248; ☏212-254-3480; www.comedycellar. com; 117 MacDougal St, btwn W 3rd St & Minetta Ln, West Village; cover $8-24; ⓢA/C/E, B/D/F/M to W 4th St-Washington Sq) This long-established basement comedy club in Greenwich Village features mainstream material and a good list of regulars, plus occasional high-profile drop-ins like Dave Chappelle, Jerry Seinfeld

and Amy Schumer. Its success continues: Comedy Cellar now boasts another location at the Village Underground around the corner on W 3rd St.

Duplex — Cabaret

(Map p248; ☏212-255-5438; www.theduplex. com; 61 Christopher St, at Seventh Ave S, West Village; cover $10-25; ⊙4pm-4am; ⓢ1 to Christopher St-Sheridan Sq; A/C/E, B/D/F/M to W 4th St-Washington Sq) Cabaret, karaoke and campy dance moves are par for the course at the legendary Duplex. Pictures of Joan Rivers line the walls, and the performers like to mimic her sassy form of self-deprecation while getting in a few jokes about audience members as well. It's a fun and unpretentious place, and certainly not for the bashful.

✪ Midtown

Jazz at Lincoln Center — Jazz

(Map p254; ☏tickets to Dizzy's Club Coca-Cola 212-258-9595, tickets to Rose Theater & Appel Room 212-721-6500; www.jazz.org; Time Warner Center, 10 Columbus Circle, Broadway at W 59th St; ⓢA/C, B/D, 1 to 59th St-Columbus Circle)

Perched atop the Time Warner Center, Jazz at Lincoln Center consists of three state-of-the-art venues: the mid-sized **Rose Theater**; the panoramic, glass-backed **Appel Room**; and the intimate, atmospheric **Dizzy's Club Coca-Cola**. It's the last of these that you're most likely to visit, given its nightly shows. The talent is often exceptional, as are the dazzling Central Park views.

Jazz Standard Jazz

(Map p252; ☎212-576-2232; www.jazzstandard.com; 116 E 27th St, btwn Lexington & Park Aves; cover $25-40; [S]6 to 28th St) Jazz luminaries like Ravi Coltrane, Roy Haynes and Ron Carter have played at this sophisticated club. The service is impeccable and the food is great. There's no minimum and it's programmed by Seth Abramson, a guy who really knows his jazz.

Carnegie Hall Live Music

(Map p254; ☎212-247-7800; www.carnegiehall.org; 881 Seventh Ave, at W 57th St; ⏲tours 11:30am, 12:30pm, 2pm & 3pm Mon-Fri, 11:30am & 12:30pm Sat Oct-Jun; [S]N/R/W to 57th St-7th Ave) Few venues are as famous as Carnegie Hall. This legendary music hall may not be the world's biggest, nor its grandest, but it's definitely one of the most acoustically blessed venues around. Opera, jazz and folk greats feature in the Isaac Stern Auditorium, with edgier jazz, pop, classical and world music in the popular Zankel Hall. The intimate Weill Recital Hall hosts chamber-music concerts, debut performances and panel discussions.

Birdland Jazz, Cabaret

(Map p254; ☎212-581-3080; www.birdlandjazz.com; 315 W 44th St, btwn Eighth & Ninth Aves; cover $30-50; ⏲5pm-1am; 📶; [S]A/C/E to 42nd St-Port Authority Bus Terminal) This bird's got a slick look, not to mention the legend – its name dates from bebop legend Charlie Parker (aka 'Bird'), who headlined at the previous location on 52nd St, along with Miles, Monk and just about everyone else. The lineup is always stellar.

Upright Citizens Brigade Theatre Comedy

(UCB; Map p254; ☎212-366-9176; www.ucbtheatre.com; 555 W 42nd St, btwn Tenth & Eleventh Aves, Hell's Kitchen; free-$10; ⏲7pm-midnight;

Shara Nova performs at Le Poisson Rouge (p187)

LEV RADIN/SHUTTERSTOCK ©

S A/C/E to 42nd St-Port Authority) Comedy sketch shows and improv reign at the new location of the legendary venue, which receives drop-ins from casting directors and often features well-known figures from TV. Entry is cheap, and so are the beer and wine. You'll find quality shows happening nightly, though the Sunday-night Asssscat Improv session is always a riot.

Don't Tell Mama   Cabaret

(Map p254; ☎212-757-0788; www.donttell mamanyc.com; 343 W 46th St, btwn Eighth & Ninth Aves, Midtown West; ⊘4pm-2:30am Sun-Thu, to 3:30am Fri & Sat; S N/Q/R, S, 1/2/3, 7 to Times Sq-42nd St) Piano bar and cabaret venue extraordinaire, Don't Tell Mama is an unpretentious little spot that's been around for more than 30 years and has the talent to prove it. Its regular roster of performers aren't big names, but true lovers of cabaret who give each show their all, and singing waitstaff add to the fun.

New Victory Theater   Theater

(Map p254; ☎646-223-3010; www.newvictory. org; 209 W 42nd St, btwn Seventh & Eighth Aves; 👶; S N/Q/R/W, S, 1/2/3, 7 to Times Sq-42nd St; A/C/E to 42nd St-Port Authority Bus Terminal) The oldest operating theater in the country, the New Victory attracts budding thespians and dancers who flock to the upbeat energy of this kid-focused theater. Comedy, dance, music, puppetry and drama shows are generally for the 12-and-under set, and there are offerings for teenagers. Events also include theater workshops, ranging from acting classes to clowning and hip-hop lessons.

Magnet Theater   Comedy

(Map p252; ☎tickets 212-244-8824; www. magnettheater.com; 254 W 29th St, btwn Seventh & Eighth Aves, Midtown West; S 1/2 to 28th St; A/C/E to 23rd St; 1/2/3 to 34th St-Penn Station) Tons of comedy in several incarnations (mostly improv) lures the crowds at this theater-cum-training-ground for comics. Performances vary weekly, though regular favorites include Megawatt (featuring the theater's resident ensembles) and the Friday Night Sh*w, the latter using the audience's written rants and confessions to drive the evening's shenanigans.

🎟 Broadway & Beyond

Broadway shows are shown in one of 40 official Broadway theaters, lavish early-20th-century jewels that surround Times Square, and are a major component of cultural life in New York. If you're on a budget, look for off-Broadway productions. These tend to be more intimate, inexpensive, and often just as good.

NYC bursts with theatrical offerings beyond Broadway, from Shakespeare to David Mamet to rising experimental playwrights including Young Jean Lee. In addition to Midtown staples such as **Playwrights Horizons** (Map p252; ☎212-564-1235; www.playwrightshorizons.org; 416 W 42nd St, btwn Ninth & Tenth Aves, Midtown West; S A/C/E to 42nd St-Port Authority Bus Terminal) and **Second Stage Theater** (Tony Kiser Theater; Map p254; ☎tickets 212-246-4422; www.2st.com; 305 W 43rd St, at Eighth Ave, Midtown West; ⊘box office noon-6pm Sun-Fri, to 7pm Sat; S A/C/E to 42nd St-Port Authority Bus Terminal), the **Lincoln Center theaters** (p76) and smaller companies such as **Soho Rep** (p184) are important hubs for works by modern and contemporary playwrights. Across the East River, **Brooklyn Academy of Music** (p192) and **St. Ann's Warehouse** (p193) offer edgy programming.

Brooklyn Academy of Music

Upper East Side

Frick Collection Concerts Classical Music
(Map p254; ☎212-288-0700; www.frick.org; 1 E 70th St, cnr Fifth Ave; $45; 🕑5pm Sun; [S]6 to 68th St-Hunter College; Q to 72nd St) Once a month this opulent mansion-museum (p69) hosts a Sunday 5pm concert that brings in world-renowned performers, such as cellist Yehuda Hanani and violinist Thomas Zehetmair.

Café Carlyle Jazz
(Map p254; ☎212-744-1600; www.thecarlyle.com; Carlyle Hotel, 35 E 76th St, cnr Madison Ave; cover $95-215, food & drink min $25-75; 🕑shows at 8:45pm & 10:45pm; [S]6 to 77th St) This swanky spot at the Carlyle Hotel draws top-shelf talent. Woody Allen plays his clarinet here with the Eddy Davis New Orleans Jazz Band on Mondays at 8:45pm (September through May). Bring mucho bucks: the cover charge doesn't include food or drinks, and there's a minimum spend. The dress code is 'chic' – gentlemen, wear a jacket.

Upper West Side

Symphony Space Live Performance
(Map p254; ☎212-864-5400; www.symphonyspace.org; 2537 Broadway, at 95th St; [S]1/2/3 to 96th St) Symphony Space is a multidisciplinary gem supported by the local community. It often hosts three-day series that are dedicated to one musician, and also has an affinity for world music, theater, film, dance and literature (with appearances by acclaimed writers).

Film Society of Lincoln Center Cinema
(Map p254; ☎212-875-5367; www.filmlinc.com; Lincoln Center; [S]1 to 66th St-Lincoln Center) The Film Society is one of New York's cinematic gems, providing an invaluable platform for a wide gamut of documentary, feature, independent, foreign and avant-garde art pictures. Films screen in one of two facilities at Lincoln Center: the **Elinor Bunin Munroe**

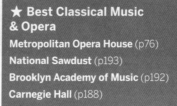

★ **Best Classical Music & Opera**

Metropolitan Opera House (p76)
National Sawdust (p193)
Brooklyn Academy of Music (p192)
Carnegie Hall (p188)

Clockwise from top left: Birdland (p188); Beacon Theatre (p192); Film Society of Lincoln Center; Carnegie Hall (p188)

DAVID SUNDBERG ESTO ©

Shakespeare's *Henry IV* performed at St. Ann's Warehouse

Film Center ([📞]212-875-5232), a more intimate, experimental venue, or the **Walter Reade Theater** ([📞]212-875-5601), with wonderfully wide, screening-room-style seats.

Beacon Theatre
Live Music

(Map p254; [📞]212-465-6500; www.beacon theatre.com; 2124 Broadway, btwn 74th & 75th Sts; [S]1/2/3 to 72nd St) This historic 1929 theater is a perfect medium-size venue with 2829 seats (not a terrible one in the house) and a constant flow of popular acts from ZZ Top to Jerry Seinfeld. A 2009 restoration left the gilded interiors – a mix of Greek, Roman, Renaissance and rococo design elements – totally sparkling.

✪ Harlem & Upper Manhattan

Marjorie Eliot's Parlor Jazz
Jazz

([📞]212-781-6595; 555 Edgecombe Ave, Apartment 3F, at 160th St, Washington Heights; ⊘3:30pm Sun; [S]A/C to 163rd St-Amsterdam Ave; 1 to 157th St) Each Sunday the charming Ms Eliot provides one of New York's most magical

experiences: free, intimate jazz jams in her own apartment. Dedicated to her two deceased sons, the informal concerts feature a revolving lineup of talented musicians, enchanting guests from all over the globe. Go early, as this event is popular (there's usually a line by 2:30pm).

✪ Brooklyn

Brooklyn Academy of Music
Performing Arts

(BAM; Map p256; [📞]718-636-4100; www.bam.org; 30 Lafayette Ave, at Ashland Pl, Fort Greene; [📶]; [S]B/D, N/Q/R, 2/3, 4/5 to Atlantic Ave-Barclays Center) Founded in 1861, BAM is the country's oldest performing-arts center. With several neighboring venues located in the Fort Greene area, the complex offers innovative and edgier works of opera, modern dance, music, cinema and theater – everything from Merce Cunningham retrospectives and multimedia shows by Laurie Anderson to avant-garde interpretations of Shakespeare and other classics.

St. Ann's Warehouse Theater
(Map p256; ☎718-254-8779; www.stannswarehouse.org; 45 Water St, at Old Dock St, Dumbo; 🚌B25 to Water/Main Sts, [S]A/C to High St; F to York St) This avant-garde performance company hosts innovative theater, music and dance happenings – everything from genre-defying music by new composers to strange and wondrous puppet theater. In 2015, St. Ann's moved from its old home several blocks away to this location in the historic Tobacco Warehouse (p108) in Brooklyn Bridge Park.

Barbès Live Music, Jazz
(Map p256; ☎718-965-9177; www.barbesbrooklyn.com; 376 9th St, at Sixth Ave, Park Slope; requested donation for live music $10; 🕒5pm-2am Mon-Thu, 2pm-4am Fri & Sat, to 2am Sun; [S]F, G to 7th Ave; R to 4th Ave-9th St) This compact bar and performance space, named after a North African neighborhood in Paris, is owned by French musician (and longtime Brooklyn resident) Olivier Conan, who sometimes plays here with his Latin-themed band Las Rubias del Norte. There's live music all night, every night: the impressively eclectic lineup includes Afro-Peruvian grooves, West African funk and gypsy swing, among other sounds.

Bell House Live Performance
(Map p256; ☎718-643-6510; www.thebellhouseny.com; 149 7th St, btwn Second & Third Aves, Gowanus; 🕒5pm-late; 📶; [S]F, G, R to 4th Ave-9th St) A large, old venue in a mostly barren area of industrial Gowanus, the Bell House features high-profile live performances, indie rockers, DJ nights, comedy shows and burlesque parties. The handsomely converted warehouse has a spacious concert area, plus a friendly little bar in the front room with flickering candles, leather armchairs and 10 or so beers on tap.

National Sawdust Live Performance
(Map p257; ☎646-779-8455; www.nationalsawdust.org; 80 N 6th St, at Wythe Ave, Williamsburg; 👪; [S]L to Bedford Ave) Covered in wildly hued murals, this arts space dedicated to cutting-edge multidisciplinary programming opened to much fanfare in 2015. You can see daring works like contemporary opera with multimedia projections, electro-acoustic big-band jazz and concerts by experimental composers, along with more globally infused performances – Inuit throat singing, African tribal funk, and the singing of Icelandic sagas, among other things.

Nitehawk Cinema Cinema
(Map p257; ☎718-782-8370; www.nitehawkcinema.com; 136 Metropolitan Ave, btwn Berry & Wythe Sts, Williamsburg; tickets adult/child $12/9; 👪; [S]L to Bedford Ave) This indie triplex has a fine lineup of first-run and repertory films, a good sound system and comfy seats…but the best part is that you can dine and drink all during the movie. Munch on hummus plates, sweet-potato risotto balls or short-rib empanadas, matched by a Blue Point toasted lager, a negroni or a movie-themed cocktail invention.

Jalopy Live Music
(Map p256; ☎718-395-3214; www.jalopy.biz; 315 Columbia St, btwn Hamilton Ave & Woodhull St, Columbia St Waterfront District; 🕒4-9pm Mon, noon-midnight Tue-Sun; 👪; 🚌B61 to Columbia & Carroll Sts, [S]F, G to Carroll St) This banjo shop and bar on the fringes of Carroll Gardens and Red Hook has a fun DIY space where it serves cold beer and stages bluegrass, country, klezmer and ukulele shows, including a no-cover feel-good Roots 'n' Ruckus show every Wednesday night at 9pm. Check the website for show schedules.

Music Hall of Williamsburg Live Music
(Map p257; ☎718-486-5400; www.musichallofwilliamsburg.com; 66 N 6th St, btwn Wythe & Kent Aves, Williamsburg; tickets $15-40; [S]L to Bedford Ave) This popular Williamsburg music venue is *the* place to see indie bands in Brooklyn – everyone from They Might Be Giants to Kendrick Lamar has played here. (For many groups traveling through New York, this is their one and only spot.) It's got an intimate feel (capacity is 550) and the almost-nightly programming is solid.

ACTIVE
NYC

Sports, biking, tours and more

Active NYC

Although hailing cabs in New York City can feel like a blood sport, and waiting on subway platforms in summer heat is steamier than a sauna, New Yorkers still love to stay active in their spare time. And considering how limited the green spaces are in the city, it's surprising for some visitors just how active the locals can be.

For those who prefer their sport sitting down, there's a packed calendar of over half a dozen pro teams playing within the metropolitan area. Football, basketball, baseball, hockey, tennis – there's lots of excitement right on your doorstep.

In This Section

Sports Seasons

In the US, the football (NFL) season generally runs from September to January; basketball (NBA) from October through May; ice hockey (NHL) from October to April; and major-league baseball from April to October. The US Open, America's biggest tennis tournament, takes place in late August/early September.

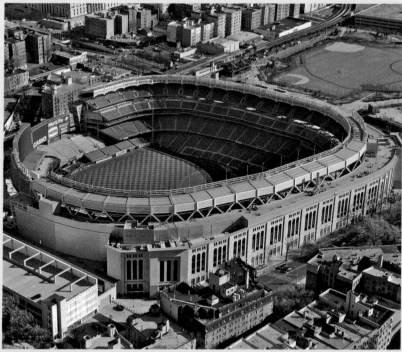

RICHARD CAVALLERI/SHUTTERSTOCK ©

Yankee Stadium (p198)

The Best...

Places to Get Active

Central Park (p36) The city's playground has forested paths and a beautiful lake.

Chelsea Piers Complex (p199) Every activity imaginable under one gigantic roof.

Brooklyn Bridge Park (p106) A beautifully designed waterfront park.

Prospect Park (p102) Brooklyn's gorgeous park has trails, hills, a lake and meadows.

New York Spa Castle (p200) A bathing behemoth with wallet-friendly prices.

Pro Sports Teams

New York Yankees The legendary baseball team battles it out in the Bronx.

New York Giants This football powerhouse actually plays in New Jersey.

New York Knicks See the Knicks get nothin' but net at Madison Square Garden.

Brooklyn Nets NYC's newest NBA team is a symbol of Brooklyn's resurgence.

New York Mets Another baseball team; plays at Citi Field in Queens.

Sports Arenas

Yankee Stadium Stadium

(☎718-293-4300, tours 646-977-8687; www.mlb.com/yankees; E 161st St, at River Ave; tours $25; [S]B/D, 4 to 161st St-Yankee Stadium) The Boston Red Sox like to talk about their record of eight World Series championships in the last 90 years...well, the Yankees have won a mere 27 in that period. The team's magic appeared to have moved with them across 161st St to the new Yankee Stadium, where they played their first season in 2009 – winning the World Series there in a six-game slugfest against the Phillies. The Yankees play from April to October.

Madison Square Garden Sport/Concert Venue

(MSG, 'the Garden'; Map p252; www.thegarden.com; 4 Pennsylvania Plaza, Seventh Ave, btwn 31st & 33rd Sts; [S]A/C/E, 1/2/3 to 34th St-Penn Station) NYC's major performance venue – part of the massive complex housing Penn Station (p237) – hosts big-arena performers, from Kanye West to Madonna. It's also a sports arena, with New York Knicks (www.nba.com/knicks.com) and New York Liberty (www.liberty.wnba.com) basketball games and New York Rangers (www.nhl.com/rangers) hockey games, as well as boxing and events like the Annual Westminster Kennel Club Dog Show.

Barclays Center Sport/Concert Venue

(Map p256; ☎917-618-6100; www.barclayscenter.com; cnr Flatbush & Atlantic Aves, Prospect Heights; [S]B/D, N/Q/R, 2/3, 4/5 to Atlantic Ave-Barclays Center) The Dodgers still play baseball in Los Angeles, but the (currently woeful) **Brooklyn Nets** in the NBA (formerly the New Jersey Nets) now hold court at this high-tech stadium that opened in 2012. Basketball aside, Barclays also stages major concerts and big shows: Bruce Springsteen, Justin Bieber, Barbra Streisand, Cirque de Soleil, Disney on Ice...

Speaking of ice, Brooklyn hockey fans now have a home team: the New York Islanders began playing their home games here in 2015. Poor sight lines and fan-base dissatisfaction mean the Islanders aren't

Chicago Bulls vs New York Knicks at Madison Square Garden

ALEX GOODLETT/STRINGER/GETTY IMAGES ©

likely to be at Barclays for long, however, and it's doubtful they'll still be playing there after 2019.

The stadium, with its futuristic design – which looks like a rusting spaceship topped by a well-kept grassy lawn – has transformed the neighborhood. A strange-looking condominium, assembled with colorful modular parts, is being built directly overhead.

Activities & Fitness

Chelsea Piers Complex Health & Fitness

(Map p252; ☎212-336-6666; www.chelseapiers.com; Pier 62, at W 23rd St, Chelsea; ⏰5:30am-11pm Mon-Fri, 5:30am-9pm Sat & Sun; 👪; 🚌M23 to Chelsea Piers, [S]1, C/E to 23rd St) This massive waterfront sports center caters to the athlete in everyone. You can hit a bucket of golf balls at the four-level driving range, skate on an indoor ice rink or rack up strikes in a jazzy bowling alley. There's basketball at Hoop City, a sailing school for kids, batting cages, a huge gym and covered swimming pool and indoor rock-climbing.

Central Park Tennis Center Tennis

(Map p254; ☎212-316-0800; www.centralparktenniscenter.com; Central Park, btwn W 94th & 96th Sts; ⏰6:30am-dusk Apr-Nov; [S]B, C to 96th St) This daylight-hours-only facility has 26 clay courts for public use and four hard courts for lessons. You can buy single-play tickets ($15; cash only) here, and can reserve a court if you pick up a $15 permit at **Arsenal** (Map p254; ☎gallery 212-360-8163; www.nycgovparks.org; Central Park, at Fifth Ave & E 64th St; ⏰9am-5pm Mon-Fri; [S]N/R/W to 5th Ave-59th St) [FREE]. The least busy times are roughly from noon to 4pm weekdays. Closest park entrance is Central Park West and 96th St.

Brooklyn Boulders Climbing

(Map p256; ☎347-834-9066; www.brooklynboulders.com; 575 Degraw St, at Third Ave, Gowanus; day pass $32, shoe & harness rental $12; ⏰7am-midnight Mon-Fri, to 10pm Sat & Sun; [S]R to Union St) Brooklyn's biggest indoor climbing arena is housed in an airy and vibrant space on an industrial block in the Gowanus neighborhood. Ceilings top out at 30ft inside this 18,000-sq-ft facility, and its caves and freestanding 17ft boulder and climbing walls offer numerous routes for both beginners and experts. There are overhangs of 15, 30 and 45 degrees. Climbing classes are available.

Jivamukti Yoga

(Map p248; ☎212-353-0214; www.jivamuktiyoga.com; 841 Broadway, 2nd fl, btwn E 13th & 14th Sts, Union Square; classes $15-22; ⏰classes 7am-8:30pm Mon-Fri, 7:45am-8pm Sat & Sun;

Biking the Big Apple

NYC has taken enormous strides in making the city more bike-friendly, adding hundreds of miles of bike lanes in recent years. That said, we recommend that the uninitiated stick to the less hectic trails in the parks and along the waterways, such as Central Park, Prospect Park, the Manhattan Waterfront Greenway and the Brooklyn Waterfront Greenway.

Citi Bike (www.citibikenyc.com) is handy for quick jaunts, but for longer rides, you'll want a proper rental. Biking tours let you cover a lot of ground and are worth considering. Try **Bike the Big Apple** (☎347-878-9809; www.bikethebigapple.com; tours incl bike & helmet $99) or Central Park Bike Tours (p203).

Cycling over the Brooklyn Bridge (p46)
DANNY THOMAS/EYEEM/GETTY IMAGES©

Running in NYC

Central Park's loop roads are best during traffic-free hours, though you'll be in the company of many cyclists and in-line skaters. The 1.6-mile path surrounding the Jacqueline Kennedy Onassis Reservoir (where Jackie O used to run) is for runners and walkers only; access it between 86th and 96th Sts. Running along the Hudson River is a popular path, best from about 30th St to Battery Park in Lower Manhattan. The Upper East Side has a path that runs along FDR Dr and the East River (from 63rd St to 115th St). Brooklyn's Prospect Park has plenty of paths (and a 3-mile loop), while 1.3-mile-long Brooklyn Bridge Park has incredible views of Manhattan (reach it via Brooklyn Bridge to up the mileage). The New York Road Runners Club (www.nyrr.org) organizes weekend runs citywide, including the New York City Marathon.

S 4/5/6, N/Q/R/W, L to 14th St-Union Sq) Considered *the* yoga spot in Manhattan, Jivamukti – in a 12,000-sq-ft locale on Union Sq – is a posh place for Vinyasa, Hatha and Ashtanga classes. The center's 'open' classes are suitable for both rookies and experienced practitioners, and there's an organic vegan cafe on-site too. Gratuitous celebrity tidbit: Uma's little bro Dechen Thurman teaches classes here.

🌀 Spas & Baths

New York Spa Castle   Spa
(☑718-939-6300; http://ny.spacastleusa.com; 131-10 11th Ave, College Point; weekday/weekend $40/50; ⊙8am-midnight; S 7 to Flushing-Main St) A slice of cutting-edge Korean bathhouse culture in an industrial corner of Queens, this 100,000-sq-ft spa complex is a bubbling dream of mineral and massage pools, saunas of dazzling variety, steam rooms and waterfalls. It also has a food court, beauty treatments and massages (30 minutes from $50). Avoid on weekends as it gets packed.

Great Jones Spa   Spa
(Map p248; ☑212-505-3185; www.gjspa.com; 29 Great Jones St, btwn Lafayette St & Bowery, NoHo; ⊙9am-10pm; S 6 to Bleecker St; B/D/F/M to Broadway-Lafayette St) Don't skimp on the services at this downtown feng shui–designed place, whose offerings include blood-orange salt scrubs and stem-cell facials. If you spend over $100 per person (not difficult), you get access to the water lounge with thermal hot tub, sauna, steam room and cold plunge pool (swimsuits required).

Russian & Turkish Baths   Bathhouse
(Map p248; ☑212-674-9250; www.russianturkish baths.com; 268 E 10th St, btwn First Ave & Ave A, East Village; per visit $45; ⊙noon-10pm Mon-Tue & Thu-Fri, from 10am Wed, from 9am Sat, from 8am Sun; S L to 1st Ave; 6 to Astor Pl) Since 1892, this cramped and grungy downtown spa has been drawing a polyglot and eclectic mix: actors, students, frisky couples, singles-on-the-make, Russian regulars and old-school locals, who strip down to their skivvies (or the roomy cotton shorts provided) and rotate between steam baths, an ice-cold plunge pool, a sauna and the sundeck.

❄ Ice Skating

Wollman Skating Rink   Ice Skating
(Map p254; ☑212-439-6900; www.wollman skatingrink.com; Central Park, btwn E 62nd & 63rd Sts; adult Mon-Thu $12, Fri-Sun $19, child

$6, skate rentals $9; ⏰10am-2:30pm Mon & Tue, to 10pm Wed & Thu, to 11pm Fri & Sat, to 9pm Sun late Oct-early Apr; 👪; [S] F to 57 St; N/Q/R/W to 5th Ave-59th St) This rink is much larger than the Rockefeller Center skating rink, and not only does it allow all-day skating, its position at the southeastern edge of Central Park offers magical views. There's locker rental for $5 and a spectator fee of $5. Cash only.

LeFrak Center at Lakeside Skating, Boating

(Map p256; ☎718-462-0010; www.lakesideprospectpark.com; 171 East Dr, Prospect Park, near Ocean & Parkside Aves; skating $6-9, skate rentals $6-7, boat rentals per hr $15-35, bike rental per hr $8-35; ⏰hours vary by season; 👪; [S] Q to Parkside Ave) This $74-million project, opened in 2013, reconfigured 26 acres of Prospect Park (p102) land into a beautiful, ecofriendly showcase. In the winter there's ice skating; in summer, roller skating and a sprinkler-filled water play area for kids to splash about in.

Rink at Rockefeller Center Ice Skating

(Map p254; ☎212-332-7654; www.therinkatrockcenter.com; Rockefeller Center, Fifth Ave, btwn W 49th & 50th Sts; adult $25-32, child $15, skate rental $12; ⏰8:30am-midnight mid-Oct–Apr; 👪; [S] B/D/F/M to 47th-50th Sts-Rockefeller Center) From mid-October to April, Rockefeller Plaza is home to New York's most famous ice-skating rink. Carved out of a recessed oval with the 70-story art deco Rockefeller Center (p84) towering above, plus a massive Christmas tree during the holiday season, it's incomparably magical. It's also undeniably small and crowded. Opt for the first skating period of the day (8:30am) to avoid a long wait. Come summer, the rink becomes a cafe.

Water Activities

Loeb Boathouse Boating

(Map p254; ☎212-517-2233; www.thecentralparkboathouse.com; Central Park, btwn 74th & 75th Sts; boating per hr $15; ⏰10am-dusk Mar or

Rink at Rockefeller Center

JEFF WHYTE/SHUTTERSTOCK ©

Loeb Boathouse

Apr–mid-Nov; 🚹; Ⓢ B, C to 72nd St; 6 to 77th St) Central Park's boathouse has a fleet of 100 rowboats, as well as a Venetian-style gondola that you can reserve for up to six people if you'd rather someone else do the paddling ($45 for 30 minutes). Rentals include life jackets and require ID and a $20 deposit. Cash only.

Downtown Boathouse Kayaking
(Map p248; www.downtownboathouse.org; Pier 26, near N Moore St; ⊘9am-5pm Sat & Sun mid-May–mid-Oct, plus 5-7:30pm Tue-Thu mid-Jun–mid-Sep; Ⓢ1 to Houston St) FREE New York's most active public boathouse offers free, walk-up, 20-minute kayaking sessions (including equipment) in a pro-tected embayment in the Hudson River on weekends and some weekday evenings. For more activities – kayaking trips, stand-up paddleboarding and classes – check out www.hudsonriverpark.org for the four other kayaking locations on the Hudson River. There's also a summer-only kayaking loca-tion on Governors Island (p109).

Manhattan Community Boathouse Kayaking
(www.manhattancommunityboathouse.org; Pier 96, at 56th St, Hudson River Park; ⊘10am-6pm Sat & Sun Jun-early Oct, plus 5:30-7:30pm Mon-Wed Jun-Aug; 🚹; 🚌M12 to 12th Ave/56th St, ⓈA/C, B/D, 1 to 59th St-Columbus Circle) FREE Fancy a quick glide on the mighty Hudson? This volunteer-run boathouse offers free kayak-ing on summer weekends. No reservations: it's first-come, first-served. It also offers free classes in kayaking technique and safety.

Expect to get wet while paddling – there are changing rooms and lockers at the pier. If you want more than a 20-minute paddle, check out the Downtown Boathouse, which offers weekend trips out on the Hudson.

⊕ Family Activities

Brooklyn Bowl Bowling
(Map p257; ☎718-963-3369; www.brooklynbowl. com; 61 Wythe Ave, btwn N 11th & N 12th Sts, Williamsburg; lane rentals per 30min $25, shoe rentals $5; ⊘6pm-2am Mon-Fri, from 11am Sat &

Sun; [icon]; [S]L to Bedford Ave; G to Nassau Ave) This incredible alley is housed in the 23,000-sq-ft former Hecla Iron Works Company, which provided ornamentation for several NYC landmarks at the turn of the 20th century. There are 16 lanes surrounded by cushy sofas and exposed brick walls. In addition to bowling, Brooklyn Bowl hosts concerts (p185) throughout the week, and there's always good food on hand.

Saturdays from 11am to 5pm and Sundays to 6pm are all-ages Family Bowl hours. (Nighttime bowling is for ages 21 and over.)

Battery Park City Parks Conservancy   Tours

([phone]212-267-9700; www.bpcparks.org) Offers a range of free and paid activities, from walking tours and chess for kids to parent/baby yoga, storytelling sessions and volunteer gardening. All are located in various parks and community centers around Battery Park City (the area between West St and the Hudson River from Chambers St down to Battery Pl). Check the website for upcoming events.

⊕ Tours

Central Park Bike Tours   Cycling

(Map p254; [phone]212-541-8759; www.centralpark biketours.com; 203 W 58th St, at Seventh Ave; rentals per 2hr/day $20/40, 2hr tours $49; [clock]8am-8pm, tours 9am-4pm; [S]A/C, B/D, 1 to 59th St-Columbus Circle) This place rents out good bikes (helmets, locks and bike map included) and leads two-hour guided tours of Central Park and the Brooklyn Bridge area. See the website for tour times.

Museum Hack   Walking

([phone]347-282-5001; https://museumhack.com; 2hr tour from $59) For a fascinating, alternative perspective of the Met, sign up for a tour with Museum Hack. Knowledgeable but delightfully irreverent guides take on topics like 'Badass Witches' (a look at the dark arts in Egypt and the Middle Ages), paradigm-shifting feminist artists and an 'Unhighlights Tour' that will take you to

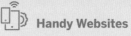
Handy Websites

NYC Parks (www.nycgovparks.org) Details on park services, including free pools and basketball courts, plus borough biking maps.

New York Road Runners Club (www. nyrr.org) Organizes weekend runs and races citywide.

Central Park (www.centralparknyc.org) Lists myriad activities and events held at NYC's best-loved green space.

NYC (www.nycgo.com/sports) Lists all the major sporting events and activities happening in town.

Central Park (p36)
A.RUIZ/SHUTTERSTOCK ©

corners of the museum few visitors know about.

Museum Hack also runs tours in the Museum of Natural History, including a family-friendly option that delves into the science behind some extraordinary animals and the captivating stories of adventurers who collected the specimens.

Big Apple Greeter   Walking

([phone]212-669-8159; www.bigapplegreeter. org) **FREE** For an inside take on the NYC experience, book a walking tour in the neighborhood of your choice led by a local volunteer who just can't wait to show off their city to you. You'll be matched with a guide who suits your needs, whether that means speaking Spanish or American Sign Language, or knowing just where to find the best wheelchair-accessible spots in the city. Reserve four weeks in advance.

REST YOUR HEAD

Top tips for the best accommodations

Rest Your Head

Like the top student in class, NYC just seems to know how to do everything well, and its lodging scene is no exception. Creative minds have descended upon New York to create memorable spaces for weary visitors, so even though the city 'never sleeps', you certainly can.

In This Section

Prices & Tipping

A 'budget hotel' in NYC generally costs up to $200 for a standard double room including breakfast. For a modest mid-range option, plan on spending $200 to $350. Luxury options run $350 and higher.

Tip the hotel housekeeper $3 to $5 per night, tip porters around $2 per bag. Staff providing service (hailing cabs, room service, concierge help) should be tipped accordingly.

DAN HALLMAN/LONELY PLANET ©

Reservations

Reservations are essential – walk-ins are practically impossible and rack rates are almost always unfavorable relative to online deals. Reserve your room as early as possible and make sure you understand your hotel's cancellation policy. Expect check-in to always be in the middle of the afternoon and check-out in the late morning. Early check-ins are rare, though high-end establishments can often accommodate with advance notice.

Useful Websites

newyorkhotels.com (www.newyorkhotels. com) The self-proclaimed official website for hotels in NYC.

NYC (www.nycgo.com/hotels) Loads of listings from the NYC Official Guide.

Lonely Planet (lonelyplanet.com/usa/ new-york-city/hotels) Accommodation reviews and online booking service.

Renting Rooms & Apartments Online

More and more travelers are bypassing hotels and staying in private apartments listed online through companies such as Airbnb. The wealth of options is staggering, with more than 25,000 listings per night scattered in every corner of New York City. If you want a more local, neighborhood-oriented experience, then this can be a great way to go.

There are a few things, however, to keep in mind. First off: many listings are actually illegal. Laws in NYC dictate that apartments can be rented out for less than 30 days only if the occupants are present. Effects on the immediate community are another issue, with some neighbors complaining about noise, security risks and the unexpected transformation of their residence into a hotel of sorts. There are also the larger impacts on the housing market: some landlords are cashing in, knowing they can earn more from holiday rentals than with long-term tenants. Taking thousands of possible rentals off the market is only driving rental prices for NYC residents ever higher.

Booking Accommodations

In New York City, the average room rate is well over $300. But don't let that scare you, as there are great deals to be had – almost all of which can be found through savvy online snooping. To get the best deals, launch a two-pronged approach: if you don't have your heart set on a particular property, then check out the generic booking websites. If you do know where you want to stay, it might sound simple but it's best to start at your desired hotel's website – these days it's not uncommon to find deals and package rates listed there.

Room Rates

New York City doesn't have a 'high season' in the common way that beach destinations do. Sure, there are busier times of the year when it comes to tourist traffic, but, with more than 50 million visitors per annum, the Big Apple never needs to worry when it comes to filling up beds. As such, room rates fluctuate based on availability; in fact, most hotels have a booking algorithm in place that spits out a price quote relative to the number of rooms already booked on the same night, so the busier the evening the higher the price goes.

If you're looking to find the best room rates, then flexibility is key – weekdays are often cheaper, and you'll generally find that accommodations in winter months have smaller price tags. If you are visiting over a weekend, try for a business hotel in the Financial District, which tends to empty out when the work week ends.

Accommodation Types

B&Bs & Family-Style Guesthouses

Offer mix-and-match furnishings and some serious savings (if you don't mind eating breakfast with strangers).

Boutique Hotels

Usually have tiny rooms decked out with fantastic amenities and at least one celebrity-filled basement bar, rooftop bar or hip, flashy eatery on-site.

Classic Hotels

Typified by old-fashioned, small-scale European grandeur; these usually cost the same as boutiques and aren't always any larger.

European-Style Travelers' Hotels

Have creaky floors and small, but cheap and clean (if chintzily decorated), rooms, often with a shared bathroom.

Hostels

Functional dorms (bunk beds and bare walls) that are nonetheless communal and friendly. Many have a backyard garden, kitchen and lounge that make up for the soulless rooms.

Upper West Side

Upper East Side

Midtown

Greenwich Village, Chelsea & Meatpacking District

Union Square, Flatiron District & Gramercy

SoHo & Chinatown

East Village & Lower East Side

Financial District & Lower Manhattan

Brooklyn

Neighborhood	For	Against
Financial District & Lower Manhattan	Convenient to Tribeca's nightlife and ferries. Cheap weekend rates at business hotels.	The area can feel impersonal, corporate and even a bit desolate after business hours.
SoHo & Chinatown	Shop to your heart's content right on your doorstep.	Crowds swarm the commercial streets of SoHo almost any time of day.
East Village & Lower East Side	Funky and fun, the area feels the most 'New York' to visitors and Manhattanites alike.	Not a great deal to choose from when it comes to hotels.
Greenwich Village, Chelsea & Meatpacking District	Brilliantly close-to-everything feel in a thriving part of town that has an almost European feel.	Prices soar for traditional hotels, but remain reasonable for B&Bs. Rooms can sometimes be on the small side, even for NYC.
Union Square, Flatiron District & Gramercy	Convenient subway access to anywhere in the city. You're also steps away from the Village and Midtown in either direction.	Prices are high and there's not much in the way of neighborhood flavor.
Midtown	In the heart of the postcard's version of NYC: skyscrapers, museums, shopping and shows.	One of the most expensive areas in the city; expect small rooms. Midtown can often feel touristy and impersonal.
Upper East Side	You're a stone's throw from top-notch museums and the rolling hills of Central Park.	Options are scarce and wallet-busting prices are not uncommon; also not particularly central.
Upper West Side	Convenient access to Central Park and the Museum of Natural History.	Tends to swing in the familial direction if you're looking for a livelier scene.
Brooklyn	Better prices; great for exploring some of NYC's most creative neighborhoods.	It can be a long commute to Midtown Manhattan and points north.

In Focus

New York City Today

*New York remains an economic dynamo with record-low
unemployment, overflowing city coffers and a building
boom across the five boroughs. Beneath the veneer,
however, are plenty of challenges, including an aging
transit system, rising homelessness and the ongoing
threat of terrorism. But this is a city that takes
everything in stride. As former president Barack Obama
once said, 'New Yorkers are as tough as they come.'*

Tale of Two Cities

In many ways, New York is becoming ever more divided between the haves and the have-nots. Staggering development projects and high-priced apartments litter the landscape, from the $4.5 billion Hudson Yards to 432 Park, the Rafael Viñoly–designed, superslim tower with a penthouse that recently listed for $82 million. For the wealthy, New York is the ultimate playground. One Upper East Side property, selling for $85 million, also came with a $1 million yacht and two Rolls-Royce Phantoms.

Meanwhile the ranks of the homeless continue to grow, with more than 63,000 homeless New Yorkers today, over twice as many as in 2002. Stagnant wages and skyrocketing rents have fueled the crisis: from 2000 to 2014, the median NYC rent increased by nearly 20% while incomes rose by just 5%.

Most New Yorkers live between these two extremes, though lack of affordable housing has placed a huge strain on residents. As more neighborhoods undergo gentrification, prices go up and landlords chip away at rent-stabilized apartments to command ever higher returns, leaving many New Yorkers to pay unsustainably high rents – which costs residents an average 60% of their income. Of the families living in NYC's homeless shelters, one-third of the adults have a job.

A Progressive Mayor

Mayor Bill de Blasio came into office in 2014 aiming to address the egregious inequalities in New York. One of his early successes was the creation of free, universal pre-kindergarten for all New Yorkers. By September 2015, some 68,000 four-year-olds were enrolled in a free, one-year head start on their educational path. In 2015 and 2016, under de Blasio, the city also instituted a rent-freeze, which benefited more than two million people living in rent-controlled apartments. Another main goal was the creation or preservation of 200,000 units of affordable housing by 2024; by the end of his first term, the city had created 77,000 affordable housing units.

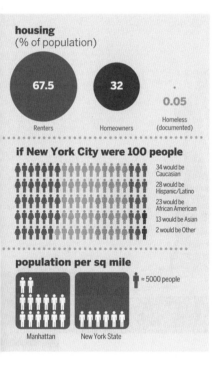

housing
(% of population)

67.5 — Renters
32 — Homeowners
0.05 — Homeless (documented)

if New York City were 100 people

34 would be Caucasian
28 would be Hispanic/Latino
23 would be African American
13 would be Asian
2 would be Other

population per sq mile

≈ 5000 people

Manhattan   New York State

De Blasio gave all 50,000 city workers a raise, increasing the minimum wage to $15 an hour. Unemployment also reached a record low of 4.3% – its lowest in nearly 40 years – with the private sector adding 100,000 new jobs a year during his first term. The city has also seen record-low crime rates under de Blasio.

With his many successes, Bill de Blasio coasted to victory during his bid for re-election in 2017, winning handily his second term as the head of America's largest city.

Subway Blues

One of New York's big challenges is maintaining its century-old subway system. Severely overcrowded trains and the increasing frequency of breakdowns have led to much public resentment toward the MTA (Metropolitan Transit Authority). During rush hour, some trains are so crowded that commuters must wait for one or two more to pass by before they can jam themselves inside. Part of the problem stems from the 1930s-era signal system, which according to officials would take decades and cost billions of dollars to update.

Adding to the woes is the planned shutdown of the L train for much-needed repairs. During Hurricane Sandy in 2012, its East River tunnel was flooded with seawater, causing serious damage. This key route provides service for some 400,000 riders daily, who'll have to find alternate means of transport when the Manhattan-to-Brooklyn section is shut down for a scheduled 15 months, starting in April 2019.

History

This is the tale of a city that never sleeps, of a kingdom where tycoons and world leaders converge, of a place that's seen the highest highs and the most devastating lows. Yet through it all, it continues to reach for the sky (both figuratively and literally). And to think it all started with $24 and a pile of beads...

c AD 1500

About 15,000 Native Americans live in 80 sites around the island. The groups include the feuding Iroquois and Algonquins.

1625–26

The Dutch West India Company imports slaves from Africa to work in the fur trade and construction.

1646

The Dutch found the village of Breuckelen (Brooklyn) on the eastern shore of Long Island, naming it after Breukelen in the Netherlands.

⅃ying Manhattan

ₑ Dutch West India Company sent 110 settlers to begin a trading post here in 1624.
ₑy settled in Lower Manhattan and called their colony New Amsterdam, touching off
ₒody battles with the unshakable Lenape, a people who had roots on the island dating
ₐck 11,000 years. It all came to a head in 1626, when the colony's first governor, Peter
linuit, became the city's first (but certainly not the last) unscrupulous real estate agent
y purchasing Manhattan's 14,000 acres from the Lenape for 60 guilders ($24) and some
ₗlass beads.

By the time Peter Stuyvesant arrived to govern the colony in 1647, the Lenape population had dwindled to about 700. In 1664 the English arrived in battleships; Stuyvesant avoided bloodshed by surrendering without a shot. King Charles II renamed the colony after his brother the Duke of York. New York became a prosperous British port and the population rose to 11,000 by the mid-1700s; however, colonists started to become resentful of British taxation.

1784	**1811**	**1853**
Alexander Hamilton founds America's first bank, the Bank of New York, with holdings of $500,000.	Manhattan's grid plan is developed by Mayor DeWitt Clinton, reshaping the city and laying plans for the future.	The State Legislature authorizes the allotment of public lands for what will later become Central Park.

Ellis Island (p41)

Revolution & War

By the 18th century the economy was so robust that the locals were improvising ways to avoid sharing the wealth with London, and New York became the stage for a fatal confrontation with King George III. Revolutionary battles began in August of 1776, when General George Washington's army lost about a quarter of its men in just a few days. The general retreated, and fire engulfed much of the colony. But soon the British left and Washington's army reclaimed the city. In 1789 the retired general found himself addressing crowds at Federal Hall, gathered to witness his presidential inauguration. Alexander Hamilton, as Washington's secretary of the treasury, began rebuilding New York and working to establish the New York Stock Exchange.

Population Bust, Infrastructure Boom

There were setbacks in the 19th century: the bloody Draft Riots of 1863, cholera epidemics, tensions among 'old' and 'new' immigrants, and poverty and crime in Five Points, the city's first slum. But the city prospered and found resources for mighty public works. Begun in 1855, Central Park was a vision of green reform and a boon to real-estate speculation. It also offered work relief when the Panic of 1857 shattered the nation's finance system. Another vision was realized by German-born engineer John Roebling who designed the Brooklyn Bridge, spanning the East River and connecting lower Manhattan and Brooklyn.

The Burgeoning Metropolis

By the start of the 20th century, elevated trains carried a million people a day in and out of the city. Rapid transit opened up areas of the Bronx and Upper Manhattan. Tenements were overflowing with immigrants arriving from southern Italy and Eastern Europe, who

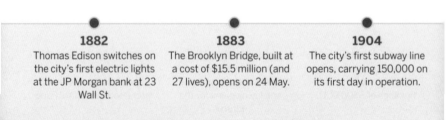

1882
Thomas Edison switches on the city's first electric lights at the JP Morgan bank at 23 Wall St.

1883
The Brooklyn Bridge, built at a cost of $15.5 million (and 27 lives), opens on 24 May.

1904
The city's first subway line opens, carrying 150,000 on its first day in operation.

increased the metropolis to about three million. Newly wealthy folks – boosted by an economy jump-started by financier JP Morgan – built splendid mansions on Fifth Ave. Reporter and photographer Jacob Riis illuminated the widening gap between the classes, leading the city to pass much-needed housing reforms.

Rights for Women & Workers

Wretched factory conditions – low pay, long hours, abusive employers – in the early 20th century were highlighted by a tragic event in 1911. The infamous Triangle Shirtwaist Company fire saw rapidly spreading flames catch onto the factory's piles of fabrics, killing 146 of the 500 female workers who were trapped behind locked doors. The event led to sweeping labor reforms after 20,000 female garment workers marched to City Hall. Nurse and midwife Margaret Sanger opened the first birth-control clinic in Brooklyn and suffragists held rallies to obtain the vote for women.

Move to the Beats

The 1960s ushered in an era of legendary creativity and anti-establishment expression, with many of its creators centered right downtown in Greenwich Village. One movement was abstract expressionism, a large-scale outbreak of American painters – Mark Rothko, Jackson Pollock, Lee Krasner, Helen Frankenthaler and Willem de Kooning among them – who offended and intrigued with incomprehensible squiggles and blotches and exuberant energy. Then there were the writers, such as Beat poets Allen Ginsberg and Jack Kerouac and novelist/playwright Jane Bowles. They gathered in Village coffeehouses to exchange ideas and find inspiration, which was often discovered in the form of folk music from burgeoning big names, such as Bob Dylan.

The Jazz Age

The 1920s saw the dawning of the Jazz Age, when Prohibition outlawed the sale of alcohol, encouraging bootlegging and speakeasies, as well as organized crime. Congenial mayor James Walker was elected in 1925, Babe Ruth reigned at Yankee Stadium and the Great Migration from the South led to the Harlem Renaissance, when the neighborhood became a center of African American culture and society. Harlem's nightlife attracted the flappers and gin-soaked revelers that marked the complete failure of Prohibition.

Hard Times

The stock market crashed in 1929 and the city dealt with the Great Depression through grit, endurance, rent parties, militancy and public works projects. Texas-born, Yiddish-speaking Mayor Fiorello La Guardia worked to bring relief in the form of New Deal–funded projects. WWII brought troops to the city, ready to party in Times Square before shipping

1939

The World's Fair opens in Queens. With the future as its theme, the exposition invites visitors to take a look at 'the world of tomorrow.'

1969

Police officers raid the gay-friendly Stonewall Inn, sparking days of rioting and the birth of the modern LGBT+ rights movement.

1977

A summer blackout leaves New Yorkers in the dark for 24 sweltering hours, which leads to rioting around the city.

September 11

On September 11, 2001, terrorists flew two hijacked planes into the World Trade Center's Twin Towers, turning the whole complex to dust and rubble and killing nearly 3000 people. Downtown Manhattan took months to recover from the ghastly fumes wafting from the ruins as forlorn missing-person posters grew ragged on brick walls. While the city mourned its dead and recovery crews coughed their way through the debris, residents braved constant terrorist alerts and an anthrax scare. Shock and grief drew people together, uniting the oft-fractious citizenry in a determined effort not to succumb to despair.

off to Europe. Converted to war industries, factories hummed, staffed by women and African Americans who had rarely before had access to good, unionized jobs. With few evident controls on business, Midtown bulked up with skyscrapers after the war.

Enter Robert Moses

Working with Mayor La Guardia to usher the city into the modern age was Robert Moses, an urban planner who would influence the physical shape of the city more than anyone else in the 20th century. He was the master-mind behind the Triborough Bridge (now the Robert F Kennedy Bridge), Jones Beach State Park, the Verrazano–Narrows Bridge, the West Side Hwy and the Long Island parkway system – not to mention endless highways, tunnels and bridges, which shifted this mass-transit area into one largely dependent on the automobile.

'Drop Dead'

By the early 1970s deficits had created a fiscal crisis. President Gerald Ford refused to lend federal aid – summed up by the *Daily News* headline 'Ford to City, Drop Dead!' Massive lay-offs decimated the working class; untended bridges, roads and parks reeked of hard times. The traumatic '70s – which reached a low point in 1977 with a citywide blackout and the existence of serial killer Son of Sam – drove down rents, helping to nourish an alternative culture that transformed the former industrial precincts of SoHo and Tribeca into energized nightlife districts.

Out of the Ashes

While the stock market boomed for much of the 1980s, neighborhoods struggled with the spread of crack cocaine; the city reeled from the impact of addiction, crime and AIDS. Squatters in the East Village fought back when police tried to clear a big homeless encampment, leading to the Tompkins Square Park riots of 1988. In South Bronx, a wave of arson reduced blocks of apartments to cinders. But amid the smoke, an influential hip-hop culture was born there and in Brooklyn.

1988
Squatters riot when cops attempt to remove them from their de facto home in the East Village's Tompkins Square Park.

2001
On September 11, terrorist hijackers fly two planes into the Twin Towers, destroying the World Trade Center and killing nearly 3000 people.

2008–09
The stock market crashes due to mismanagement by major American financial institutions.

Still convalescing from the real-estate crash of the late 1980s, the city faced crumbling infrastructure, jobs leaking south and Fortune 500 companies leaving for suburbia. Then the dot-com market roared in, turning the New York Stock Exchange into a speculator's fun park, and the city launched a frenzy of building and partying unparalleled since the 1920s.

With pro-business, law-and-order Rudy Giuliani as mayor, the dingy and destitute were swept from Manhattan's yuppified streets to the outer boroughs, leaving room for the well-off to live the high life. Giuliani grabbed headlines with his campaign to stamp out crime, even kicking the sex shops off notoriously seedy 42nd St.

The New York Naughts

The 10 years after 9/11 were a period of rebuilding – both physically and emotionally. In 2002 Mayor Michael Bloomberg began the unenviable task of picking up the pieces of a shattered city. Much to Bloomberg's pleasure, New York did see a great deal of renovation and reconstruction, especially after the city hit its stride with spiking tourist numbers in 2005. By the latter part of Bloomberg's second term as mayor, the entire city seemed to be under construction, with luxury high-rise condos sprouting up in every neighborhood.

Soon the economy buckled under its own weight in what has largely become known as the Global Financial Crisis (GFC). The city was paralyzed as the cornerstones of the business world were forced to close shop. Although hit less badly than many pockets of the country, NYC still saw a significant dip in real-estate prices and many cranes became frozen monuments of a broken economy.

In 2011 the city commemorated the 10th anniversary of the 9/11 attacks with the opening of a remembrance center, while the half-built Freedom Tower – a new corporate behemoth – loomed overhead.

Storms & Political Change

New York's resilience would be tested again in 2012 by superstorm Hurricane Sandy. On October 29, cyclonic winds and drenching rain pounded the city, causing severe flooding and property damage in all five boroughs, including to the NYC subway system, the Hugh L Carey Tunnel to Brooklyn and the World Trade Center site. A major power blackout plunged much of Lower Manhattan into surreal darkness, while trading at the New York Stock Exchange was suspended for two days in its first weather-related closure since 1888. In the neighborhood of Breezy Point, Queens, a devastating storm surge hindered the efforts of firefighters confronted with a blaze that reduced over 125 homes to ashes. The fire went down as one of the worst in NYC's history, while the storm itself claimed 44 lives in the city alone.

The winds of political change swept through the city in November 2013, when Bill de Blasio became the city's first Democrat mayor since 1989. The 52-year-old self-proclaimed progressive also became the first white mayor of NYC with an African American spouse.

2012
Superstorm Sandy hits NYC in October, cutting power and causing major flooding and property damage.

2016
Architect Santiago Calatrava's landmark World Trade Center Transportation Hub officially opens in Lower Manhattan.

2017
Massive projects continue, with ongoing work on the 28-acre Hudson Yards, and the opening of the Second Ave subway line.

Arts & Architecture

Peel back the concrete urban landscape, and you discover one of the world's great artistic centers. New York City has been a showcase for talents great and small, who've added their mark to the city's canvas – both on its gallery walls and onto its gritty streets in the form of architectural icons that soar above the crowded sidewalks.

An Artistic Heavyweight

That New York claims some of the world's mightiest art museums attests to its enviable artistic pedigree. From Pollock and Rothko, to Warhol and Rauschenberg, the city has nourished many of America's greatest artists and artistic movements.

The Birth of an Arts Hub

In almost all facets of the arts, New York really got its sea legs in the early 20th century, when the city attracted and retained a critical mass of thinkers, artists, writers and poets. It was at this time that the homegrown art scene began to take shape. In 1905 photographer (and husband of artist Georgia O'Keeffe) Alfred Stieglitz opened 'Gallery 291,' a Fifth Ave space that provided a vital platform for American artists and helped establish photography as a credible art form.

In the 1940s, an influx of cultural figures fleeing the carnage of WWII saturated the city with fresh ideas – and New York became an important cultural hub. Peggy Guggenheim established the Art of this Century gallery on 57th St, a space that helped launch the careers of painters such as Jackson Pollock, Willem de Kooning and Robert Motherwell. These Manhattan-based artists came to form the core of the abstract expressionist movement – also known as the New York School – creating an explosive and rugged form of painting that changed the course of modern art as we know it.

An American Avant-Garde

The abstract expressionists helped establish New York as a global arts center. Another generation of artists then carried the ball. In the 1950s and '60s, Robert Rauschenberg, Jasper Johns and Lee Bontecou turned paintings into off-the-wall sculptural constructions that included everything from welded steel to taxidermy goats. By the mid-1960s, pop art – a movement that utilized the imagery and production techniques of popular culture – had taken hold, with Andy Warhol at the helm.

By the '60s and '70s, when New York's economy was in the dumps and much of SoHo lay in a state of decay, the city became a hotbed of conceptual and performance art. Gordon Matta-Clark sliced up abandoned buildings with chainsaws and the artists of Fluxus staged happenings on downtown streets. Carolee Schneemann organized performances that utilized the human body; at one famous 1964 event, she had a crew of nude dancers roll around in an unappetizing mix of paint, sausages and dead fish in the theater of a Greenwich Village church.

Art Today

New York remains the world's gallery capital, with more than 800 spaces showcasing all kinds of art all over the city. The blue-chip dealers can be found clustered in Chelsea and the Upper East Side. Galleries that showcase emerging and mid-career artists dot the Lower East Side, while prohibitive rents have pushed the city's more emerging and experimental scenes further out, with current hot spots including Harlem and the Brooklyn neighborhoods of Bushwick, Greenpoint, Clinton Hill and Bedford-Stuyvesant (Bed-Stuy).

Graffiti & Street Art

Contemporary graffiti as we know it was cultivated in NYC. In the 1970s the graffiti-covered subway train became a potent symbol of the city and work by figures such as Dondi, Blade and Lady Pink became known around the world. In addition, fine artists such as Jean-Michel Basquiat, Kenny Scharf and Keith Haring began incorporating elements of graffiti into their work.

The movement received new life in the late 1990s when a new generation of artists – many with art-school pedigrees – began using materials such as cut paper and sculptural elements (all illicitly). Well-known New York City artists working in this vein include John Fekner, Stephen 'Espo' Powers, Swoon and the twin-brother duo Skewville.

These days, spray-can and stencil hot spots include the Brooklyn side of the Williamsburg Bridge and the corner of Troutman St and St Nicholas Ave in Bushwick, also in Brooklyn. In Astoria, Queens, explore the technicolor artworks around Welling Ct and 30th Ave.

Grand Central Terminal

LIFE IN PIXELS/SHUTTERSTOCK ©

Architecture

New York's architectural history is a layer cake of ideas and styles – one that is literally written on the city's streets. Humble colonial farmhouses and graceful Federal-style buildings can be found alongside ornate beaux-arts palaces from the early 20th century. There are the unadorned forms of the International Style, and, in recent years, there has been the addition of the torqued forms of deconstructivist architects. For the architecture buff, it's a bricks-and-mortar bonanza.

Beaux-Arts Blockbusters

At the turn of the 20th century, New York entered a gilded age. Architects, many of whom trained in France, came back with European design ideas. Gleaming white limestone began to replace all the brownstone, first stories were elevated to allow for dramatic staircase entrances, and buildings were adorned with sculptured keystones and Corinthian columns.

McKim Mead & White's Villard Houses, from 1884 (now the Palace Hotel), show the movement's early roots. Loosely based on Rome's Palazzo della Cancelleria, they channeled the symmetry and elegance of the Italian Renaissance. Other classics include the central branch of the New York Public Library (1911) designed by Carrère and Hastings, the 1902 extension of the Metropolitan Museum of Art by Richard Morris Hunt, and Warren and Wetmore's stunning Grand Central Terminal (1913), which is capped by a statue of Mercury, the god of commerce.

Reaching Skyward

By the time New York settled into the 20th century, elevators and steel-frame engineering had allowed the city to grow up – literally. This period saw a building boom of skyscrapers, starting with Cass Gilbert's neo-Gothic 57-story Woolworth Building (1913). To this day it remains one of the 50 tallest buildings in the United States.

Others soon followed. In 1930, the Chrysler Building, the 77-story art-deco masterpiece designed by William Van Alen, became the world's tallest structure. The following year, the record was broken by the Empire State Building, a clean-lined moderne monolith crafted from Indiana limestone. Its spire was meant to be used as a mooring mast for dirigibles (airships) – an idea that made for good publicity, but which proved to be impractical and unfeasible.

The influx of displaced European architects and other thinkers who had resettled in New York by the end of WWII fostered a lively dialogue between American and European architects. This was a period when urban planner Robert Moses furiously rebuilt vast swaths of New York – to the detriment of many neighborhoods – and designers and artists became obsessed with the clean, unadorned lines of the International Style.

One of the earliest projects in this vein were the UN buildings (1948–52), the combined effort of a committee of architects, including the Swiss-born Le Corbusier, Brazil's Oscar Niemeyer and America's Wallace K Harrison. The Secretariat employed New York's first glass curtain wall – which looms over the ski-slope curve of the General Assembly. Other significant modernist structures from this period include Gordon Bunshaft's Lever House (1950–52), a floating, glassy structure on Park Ave and 54th St, and Ludwig Mies van der Rohe's austere, 38-story Seagram Building (1956–58), located just two blocks to the south.

The New Guard

By the late 20th century, numerous architects began to rebel against the hard-edged, unornamented nature of modernist design. Among them was Philip Johnson. His pink granite AT&T Building (now Sony Tower; 1984) – topped by a scrolled, neo-Georgian pediment – has become a postmodern icon of the Midtown skyline.

What never became an icon was Daniel Libeskind's twisting, angular design for the One World Trade Center (2013) tower, replaced by a boxier architecture-by-committee glass obelisk. On the same site, budget blowouts led to tweaks of Santiago Calatrava's luminous design for the World Trade Center Transportation Hub (2016). According to critics, what should have looked like a dove in flight now resembles a winged dinosaur.

Sir Norman Foster has also bequeathed his cutting-edge style upon the city. The British architect's Hearst Tower (2006) – a glass skyscraper zigzagging its way out of a 1920s sandstone structure – remains a Midtown trailblazer. The building is one of numerous daring 21st-century additions to the city's architectural portfolio, among them Brooklyn's sci-fi arena Barclays Center (2012), Thom Mayne's folded-and-slashed 41 Cooper Square (2009) in the East Village, and Frank Gehry's rippling, 76-story apartment tower New York by Gehry (2011) in the Financial District.

Starchitects on the Line

Frank Gehry's IAC Building (2007) – a billowing, white-glass structure often compared to a wedding cake – is one of a growing number of 'starchitect' creations appearing around railway-turned-urban-park, the High Line. The most prominent of these is Renzo Piano's new Whitney Museum of American Art (2015). Dramatically asymmetrical and clad in blue-gray steel, the building has received significant praise for melding seamlessly with the elevated park. Turning heads eight blocks to the north is 100 Eleventh Ave (2010), a 23-story luxury condominium by French architect Jean Nouvel. Its exuberant arrangement of angled windows is nothing short of mesmerizing, both cutting-edge in its construction and sensitive to the area's heritage. That the facade's patterning evokes West Chelsea's industrial masonry is not coincidental.

The area's latest darling is the late Dame Zaha Hadid's apartment complex at 520 W 28th St (2017). Rising 11 stories, the luxury structure was one of the Iraqi-British architect's last projects, and her only one in New York. Its voluptuous, sci-fi curves are complemented by a 2500-sq-ft sculpture deck showcasing art presented by Friends of the High Line.

ANDREI ORLOV/SHUTTERSTOCK ©

LGBTIQ+ New York City

*New York City is out and damn proud. It was here that
the modern gay rights movement bloomed and that
America's first Pride march hit the streets. Yet even
before the days of 'Gay Lib,' the city had a knack for all
things queer and fabulous, from Bowery sex saloons and
Village Sapphic poetry to drag balls in Harlem.*

Subversion in the Villages

In the 1890s New York City's rough-and-ready Lower East Side established quite a reputation for being home to venues offering everything from cross-dressing spectaculars to back rooms for same-sex shenanigans. As the city strode into the 20th century, free-thinking bohemians began stepping into Greenwich Village, turning it into a place with no shortage of bachelor pads, more tolerant attitudes and – with the arrival of Prohibition – an anything-goes speakeasy scene. A number of gay-owned businesses lined MacDougal St, among them the legendary Eve's Hangout at number 129, which was famous for two things: poetry readings and a sign on the door that read 'Men are admitted but not welcome.' Police raided the place in June 1926, charging the owner, Polish Jewish immigrant Eva Kotchever (Eve Addams), with 'obscenity' for penning her *Lesbian Love* anthology, and deporting her back to Europe.

Divas, Drag & Harlem

While Times Square had developed a reputation for attracting gay men (many of them working in the district's theaters, restaurants and speakeasy bars), another hot scene in the 1920s was found in Harlem, where drag balls were a hit with both gay and straight New Yorkers. The biggest of the lot was the Hamilton Lodge Ball, held annually at the swank Rockland Palace on 155th St. It was a chance for gay men and women to (legally) cross-dress and steal a same-sex dance. The evening's star attraction was the beauty pageant, which saw the drag-clad competitors compete for the title of 'Queen of the Ball.' Even the papers covered the extravaganza, with its outrageous frocks the talk of the town.

The Stonewall Revolution

The relative transgression of the early 20th century was replaced with a new conservatism in the following decades, as the Great Depression, WWII and the Cold War took their toll. Conservatism was helped along by Senator Joe McCarthy, who declared that homosexuals in the State Department threatened America's security and children. Tougher policing aimed to eradicate queer visibility in the public sphere, forcing the scene further underground in the 1940s and '50s. Yet on June 28, 1969, when eight police officers raided the Stonewall Inn – a gay-friendly watering hole in Greenwich Village – patrons did the unthinkable: they revolted. Fed up with both the harassment and corrupt officers receiving payoffs from the bars' owners (who were mostly organized crime figures), they began bombarding the officers with coins, bottles, bricks and chants of 'gay power' and 'we shall overcome'. Their collective anger and solidarity was a turning point, igniting intense and passionate debate about discrimination and forming the catalyst for the modern gay rights movement, not just in New York, but across the US and in countries from the Netherlands to Australia. In 2019 New York will host the international WorldPride celebration for the 50th anniversary of the Stonewall riots.

In the Shadow of AIDS

LGBT activism intensified as HIV and AIDS hit world headlines in the early 1980s. Faced with ignorance, fear and the moral indignation of those who saw AIDS as a 'gay cancer,' activists such as writer Larry Kramer set about tackling what was quickly becoming an epidemic. Out of his efforts was born ACT UP (AIDS Coalition to Unleash Power) in 1987, an advocacy group set up to fight the perceived homophobia and indifference of then President Ronald Reagan, as well as to end the price gouging of AIDS drugs by pharmaceutical companies.

The epidemic itself had a significant impact on New York's artistic community. Among its most high-profile victims were artist Keith Haring, photographer Robert Mapplethorpe and fashion designer Halston. Yet out of this loss grew a tide of powerful AIDS-related plays and musicals that would not only win broad international acclaim, but would become part of America's mainstream cultural canon. Among these are Tony Kushner's political epic *Angels in America* and Jonathan Larson's rock musical *Rent*.

Marriage & the New Millennium

The fight for complete equality took two massive steps forward in recent years. In 2011, a federal law banning LGBT military personnel from serving openly – the so-called 'Don't Ask, Don't Tell' policy – was repealed after years of intense lobbying. Also in 2011, persistence led to an even greater victory – the right to marry. The New York State Assembly passed the Marriage Equality Act, and it was signed into law on June 24, the very eve of New York City Gay Pride. State victory became a national one on June 26, 2015, when the US Supreme Court ruled that same-sex marriage is a legal right across the country, striking down the remaining marriage bans in 13 US states.

Tom's Restaurant, featured in *Seinfeld*

NYC on Screen

New York City has a long and storied life on screen. It was on these streets that a bumbling Woody Allen fell for Diane Keaton in Annie Hall, *that Meg Ryan faked her orgasm in* When Harry Met Sally, *and that Sarah Jessica Parker philosophized about the finer points of dating and Jimmy Choos in* Sex and the City. *To fans of American film and television, traversing the city can feel like one big déjà vu of memorable scenes, characters and one-liners.*

Landmarks on Screen

It's not surprising that NYC feels strangely familiar to many first-time visitors – the city itself has racked up more screen time than most Hollywood divas put together and many of its landmarks are as much a part of American screen culture as its red-carpet celebrities. Take the Staten Island Ferry (p238), which takes bullied secretary Melanie Griffith from suburbia to Wall St in *Working Girl* (1988); Battery Park (p41), where Madonna bewitches Aidan Quinn and Rosanna Arquette in *Desperately Seeking Susan* (1985); or the New York County Courthouse, where villains get what they deserve in *Wall Street* (1987) and *Goodfellas* (1990), as well as in small-screen classics such as *Cagney & Lacey*, *NYPD Blue* and *Law & Order*. The latter show, famous for showcasing New York and its characters, is honored with its own road – Law & Order Way – that leads to Pier 62 at Chelsea Piers.

Few landmarks can claim as much screen time as the Empire State Building (p70), famed for its spire-clinging ape in *King Kong* (1933, 2005), as well as for the countless romantic encounters on its observation decks. One of its most famous scenes is Meg Ryan and Tom Hanks' after-hours encounter in *Sleepless in Seattle* (1993). The sequence – which uses the real lobby but a studio-replica deck – is a tribute of sorts to *An Affair to Remember* (1957), which sees Cary Grant and Deborah Kerr make a pact to meet and (hopefully) seal their love atop the skyscraper.

Sarah Jessica Parker is less lucky in *Sex and the City* (2008), when a nervous

Hollywood Roots & Rivals

Believe it or not, America's film industry is an East Coast native. Fox, Universal, Metro, Selznick and Goldwyn all originated here in the early 20th century, and long before Westerns were shot in California and Colorado, they were filmed in the (now former) wilds of New Jersey. Even after Hollywood's year-round sunshine lured the bulk of the business west by the 1920s, 'Lights, Camera, Action' remained a common call in Gotham. The heart of the local scene was Queens' still-kicking Kaufman Astoria Studios.

Chris Noth jilts her and her Vivienne Westwood wedding dress at the New York Public Library (p74). Perhaps he'd seen *Ghostbusters* (1984) a few too many times, its opening scenes featuring the haunted library's iconic marble lions and Rose Main Reading Room. The library's foyer sneakily stands in for the Metropolitan Museum of Art in *The Thomas Crown Affair* (1999), in which thieving playboy Pierce Brosnan meets his match in sultry detective Rene Russo. It's at the fountain in adjacent Bryant Park that DIY sleuth Diane Keaton debriefs husband Woody Allen about their supposedly bloodthirsty elderly neighbor in *Manhattan Murder Mystery* (1993).

Across Central Park (p36) – whose own countless scenes include Barbra Streisand and Robert Redford rowing on its lake in clutch-a-tissue *The Way We Were* (1973) – stands the Dakota Building, used in the classic thriller *Rosemary's Baby* (1968). The Upper West Side is also home to Tom's Restaurant, whose facade was used regularly in *Seinfeld*. Another neighborhood star is the elegant Lincoln Center (p76), where Natalie Portman slowly loses her mind in the psychological thriller *Black Swan* (2010), and where love-struck Brooklynites Cher and Nicolas Cage meet for a date in *Moonstruck* (1987).

The more recent Oscar-winner *Birdman* (2014) shines the spotlight on Midtown's glittering Theater District, in which a long-suffering Michael Keaton tries to stage a Broadway adaptation at the St James Theatre on W 44th St.

Dancing in the Street

Knives make way for leotards in the cult musical *Fame* (1980), in which New York High School of Performing Arts students do little for the city's traffic woes by dancing on Midtown's streets. The film's graphic content was too much for the city's Board of Education, who banned shooting at the real High School of Performing Arts, then located at 120 W 46th St. Consequently, filmmakers used the doorway of a disused church on the opposite side of the street for the school's entrance, and Haaren Hall (Tenth Ave and 59th St) for interior scenes.

Fame is not alone in turning Gotham into a pop-up dance floor. In *On the Town* (1949), starstruck sailors Frank Sinatra, Gene Kelly and Jules Munshin look straight off a Pride float as they skip, hop and sing their way across this 'wonderful town,' from the base of Lady Liberty (p40) to Rockefeller Plaza (p84) and the Brooklyn Bridge (p47). Another

NYC on TV

Over 70 TV shows are filmed in NYC, from hit series such as *Law & Order: Special Victims Unit* and *The Good Wife* and quirky comedies like *Broad City*, to long-standing classics including *The Tonight Show Starring Jimmy Fallon* and *Saturday Night Live*. Combined, the city's TV and film industries spend over $8 billion on production annually and support 104,000 jobs. Over a third of professional actors in the US are based here.

wave of campness hits the bridge when Diana Ross and Michael Jackson cross it in *The Wiz* (1978), a bizarre take on *The Wizard of Oz*, complete with munchkins in Flushing Meadows Corona Park and an Emerald City at the base of the WTC Twin Towers. The previous year, the bridge provided a rite of passage for a bell-bottomed John Travolta in *Saturday Night Fever* (1977), who leaves the comforts of his adolescent Brooklyn for the bigger, brighter mirror balls of Manhattan. Topping them all, however, is the closing scene in Terry Gilliam's *The Fisher King* (1991), which sees Grand Central Terminal's Main Concourse (p113) turned into a ballroom of waltzing commuters.

NYC on Film

It would take volumes to cover all the films tied to Gotham, so fire up your imagination with the following celluloid hits:

Taxi Driver (Martin Scorsese, 1976) Robert De Niro plays a mentally unstable Vietnam War vet whose violent urges are heightened by the city's tensions.

Manhattan (Woody Allen, 1979) A divorced New Yorker dating a high-school student falls for his best friend's mistress in what is essentially a love letter to NYC. Catch romantic views of the Queensboro Bridge and the Upper East Side.

Desperately Seeking Susan (Susan Seidelman, 1985) A case of mistaken identity leads a bored New Jersey housewife on a wild adventure through Manhattan's subcultural wonderland. Relive mid-1980s East Village and long-gone nightclub Danceteria.

Summer of Sam (Spike Lee, 1999) Spike Lee puts NYC's summer of 1977 in historical context by weaving together the Son of Sam murders, the blackout, racial tensions and the misadventures of one disco-dancing Brooklyn couple, including scenes at CBGB and Studio 54.

Angels in America (Mike Nichols, 2003) This movie version of Tony Kushner's Broadway play recalls 1985 Manhattan: crumbling relationships, AIDS out of control and a closeted Roy Cohn – advisor to President Ronald Reagan – doing nothing about it except falling ill himself. Follow characters from Brooklyn to Lower Manhattan to Central Park.

Party Monster (Fenton Bailey, 2003) Starring Macaulay Culkin, who plays the famed, murderous club kid Michael Alig, this is a disturbing look into the drug-fueled downtown clubbing culture of the late '80s. The former Limelight club is featured prominently.

Precious (Lee Daniels, 2009) This unflinching tale of an obese, illiterate teenager who is abused by her parents takes place in Harlem, offering plenty of streetscapes and New York–ghetto 'tude.

Birdman (Alejandro G Iñárritu, 2014) Oscar-winning black-comedy/drama *Birdman* documents the struggles of a has-been Hollywood actor trying to mount a Broadway show.

OPUSNY/GETTY IMAGES ©

Survival Guide

Directory A–Z

Customs Regulations

US Customs allows each person over the age of 21 to bring 1L of liquor and 200 cigarettes into the US duty free. Agricultural items including meat, fruits, vegetables, plants and soil are prohibited. US citizens are allowed to import, duty free, up to $800 worth of gifts from abroad, while non-US citizens are allowed to import $100 worth. For updates, check www.cbp.gov.

Discount Cards

If you plan on blitzing the major sights, consider buying one of the numerous multi-attraction passes (see www.nycgo.com/attraction-passes). Getting one of these discount cards will save you a wad of cash. Go online for more details.

Electricity

The US electric current is 110V to 120V, 60Hz AC. Outlets are made for flat two-prong plugs (which often have a third, rounded prong for grounding). If your appliance is made for another electrical system (eg 220V), you'll need a step-down converter, which can be bought at hardware stores and drugstores. Most electronic devices (laptops, camera-battery chargers etc) are built for dual-voltage use, however, and will only need a plug adapter.

Type A
120V/60Hz

Type B
120V/60Hz

Health

Emergency services can be stress-inducing and slow (unless your medical condition is absolutely dire); a visit should be avoided if other medical services can be provided to mitigate the situation.

Travel MD (✆212-737-1212; www.travelmd.com)

Bellevue Hospital Center (✆212-562-4141; www.nyc healthandhospitals.org/ bellevue; 462 First Ave, at 27th St, Midtown East; S6 to 28th St)

Tisch Hospital (New York University Langone Medical Center; ✆212-263-5800; www. nyulangone.org/locations/tisch-hospital; 550 First Ave; ⊙24hr)

Lenox Hill Hospital (✆212-434-2000; www.northwell. edu/find-care/locations/lenox-hill-hospital; 100 E 77th St, at Lexington Ave; ⊙24hr; S6 to 77th St)

Insurance

Before traveling, contact your health-insurance provider to find out what types of medical care will be covered outside your hometown (or home country). Overseas visitors should acquire travel insurance that covers medical situations in the US, as nonemergency care for uninsured patients can be very expensive. For non-emergency appointments at hospitals, you'll need proof of insurance or cash.

Even with insurance, you'll most likely have to pay up front for nonemergency care and then wrangle with your insurance company afterwards in order to get your money reimbursed.

Tipping

Tipping is *not* optional; only withhold tips in cases of outrageously bad service.

Restaurant servers 18% to 20%, unless a gratuity is already charged on the bill (usually only for groups of five or more).

Bartenders 15% to 20% per round, minimum per drink $1 for standard drinks, and $2 per specialty cocktail.

Taxi drivers 10% to 15%, rounded up to the next dollar.

Airport & hotel porters $2 per bag, minimum per cart $5.

Hotel maids $2 to $4 per night, left in envelope or under the card provided.

Internet Access

Most public parks in the city now offer free wi-fi. Some prominent ones include the High Line, Bryant Park, Battery Park, Central Park, City Hall Park, Madison Square Park, Tompkins Square Park and Union Square Park (Brooklyn and Queens are also well covered). Check out www.nycgovparks.org/facilities/wifi.

Even underground subway stations now offer free wi-fi, offering a way to pass time or get work done while waiting for signal problems or other delays to be resolved. **LinkNYC** (www.link.nyc), rolled out in 2016 to replace anachronistic pay phones (once iconic symbols of the city and where Superman changed into his suit), has installed free internet-connected kiosks, replete with charging stations and wi-fi access. The network aims to install some 7500 of these structures throughout the five boroughs.

It's rare to find accommodations in New York City that don't offer wi-fi, though it isn't always free. Most cafes offer wi-fi for customers, as do the ubiquitous Starbucks around town.

Legal Matters

If you're arrested, you have the right to remain silent. There is no legal reason to speak to a police officer if you don't wish to – especially since anything you say 'can and will be used against you' – but never walk away from an officer until given permission. All persons who are arrested have the legal right to make one phone call. If you don't have a lawyer or family member to help you, call your consulate. The police will give you the number upon request.

LGBTIQ+ Travelers

One of the largest centers of its kind in the world, the **LGBT Community Center** (Map p248; ☎212-620-7310; www.gaycenter.org; 208 W 13th St, btwn Seventh & Greenwich Aves, West Village; suggested donation $5; ⏰9am-10pm Mon-Sat, to 9pm Sun; [S]A/C/E, L to 8th Ave-14th St; 1/2/3 to 14th St) provides a ton of regional publications about gay events and nightlife, and hosts frequent special events – dance parties, art exhibits, Broadway-caliber performances, readings and political panels.

Plus it's home to the National Archive for Lesbian, Gay, Bisexual & Transgender History (accessible to researchers by appointment); a small exhibition space, the Campbell-Soady Gallery; and a cyber center.

There are tons of websites geared toward the goings-on of the city's gay community, such as:

Get Out! (www.getoutmag.com) Online version of a print guide to all things queer.

Gayletter (www.gayletter.com) E-newsletter covering queer-related culture.

Gay City News (www.gaycitynews.nyc) News and current affairs with a queer bent, as well as arts and travel reviews.

Practicalities

Newspapers

New York Post (www.nypost.com) The *Post* is known for screaming headlines, conservative political views and its popular Page Six gossip column.

New York Times (www.nytimes.com) 'The gray lady' is far from staid, with hard-hitting political coverage, and sections on technology, arts and dining out.

Magazines

New York Magazine (www.nymag.com) A biweekly magazine with feature stories and great listings about anything and everything in NYC, plus an indispensable website.

New Yorker (www.newyorker.com) This highbrow weekly covers politics and culture through its famously lengthy works of reportage; it also publishes fiction and poetry.

Time Out New York (www.timeout.com/newyork) A weekly magazine with event listings and restaurant and nightlife round-ups.

Radio

WNYC (820AM and 93.9FM; www.wnyc.org) NYC's public radio station is the local NPR affiliate and offers a blend of national and local talk and interview shows.

Smoking

Strictly forbidden in any location that's considered a public place, including subway stations, restaurants, bars, taxis and parks.

Metrosource (www.metrosource.com) Bimonthly publication with a focus on culture, entertainment and travel.

Money

ATMs

ATMs are on practically every corner. You can either use your card at banks – usually in a 24-hour-access lobby – or you can opt for the lone wolves, which sit in delis, restaurants, bars and grocery stores, charging fierce service fees that average $3 but can go as high as $5.

Changing Money

Banks and moneychangers, found all over New York City (including all three major airports), will give you US currency based on the current exchange rate. **Travelex** (☎212-265-6063; www.travelex.com; 1578 Broadway, btwn 47th & 48th Sts, Midtown West; ☺9am-10pm Mon-Sat, to 7pm Sun; ⓢN/Q/R to 49th St) has a branch in Times Square.

Credit Cards

Major credit cards are accepted at most hotels, restaurants and shops throughout New York City. In fact, you'll find it difficult to perform certain transactions, such as purchasing tickets to performances and renting a car, without one.

Opening Hours

Standard business hours are as follows:

Banks 9am to 6pm Monday to Friday, some also 9am to noon Saturday

Bars 5pm to 4am

Businesses 9am to 5pm Monday to Friday

Clubs 10pm to 4am

Restaurants Breakfast 6am to 11am, lunch 11am to around 3pm, and dinner 5pm to 11pm. Weekend brunch 11am to 4pm.

Shops 10am to around 7pm weekdays, 11am to around 8pm Saturday, and Sunday can be variable – some stores stay closed while others keep weekday hours. Stores tend to stay open later downtown.

Public Holidays

Major NYC holidays and special events may force the closure of many businesses or attract crowds, making dining and accommodations reservations difficult.

New Year's Day January 1

Martin Luther King Day Third Monday in January

Presidents' Day Third Monday in February

Easter March/April

Memorial Day Late May

Gay Pride Last Sunday in June

Independence Day July 4

Labor Day Early September

Rosh Hashanah and Yom Kippur Mid-September to mid-October

Halloween October 31

Thanksgiving Fourth Thursday in November

Christmas Day December 25

New Year's Eve December 31

Safe Travel

New York City is one of the safest cities in the USA – in 2017 homicides fell to a record low of fewer than 300 and overall violent crime statistics declined for the 27th straight year. Still, it's best to take a common-sense approach to the city.

○ Don't walk around alone at night in unfamiliar, sparsely populated areas.

○ Carry your daily walking-around money somewhere inside your clothing or in a front pocket rather than in a handbag or a back pocket.

○ Be aware of pickpockets, particularly in mobbed areas, like Times Square or Penn Station at rush hour.

○ While it's generally safe to ride the subway after midnight, you may want to skip going underground and take a taxi instead, especially if traveling alone.

Taxes

Restaurants and retailers never include the sales tax – 8.875% – in their prices, so beware of ordering the $4.99 lunch special when you only have $5 to your name. Clothing and footwear purchases under $110 are tax free; anything over that amount has a sales tax. Hotel rooms in New York City are subject to a 14.75% tax, plus a flat $3.50 occupancy tax per night.

Since the US has no nationwide value-added tax (VAT), there is no opportunity for foreign visitors to make 'tax-free' purchases.

Telephone

Phone numbers within the US consist of a three-digit area code followed by a seven-digit local number. In NYC, you will always dial 10 numbers: ☏1 + the three-digit area code + the seven-digit number. To make an international call from NYC, call ☏011 + country code + area code + number. When calling Canada, there is no need to use the ☏011.

No matter where you're calling within New York City, even if it's just across the street in the same area code, you must always dial ☏1 + the area code first.

Cell Phones

International travelers can use local SIM cards in a smartphone provided it is unlocked. Alternatively, you can buy a cheap US phone and load it up with prepaid minutes.

Emergency & Important Numbers

Local directory	☏411
Municipal offices & information	☏311
National directory information	☏212-555-1212
Operator	☏0
Fire, police & ambulance	☏911

Time

Almost all of the USA observes daylight-saving time: clocks go forward one hour from the second Sunday in March to the first Sunday in November, when the clocks are turned back one hour (remember by the phrase 'spring ahead, fall back').

Toilets

Considering the number of pedestrians, there's a noticeable lack of public restrooms around the city. You'll find spots to relieve yourself in Grand Central Terminal, Penn Station and Port Authority Bus Terminal, and in parks, including

Madison Square Park, Battery Park, Tompkins Square Park, Washington Square Park and Columbus Park in Chinatown, plus several places scattered around Central Park. The good bet, though, is to pop into a Starbucks (there's one about every three blocks) or a department store (Macy's, Century 21, Bloomingdale's).

Tourist Information

There are infinite online resources to get up-to-the-minute information about New York. In person, try one of the official branches of **NYC Information Center** (www.nycgo.com):

Times Square (Map p254; ☎212-484-1222; Broadway Plaza, btwn W 43rd & 44th Sts; ⏰9am-6pm Dec-Apr, 8am-8pm May-Nov; [S]N/Q/R/W, S, 1/2/3, 7, A/C/E to Times Sq-42nd St)

Macy's Herald Square (Map p252; ☎212-484-1222; 151 W 34th St, at Broadway; ⏰10am-10pm Mon-Sat, to 9pm Sun; [S]B/D/F/M, N/Q/R/W to 34th St-Herald Sq)

City Hall (Map p246; ☎212-484-1222; City Hall Park, at Broadway; ⏰9am-6pm Mon-Sun; [S]4/5/6 to Brooklyn Bridge-City Hall; R/W to City Hall; J/Z to Chambers St) and South Street Seaport.

Explore Brooklyn (www.explorebk.com) has event listings and lots of other info on this much-loved borough.

Travelers with Disabilities

Federal laws guarantee that all government offices and facilities are accessible to people with disabilities. For information on specific places, you can contact the **Office for People with Disabilities** (☎212-639-9665; www.nyc.gov/html/mopd), which will send you a free copy of its Access New York guide. Also check out www.nycgo.com/accessibility for a good list of planning tools.

Much of the city is accessible with curb cuts for wheelchair users. All the major sites (the Met museum, the Guggenheim, and Lincoln Center) are also accessible. Some, but not all, Broadway theaters are accessible. Unfortunately, only about 100 of New York's 468 subway stations are fully wheelchair accessible. In general, the bigger stations have access, such as West 4th St, 14th St-Union Sq, 34th St-Penn Station, 42nd St-Port Authority Terminal, 59th St-Columbus Circle and 66th St-Lincoln Center. For a complete list of accessible subway stations, visit http://web.mta.info/accessibility/stations.htm.

Download Lonely Planet's free *Accessible Travel* guide from http://lptravel.to/AccessibleTravel.

Climate Change & Travel

Every form of transportation that relies on carbon-based fuel generates CO_2, the main cause of human-induced climate change. Modern travel is dependent on airplanes, which might use less fuel per kilometre per person than most cars but travel much greater distances. The altitude at which aircraft emit gases (including CO_2) and particles also contributes to their climate change impact. Many websites offer 'carbon calculators' that allow people to estimate the carbon emissions generated by their journey and, for those who wish to do so, to offset the impact of the greenhouse gases emitted with contributions to portfolios of climate-friendly initiatives throughout the world. Lonely Planet offsets the carbon footprint of all staff and author travel.

Visas

The US Visa Waiver Program (VWP) allows nationals from 38 countries to enter the US without a visa, provided you are carrying a machine-readable passport. For the list of countries included in the program and current requirements, see the US Department of State (https://travel.state.gov) website.

Transportation

Getting There & Away

With its three bustling airports, two main train stations and a monolithic bus terminal, New York City rolls out the welcome mat for millions of visitors who come to take a bite out of the Big Apple each year.

Direct flights are possible from most major American and international cities. Figure six hours from Los Angeles, seven hours from London and Amsterdam, and 14 hours from Tokyo. Consider getting here by train instead of car or plane to enjoy a mix of bucolic and urban scenery en route, without unnecessary traffic hassles, security checks and excess carbon emissions.

Flights, tours and rail tickets can be booked online at www.lonelyplanet.com/bookings.

Air

JFK

John F Kennedy International Airport (JFK; ☎718-244-4444; www.kennedyairport.com; [S]A to Howard Beach or E, J/Z to Sutphin Blvd-Archer Ave then AirTrain to JFK), 15 miles from Midtown in southeastern Queens, has six working terminals, serves nearly 50 million passengers annually and hosts flights coming and going from all corners of the globe. You can use the AirTrain (free within the airport) to move from one terminal to another.

Taxi

A yellow taxi from Manhattan to the airport will use the meter; prices (often about $60) depend on traffic. Expect the ride to take 45 to 60 minutes. From JFK, taxis charge a flat rate of $52 to any destination in Manhattan (not including tolls or tip); it can take 45 to 60 minutes for most destinations in Manhattan. To/from a destination in Brooklyn, the metered fare should be about $45 (Coney Island) to $62 (downtown Brooklyn).

Shuttles & Car Services

Shared vans, like those offered by **Super Shuttle Manhattan** (www.supershuttle.com), cost around $20 to $26 per person, depending on the destination. If traveling to the airport from NYC, car services have set fares from $45.

Express Bus

The **NYC Airporter** (www.nycairporter.com) runs to Grand Central Terminal, Penn Station or the Port Authority Bus Terminal from JFK. The one-way fare is $18.

Subway

The subway is the cheapest but slowest way of reaching Manhattan. From the airport, hop on the AirTrain ($5, payable as you exit) to Sutphin Blvd-Archer Ave (Jamaica Station) to reach the E, J or Z line (or the Long Island Rail Road). To take the A line instead, ride the AirTrain to Howard Beach station. The E train to Midtown has the fewest stops. Expect the journey to take a little over an hour to Midtown.

Long Island Railroad (LIRR)

This is by far the most relaxing way to arrive in the city. From the airport, take the AirTrain ($5, as you exit) to Jamaica Station. From there, LIRR trains go frequently to Penn Station in Manhattan or to Atlantic Terminal in Brooklyn (near Fort Greene, Boerum Hill and the Barclays Center). It's about a 20-minute journey from station to station. One-way fares to either Penn Station or Atlantic Terminal cost $10.25 ($7.50 at off-peak times).

LaGuardia

Used mainly for domestic flights, **LaGuardia Airport** (LGA; ☎718-533-3400; www.panynj.gov; 🚌M60, Q70) is smaller than JFK but only 8 miles from midtown Manhattan; it sees nearly 30 million passengers per year. A much-needed $4 billion overhaul of its terminal facilities has begun and is expected to be finished in 2021.

Taxi

A taxi to/from Manhattan costs about $42 for the approximately half-hour ride; it's metered, no set fare. Fares for ride-hailing apps like Lyft and Uber vary.

Car Service

A car service to LaGuardia costs around $35.

Express Bus

The **NYC Airporter** (www.nycairporter.com) costs $15 and goes to/from Grand Central, Penn Station and the Port Authority Bus Terminal.

Public Transportation

It's less convenient to get to LaGuardia by public transportation than the other airports. The best subway link is the 74 St-Broadway station (7 line, or the E, F, M and R lines at the connecting Jackson Heights-Roosevelt Ave station) in Queens, where you can pick up the Q70 Express Bus to the airport (about 10 minutes to the airport). Or you can catch the M60 bus from several subway stops in upper Manhattan and Harlem or the N/Q stop at Hoyt Ave-31st St.

Newark

Don't write off New Jersey when looking for airfares to New York. About the same distance from Midtown as JFK (16 miles), **Newark Liberty International Airport** (EWR; 973-961-6000; www.panynj.gov) brings many New Yorkers out for flights (there are some 40 million passengers annually). It's a hub for United Airlines and offers the only non-stop flight to Havana, Cuba, in the New York City area.

Car Service

A car service runs about $50 to $70 for the 45-minute ride from Midtown – a taxi is roughly the same. You'll have to pay a whopping $15 to get into NYC through the Lincoln (at 42nd St) and Holland (at Canal St) Tunnels and, further north, the George Washington Bridge, though there's no charge going back through to NJ. There are a couple of cheap tolls on New Jersey highways, too, unless you ask your driver to take Hwy 1 or 9.

Subway & Train

NJ Transit (www.njtransit.com) runs a rail service (with a $5.50 AirTrain connection) between Newark airport (EWR) and New York's Penn Station for $13 each way. The trip takes 25 minutes and runs every 20 or 30 minutes from 4:20am to about 1:40am. Hold onto your ticket, which you must show upon exiting at the airport.

Express Bus

The **Newark Liberty Airport Express** (www.newarkairportexpress.com) has a bus service between the airport and Port Authority Bus Terminal, Bryant Park and Grand Central Terminal in Midtown ($16 one-way). The 45-minute ride goes every 15 minutes from 6:45am to 11:15pm and every half hour from 4:45am to 6:45am and 11:15pm to 1:15am.

Land

Bus

For most long-distance bus trips, you'll arrive and depart from the world's busiest bus station, the **Port Authority Bus Terminal** (Map p252; 212-502-2200; www.panynj.gov; 625 Eighth Ave, at W 42nd St; A/C/E to 42nd St-Port Authority Bus Terminal), which sees more than 65 million passengers each year. Efforts to replace the aging and less than salubrious station are always on the agenda. Bus companies leaving from here include the following:

Greyhound (www.greyhound.com) Connects New York with major cities across the country.

Peter Pan Trailways (www.peterpanbus.com) Daily express services to Boston, Washington, DC, and Philadelphia.

Short Line Bus (www.shortlinebus.com) Serves northern New Jersey and upstate New York, focusing on college towns such as Ithaca and New Paltz; part of Coach USA.

Budget Buses

A number of budget bus lines operate from locations on the west side of Midtown:

BoltBus (Map p252; 877-265-8287; www.boltbus.com; W 33rd St, btwn Eleventh & Twelfth Aves;) Services from New York to Philadelphia, Boston, Baltimore and Washington, DC. The earlier you purchase tickets, the better the deal. Notable for its free wi-fi, which occasionally actually works.

Megabus (Map p252; https://us.megabus.com; 34th St, btwn 11th & 12th Aves; ; 7 to 34th St-Hudson Yards) Travels from New York to Boston, Washington, DC, and Toronto, among other destinations. Free (sometimes functioning) wi-fi.

Vamoose (Map p252; 212-695-6766; www.vamoosebus.com; cnr Seventh Ave & 30th St;

from $30; [S] 1 to 28th St; A/C/E, 1/2/3 to 34th St-Penn Station) Buses head to Arlington, Virginia and Bethesda, Maryland, both not far outside Washington, DC.

Car & Motorcycle

If you're considering traveling to NYC by car or motorcycle, be sure to have a plan for where you'll park the vehicle.

Train

Penn Station (W 33rd St, btwn Seventh & Eighth Aves; [S] 1/2/3, A/C/E to 34th St-Penn Station) The oft-maligned departure point for all **Amtrak** (www.amtrak.com) trains, including the Acela Express services to Princeton, NJ, and Washington, DC (note that this express service costs twice as much as a normal fare). All fares vary, based on the day of the week and the time you want to travel. There's no baggage-storage facility at Penn Station. Derailments and maintenance issues plagued Amtrak lines out of Penn Station in the spring of 2017; repairs mean compromised service, with no certainty of when the issues will be resolved.

Long Island Rail Road (www.mta.info/lirr) The Long Island Rail Road serves more than 300,000 commuters each day, with services from Penn Station to points in Brooklyn and Queens, and on Long Island. Prices are broken down by zones. A peak-hour ride from Penn Station to Jamaica Station (en route to JFK via AirTrain) costs $10.25 if you buy it at the station (or a whopping $16 onboard!).

NJ Transit (www.njtransit.com) Also operates trains from Penn Station, with services to the suburbs and the Jersey Shore.

New Jersey PATH (www.panynj.gov/path) An option for getting into NJ's northern points, such as Hoboken and Newark. Trains ($2.75) run from Penn Station along the length of Sixth Ave, with stops at 33rd, 23rd, 14th, 9th and Christopher Sts, as well as at the reopened World Trade Center site.

Metro-North Railroad (www.mta.info/mnr) The last line departing from the magnificent Grand Central Terminal, the Metro-North Railroad serves Connecticut, Westchester County and the Hudson Valley.

Getting Around

Check the Metropolitan Transportation Authority website (www.mta.info) for public transportation information (buses and subway), a route planner and notifications of delays and alternate travel routes during frequent maintenance.

Bicycle

Hundreds of miles of designated bike lanes have been added over the past decade. Add to this the excellent bike-sharing network **Citi Bike** (www.citibikenyc.com), and you have the makings for a surprisingly bike-friendly city. Hundreds of Citi Bike kiosks in Manhattan and parts of Brooklyn house the iconic bright blue and very sturdy bicycles, which have reasonable rates for short-term users. Nearly 14 million City Bike 'trips' were taken in 2016 and there are an estimated 12,000 bikes in the system.

To use a Citi Bike, purchase a 24-hour or three-day access pass (around $12 or $24 including tax) at any Citi Bike kiosk. You will then be given a five-digit code to unlock a bike. Return the bike to any station within 30 minutes to avoid incurring extra fees. Reinsert your credit card (you won't be charged) and follow the prompts to check out a bike again. You can make an unlimited number of 30-minute check-outs during those 24 hours or three days.

Boat

NYC Ferry (www.ferry.nyc; one-way $2.75) Operating in the East River only since May 2017 (it replaced the former East River Ferry service), these boats link Manhattan, Brooklyn, Queens and the Bronx. At only $2.75 a ride ($1 more to bring a bicycle on board) and with charging stations and mini convenience stores on board, it's an altogether more pleasurable commute than being stuck underground on the subway. Rapidly becoming a popular and scenic way to reach beach spots in Rockaway, Queens.

NY Water Taxi (www.nywatertaxi.com) Has a fleet of zippy yellow boats that provide hop-on, hop-off services with a few stops around Manhattan (Pier

79 at W 39th St; World Financial Center and Pier 11 near Wall St) and Brooklyn (Pier 1 in Dumbo), plus a **ferry service** (Ikea Express; ☏212-742-1969; www.nywatertaxi.com/ikea; 500 Van Brunt St, behind Fairway, Red Hook; adult/child $5/free, Sat & Sun free) between Pier 11 and the Ikea store in Red Hook, Brooklyn. At $35 for an all-day pass, though, it's priced more like a sightseeing cruise than practical transportation.

Staten Island Ferry (Map p246; www.siferry.com; Whitehall Terminal, 4 South St, at Whitehall St; ◷24hr; Ⓢ1 to South Ferry; R/W to Whitehall St; 4/5 to Bowling Green) ☒☒☒☒ Bright orange and large, this free commuter-oriented ferry to Staten Island makes constant journeys across New York Harbor. Even if you simply turn around to reboard in Staten Island, the views of lower Manhattan and the Statue of Liberty make this a great sightseeing experience and one of the cheapest romantic dates in the city.

Bus

Buses can be a handy way to cross town or to cover short distances when you don't want to bother going underground. Rides cost the same as subway ($2.75 per ride), and you can use your metrocard or pay in cash (exact change required) when entering the bus. If you pay with a metrocard, you get one free transfer from bus to subway, bus to bus, or subway to bus. If you pay

in cash, ask for a transfer (good only for a bus to bus transfer) from the bus driver when paying.

Car & Motorcycle

Unless you plan to explore far-flung corners of the outer boroughs, it's a bad idea to have a car in NYC. Parking garages can be quite expensive, and finding street parking can be maddeningly difficult. If you drive in from New Jersey, you'll also have to contend with high tolls. Unlike in most other parts of the US, turning right on a red light is not legal here.

Subway

The New York subway system, run by the Metropolitan Transportation Authority (www.mta.info), is iconic, cheap ($2.75 per ride, regardless of the distance traveled), round-the-clock and often the fastest and most reliable way to get around the city. It's also safer and (a bit) cleaner than it used to be. Free wi-fi is available in all underground stations. A 7-Day Unlimited Pass costs $32.

It's a good idea to grab a free map from a station attendant. If you have a smartphone, download a useful app (like the free Citymapper), with subway map and alerts of service outages.

Taxi

Hailing and riding in a cab, once rites of passage in New York, are being replaced by

the ubiquity of ride-hailing app services like Lyft and Uber. Most taxis in NYC are clean and, compared to those in many international cities, pretty cheap. When you get a driver who's a speed demon, which is often, don't forget to buckle up.

It's $2.50 for the initial charge (first one-fifth of a mile), 50¢ for each additional one-fifth mile as well as per 60 seconds of being stopped in traffic, $1 peak surcharge (weekdays 4pm to 8pm), and a 50¢ night surcharge (8pm to 6am), plus a MTA State surcharge of 50¢ per ride. Tips are expected to be 10% to 15%, but give less if you feel in any way mistreated; be sure to ask for a receipt and use it to note the driver's license number. See www.nyc.gov/taxi for more information.

Boro Taxis

Green Boro Taxis operate in the outer boroughs and Upper Manhattan. These allow folks to hail a taxi on the street in neighborhoods where yellow taxis rarely roam. They have the same fares and features as yellow cabs, and are a good way to get around the outer boroughs (from, say, Astoria to Williamsburg, or Park Slope to Red Hook). Drivers are reluctant (but legally obligated) to take passengers into Manhattan as they aren't legally allowed to take fares going out of Manhattan south of 96th St.

Behind the Scenes

Acknowledgements

Climate map data adapted from Peel MC, Finlayson BL & McMahon TA (2007) 'Updated World Map of the Köppen-Geiger Climate Classification'; *Hydrology and Earth System Sciences*, 11, 1633–44.

This Book

This 3rd edition guidebook was curated by Ali Lemer and researched and written by Regis St. Louis, Robert Balkovich, Ray Bartlett and Ali. The previous edition was was researched and written by Regis St Louis and Michael Grosberg, and the first edition was researched and written by Regis St Louis, Cristian Bonetto and Zora O'Neill. This guidebook was produced by the following:

Destination Editor Trisha Ping

Product Editors Hannah Cartmel, Kate Mathews

Senior Cartographer Alison Lyall

Book Designer Mazzy Prinsep

Assisting Editors Melanie Dankel, Bruce Evans, Jennifer Hattam, Alison Morris, Anne Mulvaney, Kristin Odijk, Christopher Pitts, Benjamin Spier

Assisting Cartographer Michael Garrett

Cover Researcher Brendan Dempsey-Spencer

Thanks to Mikki Brammer, Mark Griffiths, Anne Mason, Jenna Myers, Tony Wheeler

Send Us Your Feedback

Index

Symbols & Map Key

Look for these symbols to quickly identify listings:

◉ Sights

⊕ Activities

⊜ Courses

⊙ Tours

⊗ Festivals & Events

⊗ Eating

⊕ Drinking

✪ Entertainment

⊕ Shopping

❶ Information & Transport

These symbols and abbreviations give vital information for each listing:

🌿 Sustainable or green recommendation

FREE No payment required

☏ Telephone number

☺ Opening hours

Ⓟ Parking

⊝ Nonsmoking

❄ Air-conditioning

@ Internet access

🛜 Wi-fi access

🏊 Swimming pool

🚌 Bus

⛴ Ferry

🚊 Tram

🚆 Train

📖 English-language menu

🥄 Vegetarian selection

👪 Family-friendly

Find your best experiences with these Great For... icons.

Art & Culture

Beaches

Budget

Cafe/Coffee

Cycling

Detour

Drinking

Entertainment

Events

Family Travel

Food & Drink

History

Local Life

Nature & Wildlife

Photo Op

Scenery

Shopping

Short Trip

Sport

Walking

Winter Travel

Sights

🏖 Beach

🐦 Bird Sanctuary

☸ Buddhist

🏰 Castle/Palace

✝ Christian

卍 Confucian

🕉 Hindu

☪ Islamic

卍 Jain

✡ Jewish

❶ Monument

🏛 Museum/Gallery/ Historic Building

🏚 Ruin

⛩ Shinto

☬ Sikh

☯ Taoist

🍷 Winery/Vineyard

🐾 Zoo/Wildlife Sanctuary

◉ Other Sight

Points of Interest

🏄 Bodysurfing

⛺ Camping

☕ Cafe

🛶 Canoeing/Kayaking

● Course/Tour

🤿 Diving

🍸 Drinking & Nightlife

🍴 Eating

🎭 Entertainment

♨ Sento Hot Baths/ Onsen

🛍 Shopping

⛷ Skiing

🛏 Sleeping

🤿 Snorkelling

🏄 Surfing

🏊 Swimming/Pool

🚶 Walking

🏄 Windsurfing

⊕ Other Activity

Information

💲 Bank

🏛 Embassy/Consulate

✚ Hospital/Medical

@ Internet

⊙ Police

✉ Post Office

☎ Telephone

🚻 Toilet

❶ Tourist Information

● Other Information

Geographic

🏖 Beach

⊢⊣ Gate

⛺ Hut/Shelter

🗼 Lighthouse

🔭 Lookout

▲ Mountain/Volcano

🌴 Oasis

❶ Park

)(Pass

🧺 Picnic Area

💧 Waterfall

Transport

✈ Airport

Ⓑ BART station

⊗ Border crossing

Ⓣ Boston T station

🚌 Bus

🚡 Cable car/Funicular

🚲 Cycling

⛴ Ferry

Ⓜ Metro/MRT station

🚝 Monorail

Ⓟ Parking

⛽ Petrol station

Ⓢ Subway/S-Bahn/ Skytrain station

🚕 Taxi

🚉 Train station/Railway

🚋 Tram

⊖ Tube Station

Ⓤ Underground/ U-Bahn station

● Other Transport

PAPER CAT/SHUTTERSTOCK ©

New York City Maps

Lower Manhattan

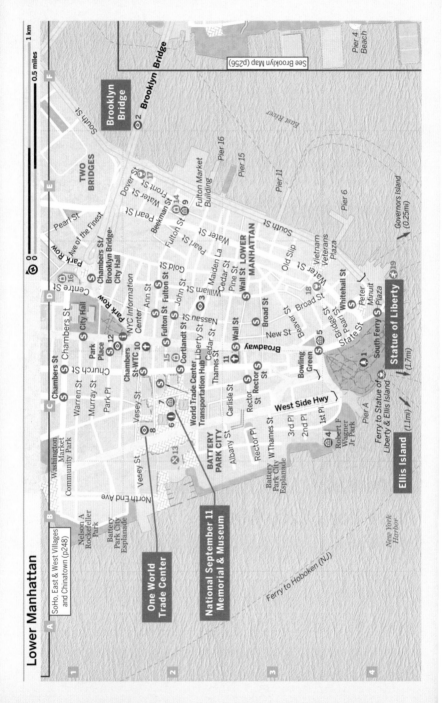

0 0.5 miles
0 1 km

SoHo, East & West Villages and Chinatown (p248)

TWO BRIDGES

Brooklyn Bridge

See Brooklyn Map (p256)

LOWER MANHATTAN

BATTERY PARK CITY

West Side Hwy

New York Harbor

Ferry to Hoboken (NJ)

Governors Island (0.25mi)

Ellis Island

Statue of Liberty

Ferry to Statue of Liberty & Ellis Island (11mi)

Ferry to Statue of Liberty & Ellis Island (1.7mi)

One World Trade Center

National September 11 Memorial & Museum

Lower Manhattan

SoHo, East & West Villages and Chinatown

Lower Manhattan (p246)

0   0
                    1 km
                    0.5 miles

E   **F**   **G**   **H**

Ⓢ 14th St-Union Sq   Ⓢ 3rd Ave ⓐ44   1st Ave   Midtown Manhattan (p252)   E 14th St

⊖58   E 13th St   E 13th St

Third Ave   Second Ave   E 12th St ⓟ76   Ave C   Ave D

E 11th St   Ave A   E 11th St

E 10th St   E 10th St

59 ⓐ   70   94 101   Tompkins Square Park
8th St-NYU Ⓢ   E 9th St   ⓐ40 ⓧ17 St Marks Pl   E 9th St
Ⓢ Astor Pl   29   E 8th St
Lafayette St   Fourth Ave   First Ave   ⓟ75

Broadway   ⓧ89   E 7th St   E 7th St   E 7th St   Ave B   E 7th St   **ALPHABET CITY**

21 ⓧ   38 ⓧ   E 6th St   E 6th St   E 5th St
E 5th St   E 5th St

NOHO   **EAST VILLAGE**   E 4th St

Great Jones St   New York City Marble Cemetery   E 3rd St   ⓧ93
99 ⓖ ⓐ ⓧ 53 25   43   E 2nd St

Bleecker St Ⓢ   ⓟ69   33 ⓧ   62 ⓟ   E Houston St

Broadway-Lafayette St Ⓢ   2nd Ave Ⓢ   E Houston St   Hamilton Fish Park   Columbia St

ⓐ41   ⓧ18   **NOLITA**   ⓟ61   54   Essex St   Norfolk St   Suffolk St   Clinton St   Stanton St   **LOWER EAST SIDE**

47 ⓐ   32   Orchard St   Allen St   Rivington St
ⓧ20   Prince St ⓐ46   ⓐ8   Eldridge St   Forsyth St   Chrystie St

37 ⓧ   83   Delancey-Essex Sts Ⓢ

Spring St Ⓢ   ⓟ77   16 ⓧ   Ⓢ Bowery   **Delancey St**   5 ⓐ   **Lower East Side Tenement Museum**
Kenmare St   Sara D Roosevelt Park   Broome St   39 ⓐ   Grand St

ⓟ71   Mott St   31   Ⓢ Grand St   Hester St   WH Seward Park   E Broadway   Henry St   Madison St

ⓧ27   68 ⓟ   **LITTLE ITALY**   92   Monroe St
48 ⓐ   ⓐ4   6 ⓐ   Canal St   Ⓢ East Broadway   Cherry St
7   Hester St
ⓐ50   Canal St Ⓢ

Lafayette St   2 ⓐ   **Chinatown**   1 ⓐ   E Broadway   Pike St   Rutgers Park
Centre St   Columbus Park   60 ⓟ   Catherine St   Madison St   Market St   **Manhattan Bridge**   South St

Federal Plaza   Park Row

SoHo, East & West Villages and Chinatown

Midtown Manhattan

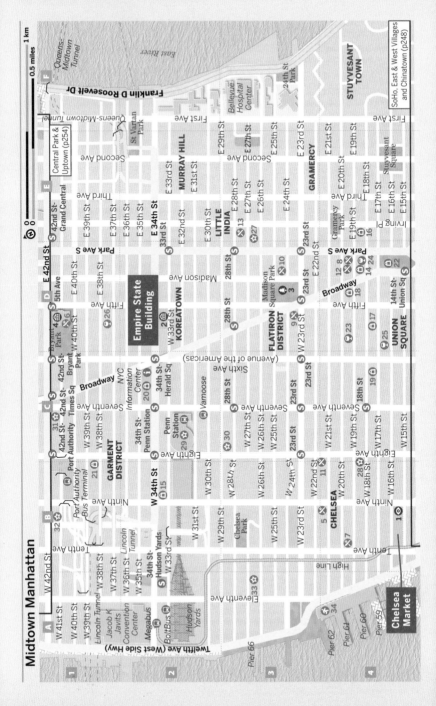

0.5 miles

1 km

Central Park & Uptown (p254)

SoHo, East & West Villages and Chinatown (p248)

Midtown Manhattan

Central Park & Uptown

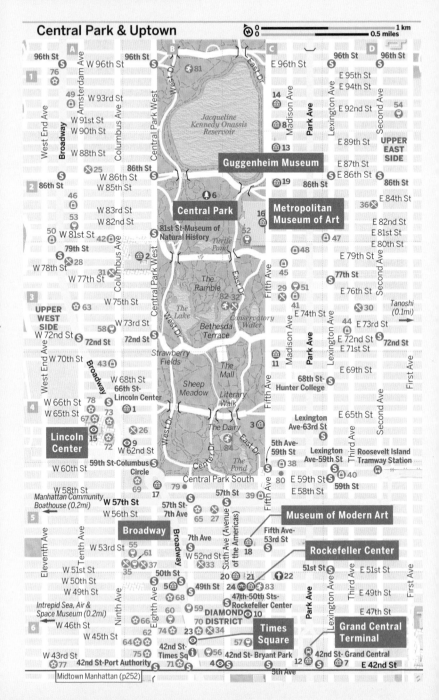

0 — 1 km
0 — 0.5 miles

Jacqueline Kennedy Onassis Reservoir

Guggenheim Museum

Central Park

Metropolitan Museum of Art

81st St-Museum of Natural History

Turtle Pond

The Ramble

The Lake

Conservatory Water

Bethesda Terrace

Strawberry Fields

The Mall

Sheep Meadow

Literary Walk

UPPER WEST SIDE

UPPER EAST SIDE

Tanoshi (0.1mi)

Lincoln Center

The Dairy

The Pond

Central Park South

66th St-Lincoln Center

68th St-Hunter College

Lexington Ave-63rd St

5th Ave-59th St

Lexington Ave-59th St

Roosevelt Island Tramway Station

59th St-Columbus Circle

Manhattan Community Boathouse (0.2mi)

Broadway

Museum of Modern Art

57th St-7th Ave

Fifth Ave-53rd St

Rockefeller Center

7th Ave

Sixth Ave (Avenue of the Americas)

Intrepid Sea, Air & Space Museum (0.2mi)

47th-50th Sts-Rockefeller Center

DIAMOND DISTRICT

Times Square

Grand Central Terminal

42nd St-Port Authority

42nd St-Times Sq

42nd St-Bryant Park

42nd St-Grand Central

Midtown Manhattan (p252)

5th Ave

Central Park & Uptown

◎ Sights

1	American Folk Art Museum	B4
2	American Museum of Natural History	B3
3	Arsenal	C4
4	Bank of America Tower	B6
5	Brill Building	B6
6	Central Park	B2
7	Chrysler Building	D6
8	Cooper-Hewitt National Design Museum	C1
9	David Rubenstein Atrium	B4
10	Diamond District	C6
11	Frick Collection	C4
12	Grand Central Terminal	C6
13	Guggenheim Museum	C2
14	Jewish Museum	C1
15	Lincoln Center	A4
16	Metropolitan Museum of Art	C2
17	Museum of Arts & Design	B5
18	Museum of Modern Art	C5
19	Neue Galerie	C2
20	Radio City Music Hall	C6
21	Rockefeller Center	C6
22	St Patrick's Cathedral	C6
23	Times Square	B6
24	Top of the Rock	C6

⊗ Eating

25	Barney Greengrass	A2
26	Boulud Sud	B4
27	Burger Joint	B5
28	Burke & Wills	A3
	Cafe 2	(see 18)
29	Café Boulud	C3
	Café Sabarsky	(see 19)
30	Candle Cafe	D3
31	Dovetail	A3
	Grand Central Oyster Bar & Restaurant	(see 12)
32	Lakeside Restaurant at Loeb Boathouse	C3
33	Le Bernardin	B5
34	Margon	B6
35	Totto Ramen	B5
36	Two Boots	D2
37	ViceVersa	B5
	Wright	(see 13)

⊕ Shopping

38	Barneys	C5
39	Bergdorf Goodman	C5
40	Bloomingdale's	D5
41	Diptyque	C3
42	Flying Tiger Copenhagen	A2
43	Icon Style	A4
44	Jacadi	D3
45	La Maison du Chocolat	C3

46	Magpie	A2
47	Mary Arnold Toys	D2
48	Michael's	C3
	MoMA Design & Book Store	(see 18)
49	Shishi	A1
50	Zabar's	A2

⊖ Drinking & Nightlife

	Bar SixtyFive	(see 24)
51	Bemelmans Bar	C3
	Caledonia	(see 36)
52	Cantor Roof Garden Bar	C2
53	Dead Poet	A2
54	Drunken Munkey	D1
55	Industry	B5
	Irving Farm Roasters	(see 28)
56	Jimmy's Corner	B6
57	Lantern's Keep	C6
58	Malachy's	A3
	Manhattan Cricket Club	(see 28)
59	R Lounge	B6
	Robert	(see 17)
60	Rum House	B6
	The Campbell	(see 12)
61	Therapy	B5

⊕ Entertainment

62	Al Hirschfeld Theatre	B6
	Ambassador Theatre	(see 5)
63	Beacon Theatre	A3
64	Birdland	B6
	Café Carlyle	(see 51)
65	Carnegie Hall	B5
66	Don't Tell Mama	B6
67	Elinor Bunin Munroe Film Center	A4
68	Eugene O'Neill Theatre	B6
	Film Society of Lincoln Center	(see 15)
	Frick Collection Concerts	(see 11)
69	Jazz at Lincoln Center	B5
70	Lyceum Theatre	B6
	Metropolitan Opera House	(see 15)
71	New Victory Theater	B6
72	New York City Ballet	A4
73	New York Philharmonic	A4
74	Richard Rodgers Theatre	B6
75	Second Stage Theatre	B6
76	Symphony Space	A1
77	Upright Citizens Brigade Theatre	A6
78	Walter Reade Theater	A4

⊕ Activities, Courses & Tours

79	Central Park Bike Tours	B5
80	Central Park Conservancy	C5
81	Central Park Tennis Center	B1
82	Loeb Boathouse	C3
83	Rink at Rockefeller Center	C6
84	Wollman Skating Rink	C4

Brooklyn

Williamsburg

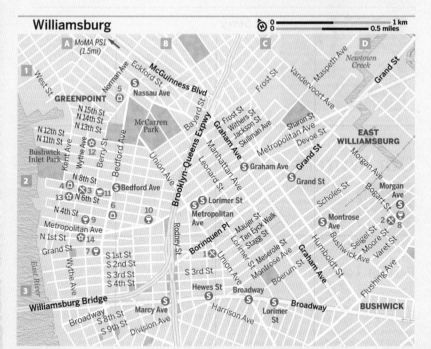

0   1 km
0   0.5 miles

Our Story

A beat-up old car, a few dollars in the pocket and a sense of adventure. In 1972 that's all Tony and Maureen Wheeler needed for the trip of a lifetime – across Europe and Asia overland to Australia. It took several months, and at the end – broke but inspired – they sat at their kitchen table writing and stapling together their first travel guide, *Across Asia on the Cheap*. Within a week they'd sold 1500 copies. Lonely Planet was born. Today, Lonely Planet has offices in Franklin, London, Melbourne, Oakland, Dublin, Beijing and Delhi, with more than 600 staff and writers. We share Tony's belief that 'a great guidebook should do three things: inform, educate and amuse'.

Our Writers

Ali Lemer

Ali has been a Lonely Planet writer and editor since 2007, and has authored guidebooks and travel articles on Russia, NYC, Los Angeles, Melbourne, Bali, Hawaii, Japan and Scotland. A native New Yorker and naturalized Melburnian, Ali has also lived in Chicago, Prague and the UK, and has traveled extensively around Europe and North America.

Regis St. Louis

Regis grew up in a small town in the American Midwest – the kind of place that fuels big dreams of travel – and he developed an early fascination with foreign dialects and world cultures. He spent his formative years learning Russian and a handful of Romance languages, which served him well on journeys across much of the globe. Regis has contributed to more than 50 Lonely Planet titles, covering destinations across six continents. His travels have taken him from the mountains of Kamchatka to remote island villages in Melanesia, and to many grand urban landscapes. When not on the road, he lives in New Orleans. Follow him on Instagram @regisstlouis.

Robert Balkovich

Robert was born and raised in Oregon, but has called New York City home for almost a decade. When he was a child and other families were going to theme parks and grandma's house he went to Mexico City and toured Eastern Europe by train. He's now a writer and travel enthusiast seeking experiences that are ever so slightly out of the ordinary to report back on. Follow him on Instagram @oh_balky.

Ray Bartlett

Ray has been travel writing for nearly two decades, bringing Japan, Korea, Mexico, and many parts of the United States to life in rich detail for publishers, newspapers and magazines. His acclaimed debut novel, *Sunsets of Tulum*, set in Yucatán, was a Midwest Book Review 2016 Fiction pick. Among other pursuits, he surfs regularly and is an accomplished Argentine tango dancer. Follow him on Facebook, Twitter, Instagram, or contact him at www.kaisora.com. Ray currently divides his time between homes in the USA, Japan, and Mexico.

STAY IN TOUCH LONELYPLANET.COM/CONTACT

AUSTRALIA The Malt Store, Level 3, 551 Swanston St, Carlton, Victoria 3053 ☑03 8379 8000, fax 03 8379 8111

IRELAND Digital Depot, Roe Lane (off Thomas St), Digital Hub, Dublin 8, D08 TCV4

USA 124 Linden Street, Oakland, CA 94607 ☑510 250 6400, toll free 800 275 8555, fax 510 893 8572

UK 240 Blackfriars Road, London SE1 8NW ☑020 3771 5100, fax 020 3771 5101

twitter.com/ lonelyplanet

facebook.com/ lonelyplanet

instagram.com/ lonelyplanet

youtube.com/ lonelyplanet

lonelyplanet.com/ newsletter